By Jane Grigson

THE ART OF CHARCUTERIE (1968)

GOOD THINGS (1971)

These are Borzoi books published by Alfred A. Knopf

GOOD THINGS

JANE GRIGSON

GOOD THINGS

Edited and with American notes by Evan Jones

Drawings by M. J. Mott

Alfred A. Knopf / 1971 / New York

This is a Borzoi Book
Published by Alfred A. Knopf, Inc.

Copyright © 1971 by Jane Grigson
All rights reserved under International and
Pan-American Copyright Conventions. Published in
the United States by Alfred A. Knopf, Inc.,
New York, and simultaneously in Canada by
Random House of Canada Limited, Toronto.
Distributed by Random House, Inc., New York.
ISBN: 0–394–46997–6
Library of Congress Catalog Card Number: 74–154926
Manufactured in the United States of America

First Edition

For Geoffrey

Contents

Introduction

This is not a manual of cookery but a book about enjoying food. Few of the recipes in it will contribute much to the repertoire of those who like to produce dinner for six in thirty minutes flat. I think food, its quality, its origins, its preparation, is something to be thought about in the same way as any other aspect of human existence.

Anyone who likes to eat can soon learn to cook well. Such a range of cookery books can now be bought in cheap paperback, from basic beginners' outlines to the best and most stimulating of them all, *French Provincial Cooking*, by Elizabeth David, that there's no reason for not eating deliciously—and simply—all the time. So why don't we? After all, in the eighteenth century English food was the envy of Europe. Why isn't it now?

There are many reasons for this, social and historical as well as agricultural. For a start, we're so used to eating, why take trouble? There are enough frozen and packaged foods about for even the worst cook to keep her family alive without their ever noticing how little real skill she has and how much better their meals might be. Intelligent housewives feel they've a duty to be bored by domesticity. A fair reaction to dusting and bedmaking perhaps, but not, I think, to cooking. The great chef Carême realized this when he wrote, "From behind my ovens I regard the cooking of India and China, of Germany and Switzerland, and I feel the ugly edifice of routine crumbling away beneath my hands."

This is not to say that I resist deep-frozen and canned and packaged food. I think we should be thankful for being relieved of the famines and inconvenience that the seasons used to bring to so many communities. I have no patience with food puritanism of that kind (though I do wonder why the run of frozen food is not better—why so many tasteless sliced beans, when one could have *haricots verts?*).

Having said this, and being always grateful for the background of an unfailing larder, I feel that delight lies in the seasons and what they bring us. One does not remember the grilled hamburgers and frozen peas, but the strawberries that come in May and June straight from the fields, the asparagus of a special occasion, kippers from Craster in July and August, the first lamb of the year from Wales, in October the fresh walnuts from France, where they are eaten with new cloudy wine. This is good food. The sad thing is that, unless we fight, and demand, and complain, and reject, and generally make ourselves thoroughly unpopular, these delights may be unknown to our great-grandchildren. Perhaps even to our grandchildren. It is certainly more convenient, with growing populations, to freeze the asparagus and strawberries straight from the ground, to dye and wrap the kippers in plastic, to import hard, red frozen lamb from New Zealand, and to push the walnuts straight into drying kilns. It is easier to put no seasoning to speak of into a sausage—it offends nobody, everybody buys it. This is the theory. We're back to the primitive idea of eating to keep alive.

When one thinks of the civilization implied in the development of peaches from the wild fruit, or of apricots, grapes, pears, plums, when one thinks of those millions of gardeners from ancient China right across Asia and the Middle East to Rome, then across the Alps north to France, Holland and England of the eighteenth and nineteenth centuries, how can we so crassly, so brutishly, reduce the exquisite results of their labour to cans full of syrup and cardboard-wrapped blocks of ice? These gardeners were concerned to grow a better-tasting fruit or vegetable, a larger and more beautiful one too, but mainly a better-tasting one. Would they believe us if we told them that now tomatoes are produced to regular size and regular shape, that only two or three kinds of potato are regularly on sale, that peas taste like mealy bullets? It's odd that we should have clung on to traditions that hardly matter—beefeaters, Swiss guards, monarchies, the paraphernalia of the past, and forgotten the long labouring struggle to learn how to survive as well and as gracefully as possible.

I do get the impression, though, that many people begin to understand that the encouragement of fine food is not greed or gourmandise; it can be seen as an aspect of the antipollution movement because it indicates concern for the quality of environment. This is not the limited concern of a few cranks. Small and medium-sized firms, feeling unable to compete with the cheap products of the giants, turn to producing better food. A courageous pig-breeder in Suffolk starts a cooked-pork shop in the high charcuterie style. People in many parts of the country run restaurants specializing in locally produced food, salmon from the Tamar River, laver and sewen[1] from the Welsh sea, snails from the Mendips, venison from the moors of Inverness. I notice in the grocers' shops in our small town the increasing appearance of bags of strong flour, whole-wheat and scofa[2] meal, and the prominence given to eggs direct from the farm.

Many families, not just the housewife, now do the cooking between them, and enjoy a protracted sociable meal as an opportunity for talking and discussing with an enthusiasm that was not encouraged at dinner parties thirty years ago. Cooking something delicious is really much more satisfactory than painting pictures or making pottery. At least for most of us. Food has the tact to disappear, leaving room and opportunity for masterpieces to come. The mistakes don't hang on the walls or stand on the shelves to reproach you forever. It follows from this that the kitchen should be thought of as the centre of the house. It needs above all space for talking, playing, bringing up children, sewing, having a meal, reading, sitting and thinking. One may have to walk about a bit, but where's the harm in that? Everything will not be shipshape, galley-fashion, but it's in this kind of place that good food has flourished. It's from this secure retreat that the exploration of man's curious and close relationship with food, beyond the point of nourishment, can start.

I should like to thank Elizabeth David, and John Thompson, until recently editor of the *Observer Colour Magazine*: they first gave me the opportunity of exploring the material that follows. Then I should like to thank the many friends and readers who have sent me recipes and information, in particular Mrs. Farida Abu-Haidar of Highgate, Mrs. Bobby Freeman who ran the Compton House Hotel at Fishguard until 1970, Mr. Paul Leyton of the Miner's Arms at Priddy in Somerset, Mrs. Mary Norwak of the *Farmer's Weekly*, Mrs. B. M. Round of Lardy in the Essonne, Mrs. Charlotte Sawyer of Woodsville, New Hampshire, Mrs. Ann Irving of Littleton, Massachusetts, Mrs. Tao Tao Sanders of Oxford, who has given me the Chinese recipes in this book. Signor Adragna of the Italian Institute for Foreign Trade, Mr. Jack of Preston-next-Wingham in Kent, Mr. Paske of Kentford in Suffolk, Mr. D. Ritchie of Rothesay, Bute, and Mr. K. L. Robson of Craster in Northumberland, have all replied patiently to my requests for information. Mr. Hopkins of Macfisheries in the Parade at Swindon, and Mr. Irland of Baxter's

---

[1] Laver is seaweed or sea lettuce, and sewen is sea trout from the west coast of England and Wales and the coast of Ireland.

[2] A brown meal for making bread and scones without yeast: it contains stoneground meal, brau, soya bean flour, malt flour, skimmed milk powder, and baking powder.

(Butchers) Ltd., of Wootton Bassett, have continually and amiably produced special orders at short notice.

Last and most important of all, I should like to say thank you to my
family and friends. They have endured carrots and sweetbreads or whatever it might be for six and even eight meals at a stretch; they have
sometimes been confronted with three or four versions of a dish at one
meal. Their comments have always been interested, and usually polite. Of
my friends, I owe most to Mrs. Marjorie White; without her help,
adaptability, and kindness, I should never have had the time to write
a word of this book.

Broad Town, 1970   JANE GRIGSON

Fish

KIPPERS & OTHER CURED FISH

Over the centuries we have developed various ways of curing and keeping the herring, that splendid northern fish which Shakespeare's contemporary Thomas Nashe—loyal to his East Anglia—grandly and comically called the "Semper Augustus of the sea's finny freeholders." Our best and longest known forms are the red herring, the bloater, and the kipper—in that order of seniority.

Yarmouth, the great herring centre since the Middle Ages, founded its wealth first of all on the long-keeping, long-cured red herring. Smoked after days in brine, until very red and fairly dry, this was the ultra-strong-flavoured herring which we used to eat especially in Lent. Red herring is worth trying as an hors d'oeuvre. The trouble is to get hold of one—even in Yarmouth, which has produced red herrings for centuries, but now sends all or most of them abroad to the Mediterranean, Africa, the West Indies and South America.[1]

[1] Fish experts in the United States know "red herrings" only as the old euphemism for deception. Markets in America offer smoked herring in the form of fillets, kippers which are split, salted, and smoked, and bloaters which are older, fatter, and so perishable they should be eaten immediately.

I've tried to get red herrings from leading food departments of London stores. They thought I was being funny, but others may be lucky in finding red herrings in a Cypriot delicatessen, or in a district where West Indians do their shopping. In the end you will probably have to write to the fountainhead of supply, Henry Sutton's of Great Yarmouth. The red herrings they export to the eastern Mediterranean are soaked and cut into strips and eaten as an hors d'oeuvre or appetiser. Sometimes they're served on dry bread, as an accompaniment to Greek bean soup. Sutton's still cures a black herring, the ultimate in hardness, almost brittle. It's much in demand in very hot difficult climates such as the West Indies, Africa and South America because it will keep almost indefinitely without refrigeration. Black and red herrings used to be slave fodder, and they still tend to go to the poorer populations of these countries.

The bloater, unsplit, soft and plump (i.e., "bloated"—it used to be called the "bloat herring"), we seem to have been eating for some 400 to 500 years.[2] It is lightly salted and lightly smoked for flavour rather than long keeping. This light style of cure has best been developed in Holland and in France, where one buys the most succulent *harengs saurs* or "*bouffis*," i.e., "bloaters."

Then comes the kipper, first produced—or so it is said—on the Northumbrian coast early in the nineteenth century, split, soaked in brine, and smoked on tenterhooks for 10 to 20 hours.

Some ordinary kippers are passable, I would agree. But if you really want to know what a kipper should taste like, luscious and bland, the surest way is to order them from kipperers at Craster (L. Robson & Sons, Craster, Alnwick, Northumberland), on Loch Fyne (Ritchie Bros, 37 Watergate, Rothesay, Bute), or on the Isle of Man (T. Moore & Sons, Mill Road, Peel). Such small kippering establishments choose the best and fattest herrings at their peak (from June to October), they smoke them properly over oak fires, and they do not colour them by adding dye to the brine. One kipperer of the splendid Loch Fyne herrings told me sadly and sarcastically that the big firms are "turning kippers all into painted ladies."

A good kipper won't be thin and skimpy or dyed (to the colour of an old mahogany commode). It will be silvery brown. It will still be in

[2] *They are so deliciously plump and have had an excellent reputation for so long that even an attractive woman like Clara Peggotty in* David Copperfield *was "proud to call herself a Yarmouth bloater."*

possession of its head, tail and backbone. And, full of its own fat, it won't need to be sold with pats of butter.

The good kipper is one of Great Britain's contributions to fine food. That frozen and packaged kippers should now dominate the fish counter strikes me as a minor national disgrace. But then we so often lack piety towards our best things.

Kippers for breakfast

Everyone has a favourite way of cooking kippers, but it's worth trying a new method sometimes, even if breakfast does not seem the right meal for experiments. There are only two rules to observe: don't overcook them, and don't add butter until they are served, as good kippers cook in their own juice.

Jugged kippers are my favourite for breakfast. Put them, head down, into a 2–3-pint stoneware jug. Pour boiling water on them straight from the kettle (as if you were making tea), right up to their tails. Leave in a warm place for 5–10 minutes, drain well and serve. They can be laid in a roasting tin, instead of a jug, but this is dangerous, as the boiling water slops about if one makes a careless, half-awake movement.

Baked kippers. Wrap them loosely in aluminum foil. Bake for 10–15 minutes in a moderately hot oven. The foil preserves the juices and, incidentally, saves washing up and eliminates lingering smells in the kitchen.

Grilled kippers. 1. Place the kippers *skin side up* on a piece of foil on the grill rack. Grill gently for 5 minutes until the skin is deliciously crisp, not charred.

Or 2. Jug the kippers for 2 minutes, then grill 2 minutes on each side.

Fried kippers. Grease the frying pan lightly with butter, just enough to prevent the kippers sticking and no more (unnecessary with a nonstick pan). Fry gently for 2–3 minutes on each side.

Whether grilled, fried, baked or jugged, eat the kippers with plenty of bread and butter. Lemon quarters, pats of butter or parsley butter can be served as well.

Kippers with scrambled eggs   *(for 4)*

A good dish for late Sunday breakfasts that merge into lunch. Try it too as an hors d'oeuvre, or in sandwiches. The kippers can be cooked or not, as you please. The main thing to notice is the use of garlic—Escoffier's idea—which enhances the flavour of the eggs without stridency. The best garlic to use is the fat, white, juicy kind imported from France.

> 2 kippers
> 6 eggs
> large clove garlic
> salt, pepper
> 6 tablespoons butter

for serving: buttered toast

Divide the cooked or uncooked kippers into large flakes, or strips. Beat the eggs for 5 minutes with a fork stuck firmly into the clove of garlic. Season with salt and pepper. Melt the butter in a thick pan over a lowe heat, pour in the eggs through a strainer and cook as slowly as possible, stirring from time to time. When the eggs are beginning to solidify, but are still fairly liquid, add the kipper pieces. Don't overcook. Serve on buttered toast.

If this dish is to be served as a cold hors d'oeuvre, it's best to scramble the eggs on their own, and lay strips of kipper across them just before serving.

Craster kippers   (for 4)

Craster is a grey stone fishing village tucked down on the Northumbrian coast, half a mile below its handsome entry arch. In the small harbour are the brightly striped cobles, flat-bottomed, lug-sailed, used for lobster, crab and salmon fishing. To the north the ruins of Dunstanburgh Castle squat dramatically on a cliff; to the south lies the quiet beach of Howick with ochre rocks and grey sea buckthorn. In sheds above the harbour the Robson family cures some of the finest kippers in Great Britain. These plump, silvery brown, almost translucent fish are best eaten ungrilled, unbaked, unjugged, unfried—in other words, just as they are, like smoked salmon.

> 2–3 kippers
> 4 lemon quarters
> whole-wheat or rye bread
> unsalted butter

Slice the kippers horizontally and thinly, after removing the bones. Serve with lemon quarters and thin slices of bread and butter.

Or: 2–3 kippers
          4 slices whole-wheat or rye bread
          unsalted butter
          4 egg yolks
          lemon juice and slices

Skin and bone the kippers. Cut them with scissors into strips. Butter the bread generously, right to the edges, and trim into a neat shape. Arrange the kippers on each side to build up a nestlike circle. Using a spoon, slip an egg yolk onto each bread slice, sprinkle with a few drops of lemon juice and serve with half a slice of lemon arranged on each side of the kippers.

To eat, break the yolk with a fork and mix into the kipper pieces. Use the lemon slices for extra seasoning. This is delicious, providing the kippers are good and the eggs really fresh.

Kippers or bloaters with potato salad

(for 4)

This favourite European dish is deceptively simple to prepare. Its success depends on using ingredients of the highest quality—the finest olive oil, the best-flavoured smoked herrings (classy kippers, bloaters, *harengs saurs*,[3] maatjes herrings[4]), waxy potatoes, wine vinegar and a firm seasoning of an onion flavour.

> 6–8 fillets of kipper, soaked in olive oil 2 hours
> 1 lb. waxy potatoes
>
> *dressing:* 4 tablespoons olive oil
> 1 tablespoon red wine vinegar
> 1 teaspoon French or German mustard
> ½ teaspoon sugar
> salt, black pepper
> 1 heaping tablespoon chopped chives,
>   shallots, mild onion, or spring onion

If salty herrings are used, soak them for several hours in milk and water before drying and putting into olive oil. Because oil acts as a preservative, the fillets can be submerged in it a day or two before they are eaten; it's advisable to cover them over and store in a refrigerator.

Scrub and boil the potatoes. Mix oil, vinegar, mustard and seasonings in a bowl. Peel and cube the cooked potatoes, adding them to the dressing while still warm. When cold add the chopped chives. Chill. Arrange on a serving dish with the kippers, which should be drained of all but a teaspoonful or so of their oil.

[3] *Harengs saurs à l'Irlandaise are prepared by cutting off the heads, then splitting the smoked herring and spreading them flat in a deep dish; cover them with whiskey and set alight—when the whiskey is consumed the herrings are ready to serve.*

[4] *Maatjes—a Dutch word—means virgin herring, i.e. the best herring. Usually sold aired and marinated.*

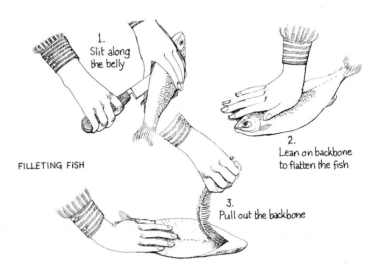

1.
Slit along
the belly

2.
Lean on backbone
to flatten the fish

FILLETING FISH

3.
Pull out the backbone

To fillet bloaters

Remove the skin, which peels off quite easily. Slit open along the belly, open out a little and put cut side down on to a board. Press firmly and steadily along the back of the fish. Turn it over and you will be able to remove the backbone quite easily, and small stray bones too. Separate the two fillets.

Kippers or salt herring fillets with dill salad

(for 4)

Dill is an underused herb in England—which is a pity. It is easy to grow, and its subtle flavour, which to my mind tastes something like caraway, goes well with fish and all kinds of vegetable dishes. Dill weed, i.e., the leaves as opposed to the seeds, which is also used as flavouring, can be bought in most groceries and supermarkets. An alternative for Britons living near the sea is the stronger, slightly liquorice-flavoured fennel, growing wild on many cliffs of England and Wales.[5]

[5] Wild fennel is a rare sight in the U.S., but Irma Goodrich Mazza in her delightful *Herbs for the Kitchen* tells of appropriating a roadside plant which so thrived in her garden that it grew seven feet in ten years.

6–8 kipper fillets, or soaked salt herring fillets
½ lb. waxy potatoes, boiled and diced
1 small beet, boiled, peeled and diced
2 medium apples, diced
1 small, mild onion, chopped

dressing: 6 tablespoons olive oil
1½ tablespoons wine vinegar
1 teaspoon French or German mustard
¾ teaspoons sugar
1½ tablespoons chopped fresh dill weed, ¾ if dried
salt, black pepper

Cut the fish fillets into strips 2 or 3 hours before the meal, and prepare each of the other main ingredients, mixing with dressing in separate bowls. Before serving, drain and arrange the ingredients on a serving dish (or on pieces of bread and butter as open sandwiches), and chill.

Alternative dressings are sour cream beaten with a little lemon juice to taste, or mayonnaise. Plus dill.

Kipper paste

Some people object to the restaurateur's habit of describing our native potted fish pastes as "pâtés." I agree. We lack a proper pride in the good food we can produce in Great Britain. It would be better if dishes like this one were given their proper names and starred as specialities. We might even begin to acquire a gastronomic reputation.

The interesting thing about potted fish—and meat—pastes is that they are becoming popular again, after half a century of neglect. When elbow-power in the kitchen was cheap, they were easy to produce. Now blenders can replace the poor slaveys of the past.

1 fat kipper
½ lb. unsalted butter
salt, cayenne pepper, lemon juice

Jug the kipper for 5 minutes (see recipe, p. 5). Drain, remove skin and bones, and cut in pieces. Melt the butter over a low heat. Put kipper pieces and butter into the jar of the blender. Whirl at top speed until they are smooth and perfectly blended. Season and put into two or three small pots. When cold and set, cover with a layer of clarified butter (butter boiled for a few seconds, then strained carefully through several layers of cheese-cloth).[6] This will keep in the refrigerator for a few weeks, if covered well with aluminum foil so that the clarified butter does not dry away from the sides of the pot.

Bloaters can be used for this paste too. About ½ lb. (or 1 cup packed) of filleted fish is required.

Kipper flan   *(for 6 to 8)*

This useful dish can be served as a first course at dinner, or as a main course at midday or for a picnic. Eat it warm for the best flavour, but it is still good when cold. When I first made the flan, I did not expect the smoky flavour of kipper to blend well with the cream and egg custard. I thought it would taste oily, particularly when cold. It is, in fact, delicious.

> *short pastry, made with 1 cup flour (see p. 57)*
> *1 fat kipper (9 oz.)*
> *1 cup heavy cream,*
> *   or ½ cup each heavy and light cream*
> *3 eggs*
> *1 tablespoon French or German mustard*
> *salt and pepper*
> *½ lemon*

Line an 8½-inch tart pan with a removable base with the pastry. Prick

---

[6] *Another method: when completely melted, remove butter from heat, letting it stand a few minutes while solids settle to bottom. Then skim the clear butter fat from the top and place in container.*

all over and bake unfilled for 5 minutes, until set but not browned. Meanwhile jug the kipper (p. 5). Remove bones and skin and arrange pieces
on the pastry case. Beat together the cream and eggs, add the mustard
gradually to your taste. Season. Pour over the kippers and bake at 350°,
for 30–40 minutes, until the filling is golden brown and puffed up. Now
quickly squeeze half a lemon over the flan.

Red herrings[7]

Need soaking, indubitably. The best way to do this is to bring
some pale ale, or water, to the boil and pour it immediately over the
fish. You will discover by tasting, and by experience, how long the fish
need to be soaked. Start by soaking them overnight.

To cook red herrings, drain them and dry them well. Brush them over
with melted butter, and grill lightly at a gentle heat (they need to be
warmed through, rather than cooked).

Serve them with hot boiled potatoes and butter. Or with melted butter
flavoured with mustard. Or with plenty of bread and butter. In the eighteenth and nineteenth centuries, buttery scrambled eggs and mashed potatoes were served with the red herrings.

Once soaked, the herrings need not be cooked. Dry them and store in
olive oil in the refrigerator, as they do in Italy. Serve them as part of an
hors d'oeuvre, with the fillets cut into small slices. Try them, too, with
Napoleon's bean salad (p. 177), instead of the usual potato salad.

Salted and spiced herrings

Preserving herrings is not at all difficult. Gut and scale them,
but leave the heads on. Soak them in ordinary distilled vinegar overnight,
then drain them well. Pack tightly together in a large pot, between layers
of salt and spices:

---

[7] *In the U.S. ask for the herring that have been most heavily smoked.*

For 50 fresh herrings
>1 lb. sea salt [or kosher]
>½ lb. sugar
>10–12 bay leaves
>2 teaspoons each black peppercorns & allspice, slightly crushed

Cover the herrings with the above and weight them until the salt turns to brine. Make sure that the herrings are always submerged. Store in a cool, dry place.[8]

Salted herrings need to be soaked before they are used. Length of time depends on the length of time they've been in salt; 8 to 10 hours is usual. It's a good idea to fillet the herrings before soaking them (see p. 9).

Danish sweet-sour herrings: soak fillets in milk and water, half and half. Meanwhile bring to the boil 1 cup granulated sugar, ⅔ cup wine vinegar, 6 peppercorns and 1 teaspoon pickling spice. Remove from the heat after boiling 3 minutes. Cool. Cut the fillets into inch strips and arrange in a plastic box or screw-top jar in layers with slices of raw onion. Pour over the marinade, cover and leave for 5 days in the refrigerator before eating.

Scottish tatties an' herrin': put a layer of evenly sized potatoes in a large pot. Lay some salt herrings, which have been soaked, on top. Put enough water in to come three-quarters of the way up the potatoes. Cover and simmer for an hour. A homely dish, requiring butter (drain off the cooking liquid before serving).

Scandinavian pickled salmon (or mackerel or trout)

Frozen Canadian salmon may be used for this delicious preparation. It's easy, and it makes a much cheaper start to a meal than smoked salmon. Everyone enjoys its fresh, unfamiliar flavour:

[8] Another way is to use quart jars. Remove backbone to fillet the soaked fish, then cut into 2-inch pieces. Pack loosely, shaking in a rounded ½ cup of salt to distribute evenly; fill with distilled white vinegar and cap. Store in refrigerator at least 6 days. Almost any fish is good for pickling in this way.

1½–2 *lb. tailpiece salmon*
1 *large tablespoon sea salt* [*or kosher*]
1 *rounded tablespoon sugar*
1 *teaspoon coarsely ground black pepper*
   plenty of dried dill weed

optional: 1 tablespoon brandy

Slice the piece of salmon in half, carefully, and remove the backbone and any little bones, but leave the skin. Rinse very quickly, dry well and put the first piece, skin side up, in a dish. Mix salt, sugar, pepper and brandy together. Rub about a quarter of this into the skin of the first piece, turn it filleted side up and rub in half the mixture; sprinkle liberally with dried dill weed and put the second piece on top, filleted side down. Rub the rest of the mixture into the skin, and sprinkle with more dill weed. Put a piece of foil on top, then a couple of cans (at least 8 ounces each) as weights. Leave for at least 12 hours, and at most 4 days, in the refrigerator or in a very cool place.

To serve, drain the pieces and slice them diagonally or horizontally starting at the tail end. Serve with thinly cut whole-wheat or rye bread, and butter, with lemon quarters. In Scandinavia this mustard sauce usually accompanies pickled salmon—and very good it is:

1 *heaping tablespoon French or German mustard*
½ *tablespoon sugar*
1 *tablespoon wine vinegar*
4 *tablespoons olive or salad oil*
   dill weed to taste

Mix all the ingredients together to a thick, smooth yellow sauce. A crushed clove of garlic, a small one, may also be added.

Mackerel (or herrings) in white wine

This popular French hors d'oeuvre tastes even better one or two days after its preparation. Muscadet is the traditional wine to use, but an ordinary dry white wine is quite satisfactory.

4 fat mackerel (or herrings), weighing ½ to ¾ pound each

Clean the fish, removing the soft roe, if there are any, for another dish.

>1½ cups dry white wine
>½ cup water
>1 medium-sized carrot, sliced
>1 medium-sized onion, sliced
>8 peppercorns, slightly crushed
>1 teaspoon pickling spices, including a red chili seed
>½ teaspoon salt

Simmer together the above ingredients for 30 minutes and then allow this *court-bouillon* to cool. Place the fish in a single layer in a saucepan or casserole, then strain the liquid over. Pick the chili and 3 slices of the carrot out of the debris from the *court-bouillon*, throwing the rest away. Bring the pan of fish slowly to the boil, bubble for 1 minute, then cover and leave to cool.

Remove skin and heads; then divide fish into fillets and discard bones. Lay them in an oval serving dish, and put the chili and carrot slices on top, plus 2 or 3 small sliced gherkins and a sliver of lemon peel. Reduce the *court-bouillon* by boiling hard, until it has a good concentrated flavour. Pour a little of it over the fish as a dressing, and keep the rest as a basis for fish soup or a sauce to go with fish.

To store for a few days, put the fish with its garnish into a jar or refrigerator box. Reduce the *bouillon* and pour over the fish to cover it. Put the lid on the jar or box and keep in the refrigerator.

NOTE: There are many British recipes of a similar kind for herrings. They make use of vinegar, malt vinegar at that, instead of wine. The result can be very aggressive.

LOBSTER

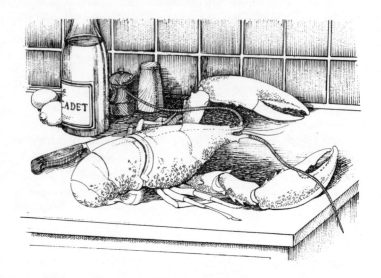

The lobster has never, it seems, been a democratic food. I mean in the way that salmon was, until our rivers were polluted. Before the industrial revolution, people used to grow tired of eating salmon. I've never heard of anyone growing tired of eating lobster.

Nowadays it's become almost exclusively a speciality of grand restaurants, an expensive dish on any menu, lobster Newberg, lobster Américaine or Armoricaine according to your fancy, *bisque de homard*.

This is not surprising, for, as the authors of one seashore guide remark, it's not so common as many would wish in spite of its wide distribution. Then there's its marvellous, daunting appearance: the blue carapace that turns fiery red when cooked; the tail fiercely flexible like fine armour (for this reason, soldiers used to be called lobsters: when armour went out, the name still did for red coats); the rapid movement of the creature, the vicious nip of its great claws; its ability to lose a limb or joint and survive. "All the ingenious men," wrote Kingsley, in *Water Babies*, "and all the scientific men, and all the imaginative men in the world could never invent, if all their wits were boiled into one, anything so curious and so ridiculous as a lobster."

Don't let price and shape put you off trying a lobster occasionally. It's worth saving for. Of all the things one can eat, it's difficult to think of anything more delicious, anything so sweet, firm and succulent. If you live at all near the sea (nowhere in Great Britain is farther than 60 miles away from it), try and discover a direct supply of lobsters. An expedition to Weymouth, say, or the western coast of Scotland, for those who have no more than 30 or 40 miles to go, can be most rewarding.[1]

The actual cooking and preparation of lobster is not difficult. Like most expensive food—steak, caviar, smoked salmon—its presentation, particularly if you are buying a ready-boiled lobster, is within the competence of a child. It's a reasonable argument that the best way of eating such a delicious substance is the simplest: that hot, lobster needs no more than melted butter and lemon juice; that cold, it needs no more than mayonnaise or vinaigrette. The raw eggs of the hen lobster are said to have a strange and delicate flavour: to the cook they are the "coral," because when the lobster is boiled they, too, turn red. When they are cooked, the flavour has gone, but they can be used to colour the sauce.

Lobster can be bought all the year round (many fishmongers and supermarkets store them ready-boiled in their freezer), but the high season runs from May to October when offshore fishing is at its peak.[2] A fisherman who has the luck to find one or two in his net or lobster pots will store them, perhaps in a crate submerged in sea water, and send a batch of lobsters off to market every so often. In France there is a scheme for sinking used cars off the shore, to provide a lobster paradise which can easily be tapped by the fishermen. Perhaps with such encouragement, lobsters will increase and the scheme will be adopted elsewhere. There's also talk of raising lobsters in plastic bags, so that they can be fattened quickly, battery style. I hope so.

If you want your lobster alive, it's best to order from your fish market several days in advance. It may seem unwise to buy lobster after it's been boiled, but a good fishmonger can be relied upon to see that you get value

[1] In America, millions who do live more than 50 miles from salt water can order large-claw lobsters from New England shippers, receiving them in their kitchens very much alive and ready for any recipe.

[2] When large-claw lobsters are not easily available, the large crayfish known as rock lobster or spiny lobster—prevalent in Pacific and southern U.S. waters—can be substituted.

for your money. He would like you to come back. Canned lobster meat is not, in my experience, worth buying: it's expensive and has a minimal flavour. As with all fish, freshness is the desirable quality.

To boil a lobster

The method of doing this in the past, and today in most professional kitchens, is to plunge the lobster into a large pan of boiling water. However, the Royal Society for the Prevention of Cruelty to Animals recommends that it should be put into a pan of cold or tepid salted water, which should then be brought slowly to the boil, thus anaesthetizing the lobster. Put a weight on the lid, whichever method you use. Lobster boiled in the first way will take 20 to 30 minutes to cook, according to size: it will require 10 to 20 minutes in the second way, once the water's come to the boil.[3] [*Usual rule of thumb in New England is 5 minutes per pound.*] Hot boiled lobster can be served with melted butter, with hollandaise or cream sauce. Cut it in half lengthways, and crack the claws before serving it.

For serving cold, lobster is usually left to cool in the cooking liquid. Mayonnaise is the most popular sauce (the coral should be pounded and beaten with the egg yolks before the oil is added). The lobster meat should be removed from the shells and mixed with the mayonnaise: use the head and the better bits of the shell as decoration, plus lettuce leaves, stuffed eggs, tomato quarters and so on.

Instead of water, a *court-bouillon* is often used to give the lobster the benefit of herbs, spices and wine. Boil the following ingredients for 1 hour:

> 2 onions, sliced
> 2 carrots, sliced
> bouquet garni (3 parsley stalks, 2 thyme sprigs, 1 bay leaf)
> ½ cup wine vinegar
> 1 cup dry white wine
> 8–9 cups water
> salt, pepper

[3] Purists disagree. "Lobsters are at their best," Michael Field said in *All Manner of Food*, "only if they breathe their last either in the dish in which they are cooked or moments before they are added to it. . . . Scientists long ago demonstrated that crustaceans have nervous systems of such simplicity that they scarcely feel pain as we do."

Put the lobster into this boiling stock; or let it cool and follow the R.S.P.C.A. method.

As a change from mayonnaise, try this way of dressing cold lobster which I've taken from Alexandre Dumas' *Grand Dictionnaire de Cuisine*. Put the cooked lobster meat into a basin. Mix it with about 5 tablespoons of olive oil, up to a tablespoon of Dijon mustard, a handful of parsley, tarragon and chives, all chopped, 1 heaped tablespoon finely chopped shallots or mild onion, 12 drops of Chinese soy sauce, and some freshly ground white pepper. The final flavouring is a glass of anisette (e.g., Pastis Ricard, Marie Brizard) and lemon juice to taste.

Homard à l'Américaine   (for 4)

The trouble about many famous lobster dishes, including this one, is that the cook is expected to cut the creature up while it's still alive. Although a first cut between tail and head kills the lobster, it's not an idea that appeals to most people. One solution is to plunge it into a pan of boiling water for exactly 2 minutes: this kills it without spoiling the flavour, which is the point of using lobster uncooked.

When cutting a lobster into pieces, start with the claws and crack the large ones after they're removed from the body. Cut the tail from the head. Divide the tail into sections across the joints; split the head down the middle. Discard the intestinal canal and the little sack of grit from the head. Take out the coral and keep to one side (the "coral" will not be coral, but a collection of black eggs), also the liver, or tomalley.

Now you are ready to start on lobster Américaine, one of the most discussed recipes in the European repertoire. The delicious flavour is not in question, it's the title that worries people. Unquestionably this is a French dish, with affinities with Provençal cooking—tomatoes, garlic and olive oil. There are early recipes of a similar kind, using a different kind of lobster, the crawfish, which is more common in the Mediterranean, before the great popularity of the dish in the late nineteenth century. It's also been suggested that the recipe has a Breton origin, that it should be called lobster Armoricaine; but the ingredients and method of the recipe don't belong to the rather humble style of Breton cooking, Brittany having been until recently one of the poorest and most neglected parts of France. One has only to read shocked nineteenth-century English accounts of the low standards of life in those parts—and remember that our middle-class travellers were used to low standards of life for the lower orders—to see that a fine recipe of this type is unlikely to have been invented in such an area, at that time.[4]

1 large lobster, cut up as above
4 tablespoons olive oil
2 tablespoons chopped onion
2 medium tomatoes, peeled and quartered
1 large clove garlic, crushed
parsley, tarragon
½ cup dry white wine
½ cup beef or fish stock
¼ cup brandy
1 teaspoon tomato paste
2 teaspoons sugar
2 tablespoons butter
1 teaspoon flour
salt, pepper

[4] In his primer written "specifically for the American cook," Gerald Maurois notes much scholarly research on the origin of this lobster dish in *La Revue Culinaire* and says Curnonsky, "prince of gourmets," credits title and invention to a chef named Fraisse who lived briefly in Chicago. One night in 1868, so the story goes, Fraisse was about to close his Paris restaurant when eight or ten people asked to be fed. Though he had little left with which to prepare a meal, Fraisse found butter, tomatoes, garlic, shallots, and lobster. In a hurry, he knew only one way to cook lobster quickly, to cut it up. He made a sauce with wine, brandy, the tomatoes and other seasonings and "threw the pieces of lobster into the savory mixture. Not long afterward it was being consumed by the hungry merrymakers to the tune of loud praise." So Fraisse named that night's dish to honor his American experience, apparently. But, wittingly or otherwise, he ignored the existence of the same concoction under two other names. Pierre Andrieu in *Fine Bouche* has written that Fraisse may have been the originator of the term "lobster à l'americaine," but not the dish itself, which was well known as *homard Bonnefoy,* after the Paris restaurant of that name; he quotes Philéas Gilbert, one of Escoffier's collaborators, as asserting that Fraisse's "lobster in the American style" was known even earlier as *langouste niçoise* and that the basic dish is of Provençal origin. That it may occasionally still be found on U.S. menus as "lobster Armoricaine" (as if it dated back to ancient Brittany) adds another touch of confusion. The fact is that the land called Armorique had no tomatoes and little if any Cognac, but the Breton spelling might indicate an effort to emphasize the recipe's genuine Gallic beginnings.

Heat the oil in a large pan, and cook the lobster for about 5 minutes (it will turn bright red). Remove and add the onion, and cook it gently until it is soft and golden. Add the tomatoes, the garlic and herbs; when they begin to boil, pour in wine, stock and brandy. (Other versions of lobster Américaine use the brandy, warm, to flambé the lobster when it has been fried in oil with the onion at the beginning of the recipe.) Season with salt, pepper, a teaspoon or more of tomato paste, depending on the flavour of the tomatoes, and the sugar. Put the lobster back in the pan to complete the cooking (10–15 minutes). Meanwhile mash the coral and liver with the butter and flour.

When the lobster is cooked, arrange it on a hot serving dish. Boil the sauce hard until it is reduced to a good flavour and consistency. Stir in the coral butter, bit by bit, and let the sauce simmer for a few moments. Strain it over the lobster. Serve with a pilaf of rice.

NOTE: The lobster meat may be removed from the shell for serving, but it's usually left to the eaters to do this for themselves.

Lobster Thermidor (for 4)

There's a story that one of Napoleon's chefs invented this dish, and that his master suggested the name Thermidor, which he'd given to the hottest month of the newly divided year. Presumably as an acknowledgement of the essential ingredient—mustard? Or of the bubbling heat of the lobster itself? But as food appreciated by Napoleon went quickly into the recipe books, and lobster Thermidor does not make much of an appearance before this century, I feel more inclined to believe a less romantic tale—that the dish was invented at the restaurant Thermidor in Paris towards the end of the nineteenth century.

There are many versions of the sauce. The simplest one is a béchamel, enriched by cream and spiced with mustard. I prefer this sharper sauce:

"Well, let the cooks and historians go on arguing . . ." says Elizabeth David in her incomparable *French Provincial Cooking*. "Let Édouard de Pomiane have the last word for now." Then she quotes the knowledgeable pre-World War II gastronome as describing *langouste à l'americaine* as a "gastronomic cacophony," and apt as not, according to Dr. de Pomiane, to bring on gout.

2 *lobsters, about* 2 *lbs. each*

sauce: 2 *tablespoons chopped onion or shallots*
¾ *cup white wine*
2 *teaspoons tarragon vinegar*
12 *peppercorns, slightly crushed*
2 *tablespoons butter*
2 *rounded tablespoons flour*
1½ *cups hot milk*
4 *tablespoons cream*
mustard powder (or French-type mustard)
salt, pepper

to finish: 1 *heaping tablespoon bread crumbs*
¼ *cup grated cheese, preferably Gruyère*
2 *tablespoons melted butter*
lemon quarters

Boil lobsters in the usual way. Remove claws, crack them and extract the meat. Split the body in half lengthways and clean; add the edible parts to the claw meat and dice it all as evenly as possible.

To make the sauce, put onion, wine, vinegar and peppercorns into a heavy pan. Boil hard until the liquid is reduced by half. Add the butter; when it has melted, stir in the flour, and, gradually, the hot milk. Let the sauce simmer until it is reduced to a thick smoothness, giving it an occasional stir. Strain it into a clean pan, add the cream, mustard to taste, salt and pepper. Start with just a little mustard, then add more; remember that English mustard powder is very fierce in flavour compared with French-made mustard of the Dijon type. You might think that this sort of flavour is too strong for the sweetness of lobster, but it isn't; it seems to emphasize it by contrast.

Pour a little of this sauce into the empty lobster shells, put the lobster dice on top, and cover with the rest of the sauce. Arrange the lobsters on a baking tray, using crumpled lengths of aluminum foil to steady them. Mix bread crumbs and cheese and sprinkle them over the top; dribble the melted butter over them as evenly as possible.

Put under a medium hot broiler to reheat and to brown. They should be served sizzling hot, garnished with lemon quarters.

This dish may conveniently be assembled several hours before it's to be eaten. In this case it's a good idea to heat the lobsters through in the oven first, at 400°, before finishing them under the broiler.

NOTE: This is a good way of serving cooked salmon and crab. The sauce can also be used with scallops in a similar way: fry them first in a little butter, until they are opaque—about 3 minutes on each side.

Bisque de homard   (for 6 to 8)

I can say without qualification of any kind that *bisque de homard* is the best of all soups. If you've only made its acquaintance canned, frozen or dehydrated, go out and buy a small lobster and make some. You can also use the shells and debris of lobster from yesterday's feast: if you intend to do this, have the forethought to hide away one or two nice pieces of lobster meat.

A consolation—if the soup is made with a whole lobster, it's a particularly filling dish. Follow it with fruit, perhaps some cheese, and most people will be well satisfied.

> 1 small lobster
> 1 large carrot, diced
> 2 heaping tablespoons chopped onion
> ½ cup butter
> ½ cup white wine
> 6 cups fish or chicken stock
> bouquet garni
> 4–7 tablespoons rice*
> ½ cup cream
> ¼ cup brandy
> salt, pepper, cayenne pepper, minced parsley

If the lobster is alive, cut it into large pieces, reserving coral (see p. 17) and liver. Simmer the vegetables in ¼ cup of butter in a frying pan, until they begin to look golden. Add the lobster and cook until it turns bright red—about 5 minutes. Pour on the wine and boil hard until the liquid is reduced by half. Add enough stock to cover the lobster; simmer until it's cooked —about 5 more minutes. Take the pieces out of the pan, set the meat aside and put the shells into a clean pan. Pour in the vegetable and wine mixture, add the rest of the stock, the bouquet garni and 4 table-spoons of rice.

In about 20 minutes, when the rice is cooked, take out the lobster shells and bouquet. Put the rest of the butter, coral, liver and contents of the saucepan—plus the lobster meat, except a nice piece or two to make a gar-nish—into the blender, or through the food mill. Pour through a strainer (to make quite sure no tiny pieces of shell remain in the soup). Wash out pan and pour strained soup into it. Reheat.

Correct the seasoning with salt, pepper, cayenne pepper. Stir in the cream and brandy, the lobster pieces cut into neat slices, and serve very hot, garnished with minced parsley.

If the lobster is already cooked, remove the meat from the shell and set it aside. Simmer the vegetables in butter in a large saucepan, add stock, shell, bouquet and 4 tablespoons of rice (use 6 or 7 tablespoons if you're short on lobster meat).* Finish as above. This is an excellent soup, which can be adapted to crab, shrimps and prawns. Sometimes a little tomato is added to improve the flavour, when one is relying mainly on shells.

Aragosta Luculliana   (for 4)

This grand recipe has been sent to me from Italy. At least I think it's grand, but I've a suspicion Lucullus would have thought it sadly simple. That Roman gourmet had a series of dining rooms, of increasing splendour. If he ordered dinner for ten friends in, say, the blue room, his slaves knew without further instruction that the meal was to cost £100. Other rooms meant far more. One day Lucullus was, exception-ally, dining at home without guests. The slave asked which room he would like the meal to be served in, expecting a £10 answer. Lucullus named the most expensive room of all.

After that, it may come as a surprise to you that the only ingredients demanded by this recipe are:

2 lobsters, about 2 lbs. each
1–2 dozen oysters
12 tablespoons bread crumbs
milk
8 anchovy fillets (canned)
½ cup butter
mustard powder, cayenne pepper, salt

Split the boiled lobsters in half down the middle. Now ease the flesh, without removing it from the shell, as if you were cutting a grapefruit. (If the lobsters are alive, split them down the middle, dot them with butter and bake in a hot oven at 400°.)

Arrange the raw oysters, removed from their shells, along the cut sides of the lobsters; pour in the oyster juice. Moisten the bread crumbs slightly with a little milk, squeezing out the surplus. Chop the anchovy fillets finely, mix into the bread and put this mixture over the oysters. Melt the butter, season it with mustard, cayenne pepper and salt. Brush this evenly over the bread crumbs. Heat for 10 minutes under the grill, or in a very hot oven, to brown the crumbs and heat the lobster.

NOTE: I suspect this recipe was intended for crawfish (see note, p. 17), which lack the large claws of the lobster. For this reason, I usually remove all the lobster meat from claws and body and throw away the inedible bits. This leaves room in the shells for all or most of the lobster meat; if there is too much keep it for another dish.

Lobster Newberg   (for 4)

This is one of the best of all lobster dishes, expensive, easy to prepare and easy to eat. It's credited to America, and it was first served at Delmonico's restaurant in New York in the early 1890's. But, like *crème vichyssoise glacée*, it was the invention of a French chef,[5] and it's

[5] *Charles Ranhofer, son and grandson of French chefs, according to Lately Thomas in* Delmonico's: A Century of Splendor, *"carried the already preeminent cuisine of Delmonico's to a summit of perfection and kept it there for nearly 34 years."*

in the purest French tradition. The proprietor first called the dish after one of his wealthy clients, Mr. Ben Wenberg, in particular because he'd popularized the use of the chafing dish, i.e., cooking done at the table as in this recipe instead of in the kitchen. Either Mr. Wenberg did not appreciate the delectable compliment, or he fell out with the proprietor for some other reason, because the name was soon altered simply but unrecognizably from lobster Wenberg to lobster Newberg, or Newburg, or Newburgh.

Original style

> 1½–2 cups cooked lobster meat, diced
> 4 tablespoons butter
> ½ cup heavy cream
> ½ cup light cream
> 3 egg yolks
> ½ cup Madeira or sherry
> salt, pepper

Using a chafing dish, or a shallow pan on a table cooker, heat the butter and the heavy cream to just under boiling point. Add the light cream beaten up with the egg yolks. When the sauce is thick (*it must on no account boil once the egg yolks are added*), pour in the Madeira, and stir in the lobster to reheat. Serve with rice.

With boiled lobster

> ingredients as above, plus 4 more tablespoons of butter

Heat lobster with 4 tablespoons of butter in a large pan. Pour in the wine and rapidly boil it down to half; draw the lobster to the side so that it doesn't overcook. Stir in the heavy cream, then the light cream beaten with the egg yolks. Thicken over a low heat. Just before serving add the extra 4 tablespoons of butter cut into little pieces: they should melt into the sauce without cooking, to give it a glaze and extra flavour.

This makes a finer-flavoured dish than the original chafing-dish recipe.

With live lobster

ingredients for boiled lobster, plus ¼ cup brandy

Pound the coral with 4 tablespoons of butter, and set it aside. Cook the lobster, cut in pieces, in 4 tablespoons of butter until they're red. Warm brandy, set it alight and pour over lobster in the pan. When flames have died away, add the Madeira. Finish the sauce as above, adding the coral butter at the end.

Best version of all. Brandy seems to have a special affinity with lobster. This recipe can be used for scallops.

MUSSELS & SCALLOPS

Scallops and mussels offer the best chance these days, the only chance for many of us, of enjoying the true shellfish quality of sweet succulence perfectly combined with salty freshness. A quality, I might say, that vinegar in the English style does nothing to improve.

Mussels, particularly, are a bargain (only the herring gives greater value for money). Scallops cost more—especially the huge ones from the Isle of Man—but they're worth the money, and are more reliable than shop-boiled crab, or shop-boiled lobster, for a special occasion.

Best of all for freshness and sweetness are the tiny mussels one eats in Normandy, often gathered straight from the rocks below the restaurant. Mussels can also be gathered from rocks and wooden posts at the seaside in Britain, but the greatest care is needed to make sure they are far from any source of pollution, such as a sewage outfall. This is so difficult nowadays that one is perhaps wise to stick to fishmongers' mussels, which have spent a few days in cleansing beds before being sold.[1]

[1] *Found in great numbers on both U.S. seacoasts, mussels cling to rocks, wharves, and mud, and are all too frequently, sadly enough, neglected by American cooks. In*

Scallops are not so gratifyingly supine to the holiday-maker's hand. They live out in deep waters, eluding their main enemy, the starfish, with strange flying leaps. Such waterjet-propelled motion must have given Venus a rough ride ashore on *her* scallop shell.[2]

The scallop has another patron as well as Venus, the Apostle St. James the Greater. The shrine at Compostela in northwestern Spain, built over what is claimed to be his body, brought the Holy Land into Europe most conveniently. Medieval pilgrims came in numbers like stars in the Milky Way (which is said to touch the earth at Compostela), wearing St. James's shell on their wide-brimmed hats. No one knows why the scallop became the badge of St. James's pilgrimage, but we've decorated our lives with its elegant shape ever since. We see it everywhere—on doorlights, fountains, silver, furniture—and petrol stations. I hope that a meal of skewered scallops, if not curried scallops, was thrown in with the price those pilgrims paid for their badges, their *coquilles St. Jacques.*

Preparation

Although mussels are best used the day they're bought, they can be kept for a couple of days in a bucket of water with a small handful of salt— preferably sea salt—added. For use later on the same day, persuade your fishmonger to put them straight into a plastic bag and leave them there until required for cleaning. Scrub them under a cold tap, with a nailbrush. Beards and barnacles should be scraped off with a sharp knife. *Any broken mussels, or any that stay open when tapped lightly, should be thrown away.*

To open mussels, put them into a large heavy pan over a moderately hot gas or electric burner. A half-cup of water or wine may be added if demanded by the recipe, but it's not necessary. Put the lid on the pan and leave for 5 minutes, shaking gently once or twice. Remove the opened mussels with a pair of kitchen tongs to a colander, and set over a bowl to drain. *Discard any mussels which obstinately refuse to open.* If the mussel

---

California it is illegal to take them from May until October, but when the season is open, cooks who gather mussels can be well rewarded by preparing them in any of the ways clams and oysters are cooked.

2 Many Americans don't seem to know that scallops are mollusks and belong to the symmetric shells bearing their names. The scallop has only one adductor muscle, proportionally huge, and it is this morsel that is the scallop of the markets. We also have two sizes—increasingly scarce bay scallops that are tiny and delicately flavored, and sea scallops, which are cheaper. Only the white muscle is sold in markets; scallops in their shells go only to those who do their own scallop hunting.

liquor is not required in the recipe, keep it in the refrigerator and use next day for fish soup or a sauce.

NOTE: 2 pounds of mussels are more or less equal to a quart. This is only a rough guide, as the size of mussels makes a difference to the measurement of capacity.

In Britain scallops are usually opened by the fishmonger. If you have to do it, the shells can be prized apart with an oyster knife (I've used a heavy screwdriver in an emergency; wrap your left hand in a cloth). Or put in a very hot oven for a few minutes. Use a knife to lever the shells apart once they've begun to open. Detach the scallops carefully from their shells, discard the black part, rinse the white part and the coral, and pat dry.

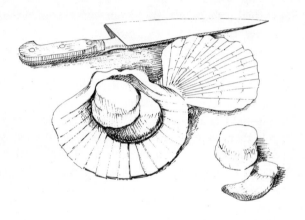

Coquilles St. Jacques à la provençale   (for 4)

The point of this dish is the crisp contrast of fried bread crumbs with garlic and moist sweet scallops. Very appetising. Don't try to do the cooking all in one pan, as the crumbs will soak up juice from the mushrooms and scallops and become soggy.

10 scallops, sliced across the grain
¼ lb. mushrooms, sliced downwards
4 large cloves garlic, chopped
2 tablespoons butter
5 tablespoons olive oil
½ cup white bread crumbs
plenty of chopped parsley
4 lemon quarters

Fry the white parts of the scallops, the mushrooms and the garlic in butter and 2 tablespoons of the olive oil for 4 or 5 minutes. Add coral, if any, and cook a further 3 minutes. Drain off any liquid. At the same time, fry the bread crumbs in another pan in remaining 3 tablespoons olive oil. Stir them around so that they brown evenly. Combine the contents of the two pans just before serving. Stir in chopped parsley. Divide between four small, heated bowls, and put a lemon quarter on top of each one.

Mussel & tomato soup   (for 4)

A soup of Provençal type, which depends for its success on well-flavoured olive oil, enough garlic, and tomatoes of quality. As far as the last ingredient is concerned, better results are obtained from canned tomatoes and a good seasoning of sugar and tomato paste than from the fresh tomatoes normally on sale.

2 lbs. mussels
2 tablespoons olive oil
2 large cloves garlic, crushed
¾ lb. peeled tomatoes,
    or drained canned tomatoes
salt, pepper
sugar and tomato paste
croutons fried in olive oil

Put ¼ inch of water in a large pan and open the mussels in it. Remove them from their shells (which should be thrown away). Strain the mussel liquor into a measuring cup, and add water to bring it up to 4 cups.

Meanwhile put the oil into another pan, add the garlic and tomatoes. Cook for 5 or 10 minutes, pressing them into a rough purée without too many large lumps. Add the 4 cups of mussel liquor and season with salt and pepper. Simmer for 15 minutes, then adjust the seasoning with sugar and tomato paste. Add the mussels to reheat for a few seconds (not for long, or they will turn rubbery), and pour into the soup tureen. Serve with the croutons, added at the last moment and sizzling on top of the soup.

Mussel or scallop chowder   *(for 4)*

Chowder sounds uncompromisingly North American to Britons—Newfoundland chowder, Manhattan chowder, New England chowder. In fact this old one-pot meal of fish, potato, onion and salt pork was taken across the Atlantic by Breton sailors, searching for cod. Like their wives at home they made it in a huge iron *chaudière* (in other words, a hot-pot or cauldron, Anglicized in the eighteenth century to "chowder").[3] Circumstances demanded the substitution of ship's biscuit for potatoes; but once the dish settled down on the eastern seaboard of Nova Scotia and New England, potatoes went back into the pot. In time a new local ingredient, milk, was added to enhance the stew, whereas a Breton cook would have used, and still uses, cider or wine.

I like these satisfying dishes of the pre-oven age. Like Lancashire hot-pot or Irish stew or Welsh cawl, fish chowders are easy to prepare and very easy on cost (what could be cheaper than this recipe?), yet they make the most of the simple ingredients. They have a basic goodness which pleases everyone.

> 2 *lbs. fish bones and trimmings*
> 2½ *cups water*

[3] *Brides leaving their old homes in seagoing New England always took with them a chowder kettle. In fact, a girl who failed to master the art of chowder making limited her chances of getting to the altar at all.*

4 oz. salt pork, or green streaky bacon, diced[4]
1 cup chopped onion
1 tablespoon flour
2 cups scalded milk
salt, cayenne pepper
1 teaspoon sugar
1 lb. potatoes, cubed
2 lbs. mussels or 4–6 sea scallops
chopped parsley
3 tablespoons heavy cream, or 6 tablespoons light cream

Most fishmongers will give you a free handful of fish bones and trimmings, or will charge you at most a few pence for them. Put them into a heavy large pan with 2 cups of water and simmer for 40 minutes without seasoning, while preparing the vegetables. Put salt pork or bacon pieces into a heavy pan on a low heat. When the fat begins to run, put in the onion and brown lightly. Stir in the flour, then, bit by bit, the strained fish stock and hot milk. Add seasoning, sugar and potatoes. Cook until potatoes are just done, but not in the least mushy.

Meanwhile open the mussels in ½ cup water, remove from their shells and keep warm. Strain the mussel liquor into the chowder, correct the seasoning with salt and cayenne pepper, and simmer for a moment or two. Just before serving add the chopped parsley, mussels and cream.

If scallops are used, slice and add to the chowder when the potatoes are almost done. Simmer for five minutes, correct seasoning, add parsley and cream and serve.

Toast or hot water biscuits are usually served with fish chowders.

---

[4] Good English bacon is usually cut from the back and has a much higher proportion of meat to fat. A cheaper cut is called fat or streaky bacon—sometimes known as "cheap streaky" when very fat—and more nearly approximates the average United States bacon. In most of these recipes that simply call for bacon, it is a good idea to use one part American bacon to one part Canadian bacon, which has almost no fat at all. The British rasher or slice is somewhat larger than the American, so a fair equivalent would be one piece of Canadian bacon plus one slice of American. "Green" bacon means fresh or uncured. When you are using American cured bacon as lardons (cut in pieces and added to a dish), it helps to simmer the pieces first in a quart of water for 10 minutes in order to reduce the fat and modify the strong flavor; then rinse, pat dry, and proceed as called for in the recipe.

Mussels on skewers

Here's quite a different combination of mussels and bacon, this time piquant and savoury. It's a good way of using large mussels.

For each person:

> 12 large mussels
> ½ cup water
> 3 rashers fat bacon (see footnote, p. 33)
> 2 teaspoons cream
> 1 teaspoon chopped parsley

for serving: plain boiled rice

Divide bacon into 14 pieces. Steam open the mussels with ½ cup of water in a heavy pan in the usual way. Discard the shells. Beginning and ending with bacon, thread mussels and bacon on two skewers (or one long one). Broil quickly, turning twice, for 5 minutes, catching the juices in the broiling pan. As the bacon browns and crisps at the edges, its fat keeps the mussels nicely basted.

Put the skewers on a bed of rice in a warm oven while making the sauce. Pour the mussel liquor into the juices in the broiling pan. Boil hard to reduce the liquid to a good flavour, and scrape in all the little brown bits and pieces. Add the cream to bind, then season to taste, and add the parsley. Serve separately in a sauce boat.

Alternatively, the skewers can be rolled in beaten egg, then in bread crumbs, and deep-fried. The sauce will then depend solely on the mussel liquor.

This dish is also very good when scallops are used instead of mussels. Slice the white scallops into two pieces (or if you are using small bay scallops, leave whole) and broil 10 minutes, about 4 inches from heat source.

Mussel omelette (for 3)

A cheap, delicious recipe.

1 quart mussels
6 tablespoons butter
3 tablespoons chopped shallots, or mild onion
2 tablespoons chopped parsley
6 eggs, beaten
salt, pepper

Put the mussels into a large pan with just enough water to cover the base. Steam over a good heat, with a lid on the pan, until they open. Remove the mussels from their shells, and keep the liquor for fish soup. Meanwhile lightly sauté the shallots or onion in the butter. When soft, add the mussels and cook for a few moments until the edges just begin to curl up. Mix into the beaten eggs and season. Make 1 large omelette or 3 small two-egg ones.

Mussels at Mesnil-Val (for 4 or 5)

One of the first things we do on arriving in France (and, sadly, one of the last before leaving) is to eat a dish of tiny Normandy mussels. The slow progress through scores of these particularly delectable mollusks is soothing after a long day's drive. Their freshness can be guaranteed as far inland as Évreux, but best of all are the mussels served in small villages on the coast, where they go from beach to table in three or four hours. At Mesnil-Val, the handsome navy-blue appearance of the mussels is set off by a yellow sauce:

1 tablespoon chopped onion
½ small bay leaf
½ cup white wine
2 quarts mussels
3 egg yolks
½ cup cream
8 tablespoons unsalted butter
salt, pepper, lemon juice, parsley

Simmer onion and bay leaf in the wine for 5 minutes. Add the mussels to the pan, and heat until they open. Drain in colander over bowl to catch the liquid and remove one half-shell from each, if they're large. Reduce the liquor by boiling hard to about 1 cup, or a little less.

Beat egg yolks and cream together in a fairly large bowl (or the top half of a double boiler). Pour in the strained mussel liquor. Set the bowl over a larger pan of simmering water, and stir gently but steadily. Add the butter in small knobs one by one. Don't hurry this part of the cooking, or the sauce will turn lumpy. Don't overheat the sauce either, or it will curdle. This may sound difficult, but it's not; it's only a question of patience. Season when the sauce is the consistency of thickish custard, with lemon juice, salt and pepper. Quickly transfer the mussels to a hot serving bowl from their colander, and pour the sauce over them. Sprinkle well with chopped parsley. Serve with plenty of good bread.

Mouclade d'Esnandes   (for 4)

This recipe shows how mussels are cooked on the Atlantic coast of France around La Rochelle. Many people there (including the inhabitants of Esnandes) work in the mussel fisheries. Miles and miles of wooden stakes, or *bouchots*, are driven into the sea bed where the water is shallow, and on these stakes mussels increase and grow fat. At low tide men come out in flat-bottomed boats to remove them for the market, and for their own *mouclade*, a version of *moules marinières* which usually includes white wine and cream. Don't omit the aniseed flavouring, which goes so well with fish.

2 quarts mussels
½ cup dry white wine
¾ cup finely chopped shallots or mild onion
2 large cloves garlic
3 tablespoons butter
1 tablespoon flour
1½ cups milk
1 star anise or aniseed to taste
2 egg yolks
generous tablespoon heavy cream
salt, pepper

Cook the mussels in the wine until they open. Drain in colander, conserving the liquid. Discard one half-shell from each, and keep warm. Heat shallots and garlic in the butter meanwhile, very gently, for 20 minutes to half an hour. Stir in the flour, strained mussel liquor, milk and the star anise or aniseed to taste (start with a pinch, then add more). Boil down a little. Beat egg yolks with heavy cream, and add to the sauce. Cook without boiling, until the sauce thickens. Correct the seasoning. Put the mussels into a soup bowl, and pour the very hot sauce over them.

Curried scallops   (for 4)

This delicious dish has no connection at all with Indian cooking. Curry powder is used as a convenient spice blend, to flavour a cream sauce in the best gastronomical tradition of France. Denmark is another country where curry powder is used in this way, again not to imitate Indian cooking: sometimes, in fact very often, it's used to flavour mayonnaise. An idea to be adopted for shellfish salads.

12 scallops
½ cup dry white wine
bouquet garni
¼ cup butter
¼ teaspoon curry powder

1 cup heavy cream
salt, pepper
2 egg yolks
2 tablespoons light cream or half-and-half

for serving: plain boiled rice

Simmer the white parts of the scallops, sliced across into two circles, in the wine flavoured with the bouquet garni. Remove and drain after 4 or 5 minutes, then sauté gently in the butter and curry powder for 4 minutes. Remove the scallops to a warm dish. Pour the wine into the butter, and boil hard to reduce. Stir in the heavy cream, and season well. Boil hard again for about 2 minutes. Beat up the egg yolks with the light cream, and amalgamate carefully with the sauce. Cook gently for a further 2 minutes, having added the scallops to reheat, *but without boiling,* or the egg yolks will curdle.

Serve with plain boiled rice.

TROUT

A good trout, rainbow or native brown trout, is one that hasn't come all flaccid out of a tank. Or frozen out of a commercial freezer. In restaurants—unless the restaurateur keeps live trout in fresh water or gets his trout straight from river or lake, and most can't—the only trout worth eating and paying for is a smoked one.

The best trout of all would be one that had jumped straight from the stream or lake or reservoir into the pan, ready to be eaten within minutes of being caught. But trout caught today should still be delicious if eaten within 24 hours—for breakfast tomorrow or even for supper.

From many people's point of view, this may seem so restrictive that there's no point in reading this bit of the book at all. But in fact more and more fresh trout are being caught by more and more people, not rich men with expensive fishing rights, but ordinary fishermen, particularly in the Midlands, who have access to the big reservoirs.[1] Needing

[1] Dams and reservoirs constructed in various parts of the U.S. since World War II are also stocked with game fish, and the number of ordinary men who set out to catch them is increasing as it is in the United Kingdom.

more water, we Britons are likely to be cooking more trout, as a bonus. And not only more, but bigger ones as well.

Trout being such a delicately flavoured fish, it follows that accompaniments should be delicate too, and of the first quality. They should be subservient, or at the most complementary, to the flavour of the fish. Avoid colourful little mounds of this and that, and serve the trout straight. As you will see from the recipes below for *truite à la meunière* and *truite au bleu*, butter is all that's required for really fresh fish. Almonds, or a few boiled new potatoes, belong to slightly less fresh fish that begin to need some help. Surplus trout can either be potted or deep-frozen, and, eventually, baked. There is an excellent cream, butter and herb sauce suitable for trout on page 211, but as a change try the less usual walnut sauce of Escoffier's given below.

NOTE: All the recipes following may be used, without adaptation, for grayling [*related to trout and more common in Europe than in the U.S.; here three slightly different types are Alaska grayling, Montana grayling and Michigan grayling*].

Truite à la meunière

I had always pictured a young miller's wife cooking trout from her husband's mill pool in this way. But it seems that the real story was quite different. At Royat, near Clermont-Ferrand in the Auvergne, a town of many streams, there is an old inn called La Belle Meunière. Its speciality used to be—perhaps still is—fresh trout, floured and fried in butter. One day Napoleon stopped there. He ate his trout with enthusiasm, declaring that this way of cooking fish should be called *à la Belle Meunière* (the "belle" has, most unfairly, been dropped with time).

It sounds to me like the apocryphal tale of Sir Loin, but perhaps it is true. I would like to think so. It's certainly true that Napoleon liked simple food of high quality. He would have enjoyed the crisp golden skin of the trout à la meunière, which sets off so well the light flavour of the flesh.

4 trout, about 8 oz. each
10 tablespoons [1¼ sticks] butter

milk
seasoned flour
pepper
lemon quarters

First clarify 6 tablespoons of the butter by bringing it to the boil in a small pan. It will separate into white froth and clear yellow oil. Strain through layers of cheesecloth or a muslin-lined strainer, directly into the frying pan. The froth will be caught in the muslin, and there will be enough clarified butter for frying the fish. This process is most important and very simple.[2] Trout or any other fish fried in unclarified butter stick to the pan, with the result that their skin (and sometimes their flesh) is broken and spoilt.

Rinse the trout quickly, wipe them dry and dip each one in milk. Turn them over firmly in the flour, while the frying pan is heating up. Shake off the surplus flour and slide them straightaway into the hot butter. Fry at a moderate heat for 5 minutes on each side, for half-pound fish. Larger fish will take longer, and the heat should be reduced after the first 2 minutes so that the fat does not blacken. The result should be golden brown fish.

Meanwhile, in a separate frying pan, bring the remaining 4 tablespoons of butter to the boil. Cook until brown, a nice golden brown, not a burnt semiblack. Put the trout on a hot serving dish, sprinkle with a seasoning of pepper, and pour over the foaming butter. Arrange the lemon quarters around the fish and rush to the table. Like a soufflé, *truite à la meunière* should not be kept waiting.

Trout with almonds

This is not entirely a dish to be despised, especially for trout eaten the day after they're caught. The flavour of almonds is welcome without being too obtrusive; their milky, mealy texture going well with firm-fleshed but delicate fish like trout and sole.

Ingredients are the same as for *truite à la meunière*, plus 1 tablespoon of almonds, blanched and split, for each fish.

[2] Or follow directions for clarified butter in footnote, p. 11.

A word about the almonds. It is not worth buying ready-blanched and split ones. Half their flavour seems to have disappeared with their skins. Buy ones with the skins still on, put them in a pan of water and bring to the boil. Drain and you'll find that the skins slip off easily. Use a sharp knife to split the almonds into halves.

Follow the method for *truite à la meunière*, but when the four tablespoons of butter are put into a separate frying pan, put in the almonds as well. By the time the butter is golden brown, the almonds will be slightly browned too.

NOTE: *Sole à la meunière* and sole with almonds are cooked in exactly the same way, except that sole should first be skinned. The fishmonger will do this for you, but if he hasn't, ease off a corner of skin at the tail end and pull. Do the same thing with the other side.

Baked trout

This excellent method of baking trout (or other whole fish such as red mullet, bass, sea bream, etc.)[3] allows none of the flavour to escape. For this reason it's the best way to cook trout from the freezer.

Incidentally, why do Britons import frozen trout from Japan? Could we not produce our own?[4] There must be a fortune in it, for some enterprising native of our islands.

> 4 trout, about 8 oz. each
> 1 small onion, finely chopped
> 1 cup bread crumbs
> ¼ lb. mushrooms, roughly chopped
> 1 lemon, grated rind & juice
> 1 heaping tablespoon chopped parsley
> salt, pepper, plenty of butter

[3] Or substitute yellow perch, calico bass, crappies, or other small fish; fillets also can be baked this way, of course.

[4] Frozen fish are becoming more and more popular and are for sale in greater variety as the U.S. frozen food industry develops. It is imperative, however, to be able to trust your supplier: no fish can survive freezing, thawing, and refreezing.

Sauté the onion gently in ¼ cup butter over a low heat. In 10 minutes it will be golden butter coloured, not brown. Mix in a bowl with bread crumbs, mushrooms, parsley and grated lemon rind. Season well with salt, pepper and lemon juice.

Cut pieces of foil about 12 inches square. In the centre of each spread a 5-inch line of butter—allow a generous tablespoon for each trout. Put the stuffing on top of the butter, dividing it among the four squares, and the trout on top of the stuffing. Twist the edges of the foil to form sealed, oblong, baggy packages. Place them on a baking sheet and put into a 350° oven, for about 30 minutes.

This method can be adapted for larger trout. A fish 2–4 pounds will take 1–1½ hours to cook.

Jellied trout

8 ½-lb. trout
1½ cups water
½ cup dry white wine
1 tablespoon wine vinegar
1 small onion, sliced
½ bay leaf
2 sprigs each parsley and thyme (or ½ teaspoon dried thyme)
scant ½ teaspoon salt
6 peppercorns

Bring to the boil in a covered pan the water, wine and seasonings and simmer for 30 minutes. Leave to cool. Place the 8 trout close together in a pan or oval casserole. Strain over them the water and wine mixture. Bring very slowly to the boil, taking about 10 minutes, either on top of the stove or in a medium oven. When the liquid boils, remove the pan from the heat and leave in a cool place. The poached trout will be firm but cooked, and of an excellent flavour. (The same method can be used for large fish; as they need more liquid to cover them, they take longer to come to the boil and longer to cool—it even works for salmon.)

When the trout are cold, place them in an oval or oblong serving dish. Boil the cooking liquor down by half, cool again, and pour over the fish.

It will set to a delicious jelly. Mayonnaise or horseradish-flavoured cream can be served with the trout, but this is not necessary. Chill the trout before serving.

Truite au bleu

If you can bring trout home alive, this is the best way of cooking them. Bring to the boil 4 cups of salted water, with 3 tablespoons of wine vinegar. Pick the trout from their bucket of water one by one, kill them humanely by banging their heads smartly on the table, and clean them quickly. *Do not rinse them.* If you do, they will fail to turn the required bluish-grey. Slip them into the boiling water, and simmer for 10 minutes. Serve with melted butter.

If you wish to eat the trout cold simmer them for 3 or 4 minutes only and leave to cool in the cooking liquid. Serve with homemade mayonnaise, or whipped cream flavoured with lemon juice and chopped parsley.

Potted trout

Any cooked, leftover trout can be broken into pieces of about ¼ inch (remove all skin and bone first). Mix with an equal weight of cool, melted butter, seasoned to taste with mace and nutmeg. Put into small pots. When firm, cover with a ¼-inch layer of clarified butter (see *truite à la meunière*). Cover with foil and store in the refrigerator.

Horseradish & walnut sauce

This unusually delicious sauce may be eaten with salmon as well as with trout. It comes from Escoffier's *Ma Cuisine,* and the only alteration I have made is to halve the quantities. There will still be plenty for six people.

> ½ cup walnuts, shelled
> 1 tablespoon grated horseradish
> pinch salt
> 1 teaspoon sugar
> 1 tablespoon white bread crumbs
> ½ cup heavy cream
> 1 teaspoon wine vinegar or lemon juice

Pour boiling water over the walnuts and leave them for a moment or two. You will then be able to remove their fine skins, which can add a bitter taste to this sauce. Chop the nuts finely, then mix with the rest of the ingredients. Add the vinegar or lemon juice gradually—the whole teaspoon may not be to your taste, or you may like to add a little more.

Meat & Game

MEAT PIES

1. RAISED PIES

Most of us have a weakness for meat pies. Or should I say for a Platonic ideal of meat pies? It's a weakness that has, surprisingly, stood firm despite some of the works of the assembly line, with their yellow-and-white cylinders of denatured egg piercing a mass of ill-seasoned pork. In our optimism (or for convenience) we Britons still buy meat pies. And of course make them. One way and another, we eat them by the million.

What is a meat pie? A hash of meat enclosed in pastry is the obvious answer. But really the matter's more complex. A pie, particularly a double-crust or raised pie, is an ingenious device whereby bird or beast (or both) develops the finest flavour possible by being cooked in its own juices. (Lidded casseroles started as a labour-saving substitute for pastry cases; many of them were, and some even nowadays are, made to imitate a raised pie.)[1]

---

[1] The art of "raising" pie crusts, dating back at least to the sixteenth century, has become outmoded in the U.S. Good cooks used to mix small amounts of lard and

Some experts may claim that the crust is unimportant once the pie is cooked, that it should be pushed to the side of the plate, but I can't agree. The right crust, succulent and crisp, is an important contribution to the success of any pie. Whether hot or cold, it sets off the meat perfectly.

The flexibility of the meat pie is another reason for its long popularity. The filling may be simply chopped pork, with a seasoning of herbs and spices, and perhaps an embellishment of hard-boiled eggs, pieces of rabbit, a few mushrooms, whatever family and local circumstances may provide. On the other hand elaborate combinations of meat and game have delighted the rich for nearly two millennia. The Roman emperor Verus, co-emperor with Marcus Aurelius, himself concocted an "amalgamation of sow's flank, pheasant, peacock, spiced ham, and wild boar's flesh . . . within the thick casing of a laboriously worked crust."

In the eighteenth century special poultry and game pies were sent to London from Yorkshire for Christmas feasting. Their pastry walls, made extra thick to withstand the jolting miles, contained a turkey stuffed with a goose, a chicken, a partridge and a pigeon, all boned and one inside the other, Russian doll fashion. The cavities round this innocent-looking creature were filled with hare, woodcock, and wild fowl, plus four pounds of butter.

We don't make such pies these days: they'd cost too much. They're not to modern taste. But when I think of their descendants, the wonderful game pies of Britain and France, I conclude that north of the Alps we've been able to bring such things to near perfection. Pies need plenty of fat in their filling: we've bred the pigs. Pies need a good crust: we've bred the pastry cooks. At this standard—let's forget the plastic and pork pies—we have achieved a certain grandeur, however elegiac and transitory that grandeur may be. "Graceful monuments, delicious fortresses, seductive ramparts, which as soon as they are on all sides attacked," wrote one great chef of the last century, "totter, crumble, and no longer present anything but glorious and ephemeral ruins, like every work of man—all pass away whether they be temples, columns, pyramids or pies."

---

boiling water with a pound of flour and, working quickly, roll out this dough while still hot and shape it into a high-walled container in which to put a meat filling. Flexible when hot, the crust hardens and retains the shape in which it was molded; a layer of additional dough is pinched on to the side walls to make the top and is ornamented with remaining bits of dough shaped like leaves, etc.

Pastry for hot-water crust
or raised pies

3½ cups (1 lb.) all-purpose flour
1 teaspoon salt
¾ cup water
¾ cup lard
beaten egg

optional: 1 scant tablespoon confectioners' sugar

Sift flour, salt and sugar if used (it gives a richness to the pastry), into a bowl. Make a well in the middle. Bring water and lard to the boil and pour into the well immediately, bringing in the flour with a wooden spoon until the dough forms a smooth ball.* Cover and leave in a warm place for the pastry, which has been rolled out, as a lid. Trim and knock up[2] the edges, a quarter for the pie lid and put the rest into a greased hinged pie mould of 4-cup capacity (or a cake tin with a removable base). Shape the dough up the sides with light firm movements, taking care to leave no cracks through which the pie juices will be able to escape. If the pastry slides down the mould, it's still a little too hot: leave it for a while, then start again.

Pack the filling gently into the corners and undulations of the pastry-lined mould, and mound it up nicely at the top to support the lid. Moisten the pastry rim with water or beaten egg, and lay on the reserved pastry, which has been rolled out, as a lid. Trim and knock up[2] the edges, make a hole in the centre and decorate with pastry leaves and roses, or whatever your fancy dictates. Cut a strip of stiff paper or use a small piece of card (a "Bristol" to the French) to roll up and push into the hole: this keeps it open during the cooking. Brush lid and decorations with beaten egg.

* As different brands of flour absorb different quantities of water, it may be necessary to add a little more flour or a little more very hot water to produce a firm but pliable consistency.

2 "Knock up" is the common British term for crimping the edge of a pie crust, making an ornamental edge by pushing up the rim with one's fingers and tapping the edge all around with the flat side of a knife. A Scotswoman transplanted to America points out how nostalgic the term is because she remembers as a child the happy sound coming from the kitchen of the knife knocking against the pie plate, indicating pie for supper.

A wooden pie mould, or a 2-pound jam jar, may be used instead of a hinged pie tin or cake tin. In this case the pastry must be shaped or "raised" on the outside. Flour the wooden mould very well before you start, or you won't be able to remove it from the pastry when it's cool. Tie a piece of thick paper (e.g., brown paper) round the warm raised pastry, which has been rolled out, as a lid. Trim and knock up[2] the edges, the wooden mould but not the paper, which should remain in place until the pie has been baked and has cooled down. Now pack the filling in gently and cover with the pastry lid. This is the way pies were and are still made in parts of the Midlands and East Anglia, but it's undeniably trickier than using a hinged pie mould, which can be bought from any good kitchen supplier.

Bake at 425° for 20 minutes, then at 325°–350° for 1½–2 hours. Test with skewer. Let the pie cool a little, remove the mould, brush sides with beaten egg and return the pie to the oven to brown (protect lid with brown paper). Pour in the runny but cool jellied stock (see p. 54) through a funnel and the hole in the middle—first removing the Bristol—and leave overnight before eating.

Making raised pies with wooden pie moulds

Raised pork pie

Unless you're a Queen's subject lucky enough to live within the delivery area of the Langroyd Pie Company, near Oakham in Rutland, who make the best pork pies I have ever eaten, it's a good idea to make your own. Anybody who has ever watched the pastry being rolled, and rerolled, and rerolled, and rerolled (and picked up off the floor and rerolled) in a greying blanket all day in a pie factory, will know what I mean.

In fact making a pork pie is not difficult. It takes time rather than any special skill. You need to remember three things: about a third of the meat must be fat to keep the filling and crust succulent; the filling must be well seasoned with herbs, spices and perhaps a dash of anchovy paste as in the Melton Mowbray area (where the local pies have found world renown); the better the pork you use, the better the pie will be—always include some bacon to improve the flavour, and to give the filling an appetising pink tinge from the saltpeter used in bacon curing.

hot-water crust as above

jelly: bones from pork, plus veal knuckle or 2 pig's trotters [feet]
  1 large carrot, sliced
  1 medium onion stuck with 2 cloves
  bouquet garni
  12 peppercorns

filling: 2 lbs. boned shoulder, throat or loin of pork, in a proportion
    of 1 part fat to 2 parts lean
  ½ lb. very thinly cut rashers of green bacon (see footnote,
    p. 33)
  1 teaspoon chopped sage
  ½ teaspoon each nutmeg, cinnamon, ground cloves, allspice
  salt, freshly ground black pepper
  1 teaspoon anchovy paste, or to taste

Make the jelly first. Put all ingredients into a large pan and fill with water to within an inch of the top. Simmer for 3–5 hours, adding no salt. Strain off the stock into a clean pan, and boil it down hard to about 1½ cups. Season with salt, and more pepper if necessary, and leave to cool. This jelly can be made a day in advance of the pie.

Next make the filling. Chop the pork, or put it through the coarse blade of the grinder. Then grind half of it finely with 2 rashers of bacon. Mix all the pork well together; add the seasonings and anchovy paste. Fry a small piece of this mixture to test the flavour, remembering that dishes to be eaten cold always need a stronger seasoning than dishes to be eaten hot.

Make the hot-water crust, and line the mould as described above. Lay the remaining rashers of bacon over the bottom and lower sides to form an inner lining. Pack in the filling and finish in the usual way (see p. 51). If the jelly has set firm, it should be melted to a state of cool runniness before being poured into a hot pie. Pour in a little of this jellied stock at a time, through the centre hole, using a kitchen funnel. Do this immediately the pie comes out of the oven, so that the stock sinks into the hot filling. Don't hurry this process, or you will flood the outer crust of the pie. The point of the jelly, flavour apart, is to fill the gap left by meat shrinkage. This will vary from one time to another, and is impossible to predict accurately, but 1½ cups of jellied stock will be more than enough. Any left over can be used for soups, sauces, and for *oeufs en gelée*, etc.

Game, chicken or rabbit pie

Follow the method in the preceding recipe, noting that jelly should be made first from the bones of the game, and make the filling of:

½ lb. hard back pork fat [fatback]
½ lb. lean pork
½ lb. thin rashers bacon (see footnote, p. 33)
½ teaspoon each nutmeg, cinnamon, ground cloves
salt, freshly ground black pepper
1 lb. game, chicken or rabbit, cut from the bone
    or 2 cups lightly packed
1 heaping tablespoon chopped parsley
3 tablespoons brandy or sherry,
    or 5 tablespoons dry white wine
½ teaspoon anchovy paste (for chicken and rabbit only)

Grind fat and lean pork together finely with 2 rashers of bacon (use the rest for lining the pastry). Season with spices, salt and pepper. Cut the game, chicken or rabbit into nice pieces, not too large (mince the trimmings and mix into the pork mixture); leave for 2 hours in a dish with the brandy or wine, and some salt and pepper and anchovy paste, if it is being used. When filling the pie, put some of the pork in first, then a layer of game pieces, then some more pork and some more game, finishing with a layer of pork. The wine should be included.

NOTE: If venison is used, port may be substituted for the brandy—or one could use them both, about ½ cup port and 1 tablespoon of brandy; the same applies to hare.

Cheshire pork & apple pie

This pork and apple pipe is at least 200 years old (Hannah Glasse gives it in her *Art of Cookery*, first edition 1747), and probably very much older than that. When pigs were killed in the autumn on Cheshire farms—and on Leicestershire farms, too—the scraps left over from preparing hams, sausages, brawn [headcheese], etc., were used up in this kind of pie. It might be made of short or hot-water pastry. The apples were usually windfalls from the dessert pippin trees (if they were sour, the deficiency was made up with more sugar). In other words, the recipe was adjusted to circumstances.

hot-water crust or short pastry, made with 1 lb. flour

filling: 1 lb. lean & 1 lb. fat pork
   or 1¼ lb. lean & ¾ lb. fat
   1½ lbs. Cox's Orange Pippins [i.e., firm crisp apples—the kind you like to eat]
   1 cup chopped onion
   brown sugar, salt, pepper, nutmeg (or sage)
   4 tablespoons butter
   ½ cup white wine, cider or light ale

optional: 2–3 rashers bacon (see footnote, p. 33)

Grind the pork coarsely (2 or 3 rashers of bacon can be included as well), and chop the onion finely. Mix them together and season well with salt, pepper and grated nutmeg. Peel, core and slice the apples; season them with sugar and nutmeg. Put a layer of pork into the pastry-lined mould, then apples, then pork, apples and pork. Dot with butter on top, pour on the wine, cider or ale. Finish in the usual way. Bake at 375° for 1¼ hours. Eat hot or cold. Sage can be used instead of nutmeg.

2. SHORTCRUST PIES

Shortcrust meat pies may not have the castellated grandeur of the chef's raised pie—the curves, the flutings, the cornice, the roses, diamonds, circles and leaves—but they're the pies that people have loved. They belong to family life, to that stage of general civilized prosperity when home cooking becomes something more than handfuls of this and that, thrown into a pot over the fire. Their success depends on a certain skill, just enough to be both challenge and pleasure. Few moments in a cook's life can be more agreeable than cutting the first wedge from a beefsteak and kidney pie (particularly if it contains oysters)—the wonderful smell, the looks of anticipation around the table, the air of restlessness until the eating may begin are the rewards of this skill.

Although these pies belong mainly to the eighteenth and nineteenth centuries, to the kitchens of farm and middle-class home, some of them are relics of a much older time. (And one, the Priddy oggy—which takes its name from a Somerset village—is a recent invention of style, in the Cornish pasty or turnover tradition.)

Ascribed now to different parts of the country, they were once eaten by everyone. Rabbit and oyster pies, for instance, are sometimes attributed to Shropshire, to Scotland, to the Kingdom of Fife, but when rabbits and oysters were abundant, the food of the poor, such pies were made everywhere. Sweetmeat mixtures surviving in the regional cookery of Pembrokeshire and northwest England were once a nationwide solution to the problem of meat that was just beginning to go off. When lamb or beef in this condition was chopped small, and dowsed in sugar, alcohol, raisins, prunes and currants, it was absorbed into stronger flavours and need not be wasted (modern mincemeats, with beef suet, are their descendants).

Of all these shortcrust pies, the masterpiece is, I think, the beefsteak, kidney and oyster pie (with Devonshire squab pie a close second). The recipe is based on one by Francatelli, Queen Victoria's French chef. He increased the flavour of our traditional recipe by browning the meat first in fat, and thickening the sauce with a roux (earlier nineteenth-century English cooks like Mrs. Isabella Beeton and Eliza Acton just floured the meat before putting it into the pie dish and adding water).

Shortcrust pastry

1 lb. (3½ cups) plain [all-purpose] flour
½ teaspoon salt
½ cup butter
1 cup lard[3]
cold water
1 egg, beaten

optional: 2 scant tablespoons confectioners' sugar

Sift flour, sugar and salt into a bowl. Rub in the lard until the mixture is crumbly. Using as little water as possible, mix to a firm dough. Leave in a cool place for an hour at least. Roll out, and line a greased loaf tin, or pie dish of about 4 cups capacity. Pack in the filling, mounding it up so that the lid will be nicely shaped, and moisten the rim of pastry. Lay on the pastry lid. Knock up the edges and make a central hole for the steam to escape (keep it open with a rolled card, or Bristol, see p. 51). Decorate with leaves and a rose (a roll of pastry rolled up, then pinched together at one side so that the other opens into a flower shape). Brush with beaten egg and bake at 300–350° for 45 minutes to 2 hours, depending on the filling.

NOTE: For single-crust pies, such as the steak and kidney and oyster pie that follows, use half the quantities given above.

---

[3] *Vegetable shortening may be used but many of us, like Mrs. Grigson, prefer the flavor of old-fashioned lard—not always so easy to find anymore in some U.S. supermarkets.*

Beefsteak, kidney & oyster pie   (for 6)

An interesting thing about Roman cookery is the ubiquity in recipes, both sweet and savoury, of a substance known as *garum* or *liquamen*. It was the monosodium glutamate of ancient times, a taste-sharpener invented by the Greeks, but developed by the Romans to the point of being produced in factories and sold in trademarked containers. The basis of this relish and its variants was the fermented liquor of salted-down fish entrails. Anchovies were used, so were mackerel and tunny, and even, in one luxurious recipe, the prized liver of red mullet.

Disgusting, you may say. But was it? I think that *liquamen* served the Romans better than monosodium glutamate serves us (it can cause head-aches when overemployed in restaurants to conceal the lack of freshness and flavour in the food). Think of beefsteak, chicken or rabbit pie, all improved by oysters until the middle of the nineteenth century, when their rising price put them out of the seasoning category. Think of anchovy paste used in meat pâtés, and in pork pies around Melton Mowbray in central England. These fishy additives lose identity in such dishes, giving up individual flavour to increase the general richness.

> shortcrust pastry as above, half quantity
> 12–18 oysters
>
> filling: 1½–2 lbs. chuck steak
> ½–¾ lb. beef kidney
> 2 tablespoons butter
> ¾ cup chopped onion
> 1 heaping tablespoon flour
> ½ lb. mushrooms, sliced
> beef stock
> Harvey's, Worcester or soy sauce
> salt, freshly ground black pepper

First open the oysters, taking the precaution of wrapping your left hand in a tea towel. Put them with their liquor into a basin. Then cut the steak into cubes and the kidney into chunky slices, discarding all fat and skin. Season the meat with salt and pepper, and brown quickly in butter with the onion. Stir in the flour and cook for a moment or two until it has taken up the fat. Add the oysters and their liquor and the mushrooms, and enough stock until the consistency of the sauce is like thick cream (the mushrooms and meat will exude a certain amount of juice, bringing the sauce to a thinner consistency). Season with salt, pepper and a dash of Harvey's, Worcester or soy sauce. Transfer to a 2–2½-pint pie dish. Roll out the pastry. Cut a strip to lay around the rim and a piece the size of the pie dish to serve as a lid. Moisten the rim piece after setting it in place, then lay on the lid. Finish in the usual way for shortcrust pies, baking for 2½ hours at 300–325°. Protect the crust with thick paper as it browns.

Alternatively the filling can be precooked for an hour, in a covered casserole, and allowed to cool a little—or completely, overnight. Transfer to the pie dish, cover with pastry and bake for 30 minutes at 400–425°. The first method is better from the point of view of flavour, I think, but the second may suit your convenience, or your stove, better. It also gives you a more exact control over the cooking meat—beef can vary a great deal in toughness, so the time required in the oven can vary.

Rabbit and some fat bacon, cut in pieces, may be substituted for steak and kidney (this used to be done in Shropshire, and is still done in Scotland, I believe). A longer cooking time will be required if the rabbit is mature; less time if it is very young and tender.

Easter pie from Berry   (for 6)

I remember once in Paris buying a wedge from a steaming wheel of pie labelled Gâteau Berrichonne. It was obviously just sausage meat in pastry, but it was cheap and we were hard up. Wandering into the Palais Royal nearby to see where Colette had lived, we started chewing unenthusiastically. We took time to appreciate how delicious that pie was. Ever since, I've had much respect for food from Berry, a province unharmed by too many visitors in spite of the reputation of George Sand, Alain-Fournier and Bourges Cathedral—and of the flinty wines of Sancerre.

The "Easter" part of the title is not obligatory—just part of the Easter egg tradition.

> shortcrust pastry, made with 1 lb. (3½ cups) flour (p. 57)

filling: 1½ lbs. pork from throat, about ⅔ lean to ⅓ fat
> 3 rashers unsmoked bacon (see footnote, p. 33)
> large clove garlic, minced or mashed
> 2 tablespoons chopped parsley
> 1 tablespoon chopped chives
> 1 teaspoon salt
> plenty of black pepper
> ¼ teaspoon each nutmeg, cinnamon, ginger & cloves
>   (or more, according to taste)
> 4 oz. mushrooms, chopped
> 6 hard-boiled eggs
> 1 egg, beaten
>   or light cream

Roll out the pastry into a rectangle a little longer than a baking sheet, but about the same width. Line a baking sheet with foil and grease it well. Cut the pastry to fit inside it, keeping the trimmings (to be used for the lid).

Now make the filling: grind pork and bacon coarsely, then grind half of it again finely. Mix and season well with garlic, herbs and spices.

Lay half this sausage meat on the pastry in a rectangle, leaving a clear 2–3-inch margin all the way round. Spread the mushrooms evenly over the meat. Cut the eggs in half and place the halves, cut side down, on top of the mushrooms to make a double row of little white domes. Tuck the remaining sausage meat in between the eggs and over the top, so that they are completely enclosed.

Nick triangles from the corners of the pastry margin to the filling, and moisten the cut edges so that you can bring them up together to make a box which encloses the sausage meat, etc. Press them firmly. Roll out all the pastry trimmings and cut an oblong lid to cover the pastry. Moisten the edges of the lid and invert it over the pie. Press the lid edges together with the box edges, making scallops with your fingers. Cut some pastry leaves and arrange in two parallel rows the length of the lid, and make some decorative slashes in the middle to let the steam escape. Brush the whole thing over with beaten egg (or light cream), and bake for 1¼ hours at 375°.

Eat cold or just warm, with a green salad.

Priddy oggies (to make 8)

The other recipes in this chapter are old, genuine antiques mostly, from well before 1820 in origin at least, even if more recent adjustments have been made to fit the recipe to life today. Here's the modern upstart referred to above—a delicious pasty with no ancestors at all, invented by Mr. Paul Leyton for the Miner's Arms, his crossroads restaurant near Priddy in Somerset. He uses local Cheddar,[4] local pork tenderloin, and his own smoked pork. The shape of it is based on the Cornish oggy or pasty, that convenient arrangement which enabled a miner —or a schoolboy—to take his lunch to work in his pocket. When, through poverty resulting from the decay of the tin mines, some or most of the original steak filling was replaced by potatoes, the Cornish pasty was often known as a tiddy oggy, tiddy being the local name for a potato. So by assonance and analogy, Mr. Leyton found a name for his invention. (If you're feeling lazy, he will supply them in special containers for storage in the freezer.)

cheese pastry: 2 cups plain [all-purpose] flour
2 tablespoons butter
2 tablespoons lard (or vegetable shortening)
1 small egg yolk
½ cup (not packed) freshly grated mature Cheddar
  or ¼ cup Parmesan, ¼ cup less-mature Cheddar
2½ tablespoons water
pinch salt

[4] Indeed, the village for which the cheese was named, after its recipe was perfected by a local farmer named Joseph Harding, is scarcely five miles from the Leytons' inn.

    meat: 1 pork tenderloin (fillet), about 1¼ lbs.
          2 generous oz. very thinly sliced smoked pork, smoked
            bacon [see footnote, p. 33] or Bayonne ham

 stuffing: 1 large egg
           ½ cup freshly grated mature Cheddar
             or ¼ cup Parmesan, ¼ cup mild Cheddar
           sprig parsley, chopped
           good pinch salt
           8 drops Tabasco
             or cayenne, or freshly ground black pepper

Make the pastry first. Mix all the pastry ingredients, *except the flour*, in a bowl. It helps to warm the butter and lard slightly. Cool the mixture in the refrigerator until firm. Sift the flour, and rub the cooled mixture in roughly. Take about one-quarter of this crumbly pastry and roll it two or three times into a half-inch slab. Repeat, placing each slab upon the other: moisten the top of the pile before putting another slab of pastry on it. Press down firmly with a knife and divide the dough into several lumps. Repeat the rolling process twice more. Leave 30 minutes in a cold place. Cut into eight pieces. Squeeze each one into a sausage shape, and roll out to measure 4 by 6 inches. Leave to rest for an hour.

Trim tenderloin of fat and skin. Slice it in half lengthways and pound gently until pieces are ¼ to ⅜ inch thick. Cut the smoked pork, ham or bacon into 8 strips.

Make the cheese stuffing. Beat the egg, and put half of it aside. Mix in the cheese, parsley, salt and Tabasco. Spread evenly over the two cut sides of the tenderloin. Roll each piece up, press down firmly, and leave in the freezer department of refrigerator to harden.

To assemble the oggies, cut each roll of tenderloin into four pieces. Wrap them round with a strip of smoked pork, ham or bacon. Lay each little parcel in the middle of a piece of pastry, which should be moistened round the edge with milk. Bring the pastry up and over the pork, pressing the two edges together in a scalloped crest, like a meat turnover or Cornish pasty. Press down to flatten the base, and trim where necessary. Brush over with the rest of the beaten egg and bake for 10 minutes at 350–375°, until the pastry begins to brown. Finish in deep fat; or fry in lard at 360–370°, turning the oggies over until they are golden brown. Before cooking they can be stored in a refrigerator for three days, or in a freezer for three months. In the latter case, give them 15–20 minutes in the oven before frying.

Sweet lamb pie, from northwest England

This recipe is based on one I heard during the war, when we were living at Casterton, in Westmorland. Our landlady was a farmer's daughter, and I remember her nostalgia when she described the pie she used to make, I think at Easter, before rationing, before the war. I remember, too, my childish, town-bred disgust at the ingredients she listed —fat and lean mutton or lamb, sugar, currants. . . . Similar recipes are found in Cumberland, and in Wales as well, where at Templeton Fair, in November, they sell Katt pies.[5] These are small raised pies, filled with layers of minced Welsh mutton, brown sugar and currants—in equal quantities.

In fact such recipes belong to the days when everybody made sweet meat pies. In two fifteenth-century cookery books there is hardly a meat pie recipe that does not contain sugar, raisins and dates, not to mention prunes and ginger, all layered with veal or chicken or pork in "coffins" of pastry. The predominantly sweet pies contain marrow and sometimes parsley. In some of these ancient recipes the sweetness was as mild as in the Devonshire squab pie on page 65, or in the fidget pie on page 61. In others—like this one—lamb or beef was so dominated by sweetness that it disappeared into a mixture we'd recognise as Christmas mincemeat.

> shortcrust pastry, made with 1 lb. (3½ cups) flour—other ingredients in proportion
>
> filling: 1 lb. mutton or lamb, weighed without bones, half lean & half fat
> ¾–1 lb. apples
> ½ lb. each currants, raisins, sultanas [smallish yellow raisins]

[5] So called in honor of Christopher Cat (or Katt), whose mutton pies caused a number of gentlemen of the court of Queen Anne to organize an eating club and name it after him.

¼ lb. candied lemon or orange peel
juice of 1 orange & 1 lemon
¼ lb. blanched almonds
¼ cup rum or brandy
½ teaspoon salt
freshly ground black pepper
1 teaspoon each mace, nutmeg, cinnamon
   (or more, to taste)

Grind lean and fat meat coarsely. Peel, core and grate the apples. Mix all the filling ingredients together, stirring well, and adding spices to taste. Use some of the mixture to make a double-crust pie (serve with light cream or a proper egg custard). Put the rest up in pots for Christmas, or the storecupboard.

NOTE: ½ lb. beef suet and ½ lb. chuck or rump steak may be substituted for the lamb. Weigh without skin in the case of the suet, and without fat and skin in the case of the steak.

Fitchet, fidget or figet pies

Before the machine age, harvest brought the farmer's wife her biggest problem of the year. She had to cope in hot, or at least warm, weather, from the farm's resources, with feeding her husband's army of reapers five times a day. Cheese was the only "convenience" food she could rely on with confidence (though cheese making could go seriously wrong, too, before the chemistry of the business was properly understood). The autumn-cured bacon might have acquired "a disagreeable rankness of Taste," it might have been spoilt by blowflies. Pork pickled in the late spring ran the risks of humidity and sudden changes of temperature. But with luck she was able to make a pie of this kind (a frugal version of the Cheshire pork and apple raised pie, p. 55) to be eaten hot at the harvest home.

shortcrust pastry to cover

filling: ¾ lb. green back rashers [see footnote, p. 33]
      1 lb. Cox's Orange Pippins [crisp eating apples]
      ½ lb. onions, chopped
      2 tablespoons stock or water
      salt, pepper and nutmeg

optional: sugar

Cut the bacon into ¼-inch dice. Peel, core and slice the apples. Put bacon, apples and onions in layers into the pie dish, seasoning with salt, pepper and nutmeg (a little sugar should be sprinkled over the apples if they are very tart). Add the stock, and a lid of shortcrust pastry. Bake in the usual way for about 40 minutes; ½ lb. very thinly sliced potatoes may be included, as in parts of Wales, but the flavour is better without them, I think.

Devonshire squab pie

The excellent flavour of this dish depends on using plenty of spices. Prunes are not always included, but I think they are important. How the pie got its name I don't know. I've tried, unsuccessfully, to find out: "squab" meaning young pigeon seems unsatisfactory, unless the pie was made with pigeons in the days of manorial dovecotes. But recipes for pigeon pies make no mention of apple and sugar. On the other hand, the recipe for pigeons and rice on page 107 does indicate some connection between mutton and pigeons—the pigeons are stewed in mutton broth. Perhaps there was felt to be a similarity between the two meats, so that the decidedly unmanorial cottager ennobled his mutton and apple pie with the name of "squab." Stories have been invented to explain the name, but they have no truth at all.

shortcrust pastry to cover, made with 1¾ cups flour (& ¼ lb.
mutton fat, if possible), p. 57

filling: 1¼ lb. of lamb or mutton chops, or 2 lbs. best end of neck
     2 lbs. tart apples
    16 unsoaked prunes
     2 medium onions, finely chopped
    ½ nutmeg, grated
     1 teaspoon each mace, cinnamon & salt
    freshly ground black pepper
    ½ cup meat stock
    brown sugar

Cut meat off the bones, into slices. Trim away bits of skin or gristle, but not fat. Peel and core the apples, then slice them. Cut the prunes into pieces, discarding the pits.

Grease a pie dish. Arrange meat, apples, prunes and onions in layers, spicing each layer well and sprinkling a little brown sugar over apple layers (if you have to make use of cookers, or windfalls, use more sugar). Add salt, pepper, stock and a pastry lid. Bake at 400° for about an hour and a quarter. Protect the crust with brown paper, if necessary. Eat this pie with clotted cream, from Devonshire.[6]

[6] An inadequate substitute but at least easily available in the U.S. is sour cream mixed with an equal amount of heavy cream and allowed to stand an hour or so at room temperature.

SALTING MEAT

England is covered with forgotten "saltways" radiating from ancient salt pans on the coast or from the salt districts of Cheshire. Along them salt merchants and trains of packhorses brought the salt that used to be needed in every household, to keep life going through the winter and spring. (The salt merchants, conveniently travelling on, became the heroes of Chaucerian episodes of love; poems recount how they outwitted watchful elderly husbands and satisfied young wives in all the bustle of a busy farm.) Cattle couldn't all be kept alive between autumn and summer, and had to be killed and salted. Mutton and fish were salted too; so was pork (think of the three little boys St. Nicholas found in the wicked innkeeper's salt tub).

This was long-term salting. Short-term salting, in the last third of the twentieth century, remains worthwhile for two reasons—it keeps meat on hand and ready to cook, and at no great cost or trouble, and I find little short of miraculous the difference it makes to taste. All cuts of pork, some of beef, and also such things as lamb and deep-frozen duckling are improved. And improvement is all the more necessary now that butchers are not hanging meat long enough to develop the flavour. Salting rescues the Sunday lunch.

If you use the brine recipe I give below, you won't find the meat salty so much as flavoured in a pleasant way. The texture will change slightly and for the better, and some of the grossness (especially of pork) will disappear. I would say that this presalting is the *sine qua non* for first-class pork cookery. Also for beef, pork or lamb you intend to eat cold.

Meat can also be cured by dry salting, but this needs more attention from the cook. It also takes longer to achieve a comparable result, brine penetrating the meat much more quickly than salt alone. The method was convenient when many hams were to be salted away—the Gauls used it for the famous hams they sent to Rome, and so did the Romans themselves.

Whichever method is used, all the home salter requires is a deep stoneware (not earthenware, which is too porous) vessel or plastic bucket, kosher or unrefined salt (preferably sea salt from health food stores), dark brown sugar and saltpeter (from the pharmacy). Saltpeter is essential: it gives an appetising rosy glow to meat, which the salting would otherwise make a dingy grey. The sugar counteracts the hardening effect of saltpeter.

In home conditions, in a cool larder, meat can be kept in brine for up to a fortnight or three weeks. Sometimes longer. The moment that islands of white mould begin to float on the surface, remove the meat and throw away the brine. The crock too will need washing with boiling soda water. The meat will be all right.

Brine

Bring to the boil:

3½ quarts water
1½ lbs. sea or coarse [kosher] salt
1 lb. dark brown sugar
scant ¼ cup saltpeter
1 bay leaf
1 sprig thyme
10 crushed juniper berries
10 crushed peppercorns

Boil hard for 5 minutes. Leave to cool. Clean crock or bucket and lid with soda dissolved in boiling water, rinse well and leave to drain dry. Pour the cold brine in, through layers of cheesecloth or a muslin-lined strainer. Immerse the meat and keep it below the surface by laying a piece of boiled wood or a scrupulously clean plate on top. Cover and keep in a dry place, at a temperature below 60°. When removing pieces of meat from brine, always use clean metal tongs; this way the brine will stay good, and other pieces of meat can be put in to salt. Keep a separate pot for pork, beef and duck, etc.; they should never be salted together, or in brine which might contain the sediments of another meat. It is possible to strain off the brine, and reboil it, adding a refresher of about half the above quantities. Naturally the crock or bucket needs a complete cleansing. This should be done before mould appears.

Salting time

Salting time depends on the thickness of the meat—pig's trotters [feet] are ready in 24 hours, a sizable leg of pork can take about 10 days. But don't worry. When salting is carried out to improve rather than to preserve meat, there is a certain amount of give and take over timing. Excess salt can always be corrected by soaking, or by changing the cooking water.

NOTE: Joints [*legs, standing ribs, shoulders, etc.*] required for roasting rather than boiling will be improved by a 12-hour soak in brine, without tasting too salty.

Duck (giblets removed): 36–48 hours.
Pork (leg, shoulder, loin): 3–10 days.
Beef (silverside or round, brisket): 7–10 days.
Lamb or, preferably, mutton (shoulder, leg, loin): 7–10 days.

Salt duck

Remove from brine, rinse quickly under the cold tap and put into a deep pan. Cover the duck with half water, half nonsweet, i.e., dry cider, and add the giblets apart from the liver (which can be used up in a pâté). Put on the lid, or cover with foil, and cook 2 hours in a slow oven (325°) or until the bird is cooked.

If, as I do, you prefer cold duck, let it cool in the water and cider. Serve it with an orange and tomato salad, seasoned with sugar, salt and pepper, and dressed with wine vinegar and olive oil.

For hot duck, serve an onion sauce in the Welsh style:

> 1 lb. onions, sliced
> about 2 cups milk
> 2 tablespoons butter
> 2 tablespoons flour
> salt, pepper, nutmeg

Cook the onions in enough milk to cover. When they are almost cooked, melt the butter in another pan, stir in the flour and cook for 2 minutes. Add 1 cup hot milk, stirring, until you have a smooth white sauce. Transfer to the onion pan. Simmer for 30 minutes, seasoning well with salt, pepper and nutmeg.

Picnic ham

Use a boned shoulder of pork, weighing up to 5 pounds, and salted for 7 to 10 days. Remove from brine, rinse quickly, dry and weigh. Calculate cooking time at 30 minutes to the pound, plus 30 minutes. Tie the meat into a firm, sausage-like shape, using plenty of string.

Put the meat into a large pan with:

> 2 onions, each stuck with 3 cloves
> 2 medium carrots, sliced
> bouquet garni
> 8 crushed peppercorns
> enough water to cover

Bring slowly to the boil. If the water tastes very much too salty, drain it off and start again. Simmer on top of the stove or in the oven until the end of cooking time. Leave the meat until next day to cool in its liquid, putting a plate and a clean stone (or some heavy cans) on top to press it lightly. Untie the ham, remove the skin and roll in hot toasted crumbs.

Glazed salted pork

Salt boned or unboned loin, shoulder or leg for 5 to 7 days. Follow cooking method for picnic ham above, but remove meat from pan 20 minutes before the end of cooking time. Remove the skin, which will peel off fairly easily, without removing the string.

Mix together:

> 1 tablespoon French mustard
> 1 tablespoon brown sugar
> 1 tablespoon heavy cream
> 1 teaspoon ground cloves or cinnamon

optional: ¼ cup white bread crumbs

Smear this paste over the pork fat; the meat should be placed in a roasting pan and put into a moderately hot oven to glaze for 20 minutes. Watch the heat—sugar catches quickly. Remove the joint when it looks glazed and brown to a warm serving dish.

Sauce can be made by stirring a ladleful of the simmering liquid into the juices left from glazing the meat. When this is bubbling nicely, add some cream and Madeira or port to finish the sauce. Let it boil down a little, then correct the seasoning and strain into a hot sauceboat.

This is just one of many possible glazes. Others, using red currant jelly or marmalade or apricot jam, etc., are easy to invent, but make sure there's a good balance of sharp (mustard, vinegar or lemon juice) to sweet.

NOTE: The liquid from boiling salt duck, pork and beef makes excellent stock for soup.

Boiled beef & carrots

Boiled beef tastes much better and is less dry if you lard it before cooking. This means drawing thin strips of bacon fat or hard back fat [fatback] through the beef by means of a long open-ended larding needle. (As these needles cost very little, it's worth buying one—steak, rabbit, hare, pheasant and pigeons and other lean meats all benefit from larding.)

A large rump roast, bottom round or brisket will benefit from 10 days' salting in brine. Then cook it as for picnic ham, page 70, putting four carrots into the pot instead of two.

Serve hot with separatedly cooked *carottes à la Vichy* (see p. 149), or red cabbage, or sauerkraut, and boiled potatoes.

To serve cold, cool the beef and press it like picnic ham; accompaniments are thinly sliced sweet-sour cucumber, sea salt and mustard, or horse-radish sauce—mix 1 tablespoon grated horseradish into about ½ cup heavy cream, season with sugar, salt and lemon juice. A potato salad, dressed with an olive oil vinaigrette and plenty of parsley, chopped chives and shallot or mild onion, is also delicious with cold salt beef (see footnote following recipe).

Salt mutton or lamb

Use a shoulder or leg; follow cooking instructions for picnic ham, page 70.

Serve hot with caper sauce:

> 2 tablespoons butter
> 2 tablespoons flour
> 1½ cups hot milk
> 3 tablespoons heavy cream
> 1 tablespoon capers

Melt the butter, stir in the flour and cook for 2 or 3 minutes. Add the hot milk gradually, until you have a smooth béchamel sauce. Cook very gently for 30 minutes, stirring from time to time, so that the sauce has a chance to develop a mellow flavour. Stir in the cream, and at the very last moment the capers. Correct the seasoning.

Serve cold (cool and press like picnic ham), sliced thin, with a green salad and new potatoes.

Salt beef sandwiches

Fourteen or fifteen years ago we often bought salt beef* sandwiches at a London Jewish restaurant at 114 Baker Street. They were the best sandwiches I've ever eaten. Thick slices of beef were cut off an immense steaming joint, slapped quickly between thick slices of rye bread, and handed out to us on the pavement.

Homemade beef sandwiches can never taste quite so good—to enjoy beef at its best, it must be cooked in huge cuts—but it's worth following that restaurant's practice of making sandwiches while the beef is still warm, and full of juice. If rye bread is unobtainable, the best substitute is a granary [or *whole-wheat*] loaf. Unsalted butter and horseradish or mustard can be spread on the slices of bread, but all that's really required is hot beef and rye bread.

THREE RECIPES FOR DRY SALTING

The Hermit of Gower's salt duck

In 1867 Lady Llanover's *Good Cookery* appeared. More of a fictionalized tract than a cookery book, it is interesting mainly for an appendix of Welsh recipes. The mouthpiece for Lady Llanover's ideas on diet (he could not be described as the hero) is an unlovable prig called the Hermit of Gower. He expounds his notions—no butter for making the soup, no strong drink to keep harvesters going, etc.—to a Traveller from our corrupt world. Fortunately for the Traveller, the Hermit supports his opinions with some excellent dishes, of which salt duck is, I think, the best:

1 duck
¼ lb. sea salt [kosher]

Lay the duck in a dish in a cool place, and rub it over with the salt. Do this twice a day for three days, turning the duck over each time. Rinse

* Corned beef in the United States.

the salt from the duck, put it into a deep pot, and add water almost to cover. Simmer for 2 hours in a moderate oven. Serve hot with onion sauce (see recipe for salt duck, p. 69) or cold with a salad.

Welsh hams

In other words, salted mutton hams. They were sold in London until nearly the end of the last century. Francatelli, in *The Cook's Guide* of 1888, gives a recipe for curing Welsh hams. Mutton hams were also made in Scotland to much the same recipe:

1 large leg of mutton cut into a ham shape

for a 6-pound joint:
        2 tablespoons black peppercorns
        2 tablespoons allspice
        3–4 coriander seeds
        1 cup sea or coarse [kosher] salt
        ½ oz. saltpeter
        ½ cup brown sugar

Crush the spices, mix with salt, saltpeter and sugar. Rub the meat all over with this mixture and put into a deep covered dish. Leave in a cool place. Every day turn the ham and rub the mixture into it well. Leave for 12 to 14 days. With a larger leg the curing mixture must be increased proportionately, and it will take up to 14 days.

It can now be covered with cold water, brought to the boil and simmered gently for 2 hours. Cool under a weight (see picnic ham, p. 70)

In the old days, the mutton would be pressed for 24 hours under a weight. Then it would be smoked over oak sawdust for 15 days. "In the Highlands," says F. Marian McNeill in *The Scots Kitchen*, "dried junipers are used in curing mutton-hams."

NOTE: A leg of pork may be cured in the same way. But cook it in the oven in a covered pot with 1½ cups water only. Turn the joint four times during cooking. Cook 45 to 50 minutes per pound at 275°.

Spiced salt beef

This used to be a great Christmas dish all over the British Isles; recipes come from Scotland, Wales, Ireland and England. The curing mixture is almost exactly the same as for Welsh hams above, but Elizabeth David adds juniper berries to the mixture itself, and has worked out an exact and successful method of cooking the beef:

> 5 or 6 lb. piece of silverside or round, cut & tied for pickling
> ⅓ cup brown sugar
> ½ oz. saltpeter
> ½ cup sea or kitchen salt
> 2 tablespoons black peppercorns
> 1 tablespoon allspice berries
> 2 tablespoons juniper berries
> shredded suet (enough to cover beef)

First rub the beef all over with the sugar. Leave it for 2 days in a deep pot. Crush the other pickling ingredients together, and rub the beef over every day for 9 days (11 in all). The salt and so on turns liquid, but continue to rub it into the meat just the same. Keep the dish covered. (A larger piece of beef will need a proportionate increase in spices and in curing time—e.g., a 12-lb. round will take 16 days in all.)

To cook the beef, rinse quickly to remove bits of spice. Put it into a close-fitting pot with about 1¼ cups water. Cover the top of the meat with shredded suet to keep it moist during cooking time. Fix on the lid with two layers of greaseproof paper or foil, so that the juices cannot evaporate. Bake in a very low oven, 275°, for 45 to 50 minutes per pound. Leave in the pot to cool undisturbed for 2 or 3 hours. Then remove it to a board (drain off all the fatty liquid first), cover it completely with greaseproof paper and put a weight on top—2–4 lbs. Leave for 24 hours. Serve with horseradish sauce (see p. 45) and a green salad, or diced avocado pears with a vinaigrette.

SNAILS

When we first went to stay in Touraine, I was amazed to see the village come alive on wet summer and autumn evenings. As the rain grew steadier, the paths of the steep cliff—the houses are layered up and into this cliff—attracted more and more people, old men and children mostly. Wrapped to pear shapes in sacking and plastic, they peered into bushes and walls. In their hands they carried sticks and those openwork globes of metal normally used for draining salad greens. The snail hunters were out.

Soon converted by the shared and savoury results, I never go out now without keeping my eyes firmly on the crevices of the lane. Returning at night to the garden, I see in the beam of the torch snail after snail moving majestically up the mint plants or over the wet gravel. When in England I hear the tap-tap-tap-tap on the paving stones outside the window, I try to startle the thrush into dropping its prey before the shell is broken.

The snail hunter's aim—and occasional prize—is the "gros Bourgogne," *Helix pomatia*, the apple or vine snail, which can measure two inches. This beautiful brown and white creature flourishes in local patches of chalk and limestone country in southern England, and is known here as the Roman snail. In spite of its name, *Helix pomatia* was not introduced by the Romans: it was here to welcome Julius Caesar when he first set his standard on the Pevensey coast in Sussex. Its most famous habitat is Burgundy, where it may be found in the vines, but more likely in *escargotières*, miniature snail farms which supply the Paris market. (The casual hunter is not likely to be very successful, though things are not as bad in Burgundy as in Neuchâtel in Switzerland, where a license is now required; it's feared that snails may become extinct without this alarming precaution. Burgundian cooks invented the best way of dressing snails. They send them to table on specially dimpled dishes of pottery, Pyrex or metal, sizzling by the dozen in garlic and parsley butter. A great treat.

Local savants, though, in our less opulent Touraine, claim that the Bourgogne's close relative, *Helix aspersa*, the common garden snail, or "petit-gris," has a better flavour. They say, too, that it's less inclined to toughness. I cannot judge between the two in this respect, as I've never cooked or had the good fortune to find Roman snails. And I can't often afford to eat them in restaurants, either. But I do notice that recipe books give a three-hour cooking time for Roman snails, whereas the common garden snail takes about forty minutes only. So local opinion may be right, as size alone would not account for the difference.

Helix aspersa is the snail most likely to be found in a garden in England.[1] Its markings are dark grey and brown, less glamourous than the Roman markings; the shell is about an inch across. It seems to have a decided penchant for walls and hard surfaces—in Bristol snails used to be sold as "wall-fish"—and I often find a dozen or eighteen of them crawling about the porch and doorstep at night.

The real devotee may profitably imitate the French *escargotière*, the snail enclosure, or snail bank if you like, into which one deposits one's find, and from which one draws a festive dozen or two or three for special occasions.

---

[1] *A number of snail varieties are native to America, but an authority at the American Museum of Natural History asserts that none are considered good to eat "except by gypsies." Only recently has the average American seemed to begin to accept imported snails as the delicious food they can be. Most snails are bought in cans, accompanied by a package of shells. In some metropolitan areas Moroccan and Tunisian snails are available fresh in markets. At the New Orleans French market, it has been reported, a basketful of imported snails some years ago escaped and inched their way across the street to Jackson Park to try their luck on American forage. Except for some victims of souvenir hunters, the immigrant snails are said to be still there, living off the city.*

The most unusual *escargotière* I've ever seen was about six yards in from the mouth of a large cave used as a general store. It consisted of a circle, about four feet in diameter, of wood ash, with a square concrete pillar about three feet high sticking up in the middle (to give the snails exercise, the farmer explained). The wood ash kept them from wandering off, without the necessity of a close-meshed wire roof. In the middle were plenty of cabbage leaves, and some thyme to improve their flavour. Naturally this is only suitable under cover, as rain would wash the wood ash away.

For temporary use, a bucket does very well. Pierce it with small air holes, and weight the lid down—it's amazing how much lifting power a determined batch of snails can muster. The idea is not only to make a collection, but also to give the snails 10 days or a fortnight to get rid of any poisonous plants they may have eaten.

Or so it's said. One friend of ours—now seventy—maintains that this is nonsense, that he's eaten snails all his life without leaving them to fast. And without feeding them on flour or bran or cabbage leaves. He also pooh-poohs the idea that snails taken from hibernation are best. Too thin, he says, no good at all.

The French think we're odd about snails. "To the Anglo-Saxon, the snail represents a curious French gastronomic habit," says a recent article in a cookery periodical. But seeing that snails are on sale in cans, with accompanying packages of Roman shells, in quite unadventurous towns, places that no one could possibly regard as swinging or avant-garde, I think the French are out of date. The 64.7 tons of snails we imported in 1970 may be the result of modern traveling, but I suspect that the habit of eating snails, in some parts of Britain at least, has never quite died out, though it has much diminished in the last hundred years.[2] Once glassblowers and glassmakers in Newcastle and Bristol used to consume them in quantity. They believed that the bubbly juice soothed their overtried lungs. This was not superstition, but the survival of a medical opinion voiced as long ago as Pliny, and still maintained in the nineteenth century.

---

[2] "The European snail was once a popular table fancy in New Orleans, but it is seldom seen on menus there today. In the old days, they were imported from Europe by the basketful, cleaned in salt water, soaked in fresh water, and boiled with herbs before being served with a sauce of wine, shallots, garlic and ham. They may still be purchased on Decatur Street today—but it is snail shells with a canned snail stuffing that today's escargot fancier buys." Mary Land in *Louisiana Cookery*, Louisiana University Press, 1954.

Doctors had for centuries forced decoctions of snails (sometimes mixed with earthworms) on delicate children and chesty patients. As late as the 1880's a recipe for "Mucilaginous Broth" appeared in Francatelli's *Cook's Guide*.[3] It included chicken, calf's foot, crawfish and a pint of snails. "This," he said, "is a powerful demulcent"—i.e., soother and loosener—"and is much in use in France, in cases of phthisis, catarrh, bronchitis, etc."

Unscrupulous dairymen of the time put these foaming gastropods to another use. They'd beat them up with milk and pass the thick result off as cream. Oh, happy days, when business initiative and individual enterprise flourished, before food adulteration laws spoilt the fun.

Whether we eat snails in England now, or whether we don't, they've been part of Europe's diet since prehistoric times. They've been eaten because they were there, and free for the gathering, and not poisonous. For thousands of years the poor have been grateful for them, and the rich resourceful with them.

The habit has been dropped here very largely, I suspect, because the English became more widely prosperous than the rest of Europe at an early stage. We've been able to buy easily prepared food for a long time; our low meat prices have appalled the rest of Europe for two centuries (pampered working classes of Britain). We've also suffered the defects of our eager adaptability in the almost complete loss of regional cooking. It's very noticeable in France, which is by no means a classless society or a particularly democratic one except in the narrowest sense of the word, that wealthy and poor in the same area eat the same food. All the grocers, for instance, are selling the same range of things whether they're supermarkets or family businesses. The wealthy eat more good things than the poor, and less bread, but their ideas of a good meal for a celebration are similar. Asparagus, cepes, morels and other mushrooms of the woods, oysters, squid, wine of quality and snails are eaten by everyone in the area in which we live in France. A contrast to England, where it seems that eating and drinking habits vary according to social class—we even give different names to our meals, or some of them, and eat them at different times. This the French would find even odder than the supposed British antagonism towards snails.

[3] *Numerous famous cookbooks were written by Charles Elmé Francatelli and they sold by the thousand. They include many recipes which are practical even today. As early as 1845 Francatelli's* The Modern Cook *was published in London, and a version designed for American kitchens was entitled* French Cookery *when it was published here.*

Preparation

Having put your snails aside for a week, as a prudent measure, move them to a large bowl or bucket of water with a handful of coarse cooking salt. Leave them for half an hour, then put on rubber gloves and swirl the water and snails about until the juice of the snails begins noticeably to thicken the water. Throw the water away, and repeat four or five times, until the water is absolutely clear.

Meanwhile make a *court-bouillon*, of 3½ cups of water and an equal amount of wine (the very luxurious use champagne, but I think that medium-priced wine is perfectly adequate, white or red), a chopped onion, a chopped carrot, bouquet garni, peppercorns and other aromatics. Let it simmer for an hour, covered, then strain into a clean large pan. When cool, add the snails and bring slowly to the boil. Simmer for 3 hours (Roman snails), or for 40 minutes (garden snails).

Take them from the *bouillon*, and, using a needle stuck eye-end into a cork, remove each snail from its shell, discarding the hard round "door" and the little black bit at the opposite end.

Now they are ready for various treatments.

Matelote of snails   (*1 dozen snails per person*)

Use red wine for the *court-bouillon*. When the snails are cooked, remove them and reduce the strained *bouillon* by hard boiling until you have 3 cups. Fork together 2 tablespoons of butter and 2 tablespoons of flour, and divide it in little bits. Add to the *bouillon*, stirring all the time, until it thickens. Put in the snails—without their shells—to reheat gently for 20 minutes. Serve with triangles of fried bread and a good sprinkling of parsley.

Snail soup   (*9 snails per person*)

Use white wine (or chicken stock plus 2 tablespoons wine vinegar) for the *court-bouillon*. Remove the snails when cooked and reduce the strained liquid to about 5 cups. Meanwhile melt 2 tablespoons of butter in a pan, stir in 2 tablespoons of flour, and add the reduced snail liquid slowly. Simmer uncovered for 15 minutes, add the snails and simmer for 5 minutes.

In a bowl, beat up 2 egg yolks and the juice of a lemon. Pour on a ladle of soup, beat well and return to the pan. Don't allow the soup to boil. Serve with a good sprinkling of parsley, and croutons.

NOTE: If you are using canned snails, make a red wine sauce in this way:

> 1 medium onion, chopped
> 1 medium carrot, chopped
> 1 clove garlic, crushed
> 2 tablespoons butter
> 2 tablespoons flour
> ¾ cup red wine
> ¾ cup chicken or beef stock
> bouquet garni
> salt, pepper

Brown onion, carrot and garlic lightly in the butter. Stir in the flour; cook for 2 minutes. Make a sauce by pouring in the red wine and stock gradually. Add the bouquet and seasoning. Simmer for 45 minutes to an hour until the sauce is reduced to the consistency of heavy cream. Put in the snails and heat through gently.

The soup recipe is not suitable for canned snails.

Escargots farcis à la bourguignonne

Allow 1 dozen snails per person. Prepare them in a *court-bouillon*, as above, using white wine, and adding 2 large cloves of garlic to the aromatics.

Snail butter for 6 dozen snails
> 1 lb. unsalted butter
> 1 large bunch parsley, chopped

¼ cup finely chopped shallots or mild onion
5 large cloves garlic
6 teaspoons salt
1¼ teaspoons freshly ground black pepper

Soften the butter in a slightly warm basin with a wooden spoon (or with an electric beater). Crush the garlic to a cream with the salt. Mix everything together well.

Put a little butter into each empty snail shell (it's sensible to wash them under the hot tap first), then the snail, and pack in some more butter until it's level with the rim of the shell.

Arrange the stuffed snails on specially dented snail plates. Or else cut slices of bread, half an inch thick, horizontally across a large loaf: in each slice, cut out 12 holes with an apple corer. Put these slices on a buttered baking tray, and rest the snails in the holes. Apart from the extra trouble required, this is a better system than snail plates, because the butter bubbles over and is efficiently soaked up by the bread, which can afterwards be eaten.

Sprinkle the snails with fine bread crumbs, and put into a moderately hot oven (375°) until they are well heated through, brown and bubbling.

If you are making use of canned snails for this recipe, very little salt will be required for the butter, as they are well salted already.

Although this is the classic butter for stuffed snails, variations of flavour are worth trying. In parts of France aniseed, fennel or thyme provides a dominant flavour. Lemon juice and spices such as nutmeg are also popular. In *Edible British Molluscs*, M. S. Lovell describes a delicious preparation of stuffed snails: "A fine stuffing is made with snails previously cooked, fillets of anchovies, nutmeg, spice, fine herbs and a liaison of yolk of eggs. The snail-shells are filled with this stuffing, then placed before the fire"—nowadays in the oven—"and served *very* hot."[4]

If you are likely to eat stuffed snails regularly, it's worth investing in snail tongs and forks (as well as in snail plates). One can manage quite efficiently, though, with a pile of paper napkins and a set of needles stuck into

[4] A New Yorker, Milo Miloradovich, combines anchovies and snails in this fashion: Mix 4 dozen cooked snails with 1 cup bread crumbs, 6 anchovy fillets, 1 beaten egg, 2 teaspoons chopped chives, 2 teaspoons chopped parsley, 2 tablespoons butter with several turns of pepper grinder. Fill shells; then melt 2 tablespoons butter in large skillet and add the stuffed shells open side down, sautéeing 3 minutes. Serve on hot plate with a dab of hot béchamel sauce into which to dip snails. Or, says Mr. Miloradovich, this dish can be served ice cold, with mayonnaise.

corks. [Small crockery snail pots are also used frequently today; they require no special utensil to extract the snail and they don't tip over as readily, to say nothing of the fact that they clean so much more easily.]

Escargots à la grand-mère

An unusual recipe from a French periodical. Very good.

4 dozen prepared snails
2 tablespoons olive oil
⅓ cup diced lean bacon [see footnote, p. 33]
⅓ cup diced cooked ham
½ cup finely chopped shelled walnuts
3–5 anchovy fillets, crushed
2 large cloves garlic, crushed
large bunch parsley, chopped
1 large teaspoon flour
1½ tablespoons fine bread crumbs
2 tablespoons butter
salt, black pepper

Brown lightly in the oil the bacon and ham. Add nuts, anchovies, garlic and parsley. Stir in the flour and cook for a moment or two. Add a bare cup of water (if canned snails are used), or of snail *bouillon*. Season. Simmer for 10 minutes, until the sauce has thickened a little. Put in the snails and simmer for about half an hour. Correct the seasoning. Divide the mixture among individual bowls and keep warm. Brown the crumbs lightly in the butter, sprinkle on top of the bowls and serve hot and bubbling.

SWEETBREADS

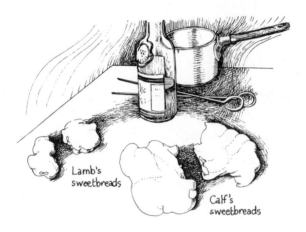

Lamb's
sweetbreads

Calf's
sweetbreads

I particularly like sweetbreads, either calf's or lamb's—it doesn't matter which. Although they come deep-frozen from New Zealand at only 5s or 6s a pound, and although they are served as greyish-white lumps in a floury sauce by hospital cooks, I persist in regarding them as a luxury. They're delicate food, to be treated with ceremony.

To start with, the name is charming: sweet describes their flavour well, and the round heart sweetbread of the calf looks like a nice round bun. Did some poetical butcher think of the name in the sixteenth century, when it was first recorded? It's unusually gracious for such a realistic trade (think of mudgeon, crow, tripe, shin, hock or ham—the only one that comes anywhere near sweetbread in feeling is tenderloin). In fact sweetbreads are the thymus gland of the animal, and the pancreas (the one that cooks prefer, for its convenient shape). They are known respectively as the throat and heart sweetbreads. One could not, I think, make a distinction in flavour between the two, or between lamb's and calf's sweetbreads.

Sweetbreads have often kept illustrious company (there is, after all, only one set to each carcass). They have made their appearance at most great European banquets of recent centuries. Along with cockscombs, truffles, and other expensive bits and pieces, they've been threaded on ornamental skewers, or arranged in little piles around some grand centerpiece.

Who ate this delicious garniture? I feel sure it wasn't always the guests. One of the greatest of all cooks, Carême, castigated those mean rich men who want to make a show—without spending too much money. Their chefs were compelled to present the identical centerpieces at dinner after dinner, and their footmen had to make sure that visitors were served from the less important dishes on the table. Economy on the grand scale. For the first few days, I expect the kitchen boys picked at the alternating piles of sweetbreads and truffles, white beside black, then rearranged them to deceive the master's eye with a dab of jelly or coating sauce.

Cooks in less princely circumstances often put sweetbreads into poultry stuffing. They would pattern a forcemeat (like the one in the sweetbread pie described later) with diced sweetbread, tongue and ham, and pistachio nuts to make a good effect when the galantine was sliced. Families in comfortable middle-class homes probably had the best of the sweetbreads, as we do now. They ate them as a course on their own, set off to advantage by a well-made sauce or a single vegetable: sweetbreads with young peas, sweetbreads creamed and scalloped, sweetbreads with a mushroom and cream sauce, or an oyster and cream sauce, sweetbreads wrapped in fat bacon and cooked on a spit in front of a lively kitchen fire.

One thing. If you are using an old recipe, or a modern French or Italian one, you'll find that sweetbreads, after their initial preparation, are sometimes baked or braised in the oven for about 30 minutes. This is because the large calf's sweetbreads are intended. Lamb's sweetbreads (for many Britons the only ones available) are tiny by comparison and they need no more than the brief cooking I've indicated in the recipes. The same applies to calf's sweetbreads, if they're sliced up.[1]

Another problem. Some recipes specify "a pair" of sweetbreads, i.e., the throat and heart sweetbread. This is muddling. A pair can vary so in weight from two to the pound in England, to one pair—or less—in France. I recently bought a pair weighing 1 pound 6 ounces in the small butcher's shop in our Touraine village. These are things to be borne

---

[1] Veal sweetbreads are most common in the U.S. and weigh about 1 pound when sold in pairs; often available in frozen packages with quality certified, and with cooking directions.

in mind. I've stuck to measurements of weight, and allowed 4 to 6 ounces per person, according to the recipe.

Preparation

Whatever size, weight or type of sweetbreads you are dealing with, the initial stages are always the same. It sounds laborious, but it isn't really. The various stages needn't be timed exactly—fit them in with your other activities. Never be tempted to skimp the preparation, whatever any recipe book may indicate. If you do, you'll end up with a rubbery, inedible mass.

Soak the sweetbreads in a bowl of cold water with a handful of salt for at least one hour, preferably three, or even longer if they are frozen solid. This removes traces of blood and any bits and pieces that shouldn't be there. Drain them, rinse them and put into a saucepan. Now, cover with water, or chicken, veal or vegetable stock and 2 teaspoons of wine vinegar or lemon juice. (Even if the dish does not require a sauce, it's worth using stock rather than water if you can: it acquires gelatin from the sweetbreads and will make beautiful soup or sauce for another meal.)

Bring to the boil slowly and simmer until the sweetbreads become firm and white, losing their raw pinkish look—2 minutes for lamb's sweetbreads, up to 20 minutes for calf's. Don't overcook them. Strain off the liquid, run the sweetbreads under the cold tap and remove hard bits, tubes, etc., as soon as they're cool enough to handle. Be careful not to take off too much of the transparent elastic skin that holds the sweetbreads together.

Put them between two boards, or plates, with a light weight on top. Leave for 1 to 2 hours in a cool place, or overnight in the refrigerator.

Sweetbreads in the English style (for 4)

Carême, who cooked for Talleyrand, Napoleon, the Rothschilds, and the Czar of Russia, also spent some time with England's Prince Regent. He was amazed at the sumptuous china and furnishings of the royal households at Brighton and London;[2] he got on well with the appreciative Prince; but in the end he returned to France, driven away from England by fogs and loneliness, the lack of conversation. However, he had come to admire quite a lot of food in our country, including the beef, a number of puddings, and sea kale.[3] In his great book on cookery, English recipes were included (and so were some of the lavish dishes he himself invented for the Prince Regent). Here's a simplified version of sweetbreads à l'anglaise, from his *Art of French Cookery in the Nineteenth Century.*

> 1 lb. prepared sweetbreads
> ½ lb. very thinly cut smoked bacon [see footnote, p. 33]
> bread sauce
> ⅓ cup bread crumbs
> 4 tablespoons butter

Cut the sweetbreads into thickish slices, suitable for threading on skewers. Cut the rashers of bacon into pieces and wrap round the slices of sweetbread. Divide between four skewers.

Prepare the bread sauce [see recipe that follows] and leave it simmering over a pan of hot water while you broil the sweetbread and bacon skewers, under a medium heat, about 10–15 minutes. Meanwhile brown the crumbs in the butter. When the skewers are cooked, roll them firmly in the bread crumbs and arrange on a serving dish, with the remaining crumbs scattered over them. Serve immediately, with the bread sauce separately in a sauceboat. This is a most felicitous combination.

Bread sauce

Bread sauce, which is invariably served with roast chicken and turkey in Britain, is the last European survivor of those medieval sauces

---

[2] In Brighton Pavilion (not Palace), the great kitchen of 1815 in which Carême worked is open to visitors, with spits turning and a batterie de cuisine of 550 copper pans on display (in fact they belonged to the Duke of Wellington, and are lent by the London Museum to give some idea of the cooking methods of the early nineteenth century).

[3] Sea kale is a plant of the European Atlantic coast. In Britain particularly it is cultivated, though sadly on a small scale, for its asparagus-like stems: sometimes it's

which were thickened with bread crumbs rather than with flour or a mixture of egg yolks and cream. It's delicious, so long as the texture retains a certain crumbiness; if it's beaten or cooked to smoothness, it turns to wallpaper paste.

> 1 cup milk
> 1 small onion, stuck with 3 cloves
> bouquet garni
> salt
> ¼ cup bread crumbs (preferably homemade type)
> 1 tablespoon butter or heavy cream
> black pepper or cayenne pepper

Bring the milk very slowly to simmering point with the onion and herbs, and a good pinch of salt. Let it take 20 minutes or even longer, so that it is well flavoured with the onion and herbs. Beat in the bread crumbs and continue to cook over a low heat, without boiling, until the sauce is thick. Add more crumbs if necessary; the better the bread, the better the flavour of the sauce will be. Fish out the onion, and bouquet, just before serving. Stir in the butter or cream, and season with more salt if necessary, and with pepper. Remember that bread-thickened sauces were popular in the days when eating irons and plates were in short supply, when a large slice of bread might be used as a plate—so the sauce had to be of a consistency which was easy to manage in such daunting circumstances. In other words it shouldn't spread much when put on the plate —yet it shouldn't be as firm as mashed potatoes.

Sweetbreads in the Italian style (for 4)

The Italians have a good way of cooking delicate pieces of lean meat such as turkey or chicken breasts, or poultry livers, or sweetbreads. The system is to brown them lightly in butter, then to stew them for a little with Marsala until they are glazed and succulent. The result is delectable, sharply stimulating to the appetite, but not in the least heavy.

---

to be found in good vegetable markets in the U.S. In either country it's a luxury worth pursuing.

    1 *lb. prepared sweetbreads*
    4 *thin slices lean smoked bacon [see footnote, p. 33],*
       or more correctly, Italian prosciutto
    6 *fresh sage leaves (1 teaspoon dried sage)*
    6 *tablespoons butter*
    scant ½ *cup Marsala (or Madeira, port, Amontillado sherry)*

for serving: 4 *large croutons of bread, fried in butter*

Divide the sweetbreads into nuggets. Cut the bacon into matchstick strips. Snip the sage into tiny pieces with scissors. Fry the sweetbreads in butter quickly until they begin to brown (be careful not to burn the butter) with the sage. Add the bacon and cook for another 2 or 3 minutes. Pour in some of the Marsala, and, as it boils down, add some more, and so on until it is used up. This takes about 10 minutes, and the heat should be turned up to evaporate the wine. Turn the sweetbreads over and over all the time, to acquire a brown, syrupy glaze. Serve them on the croutons of bread, with the small amount of sauce left in the pan poured over them.

Sweetbreads à la Castillane   *(for 6)*

    The French way of cooking sweetbreads produces a richer result, with more sauce. The usual accompaniment is mushrooms, but in this recipe (which I've adapted from one given me in Tours) the sweetbreads sit on a purée of apples and bananas. Out of the ordinary and very good.

    1½–2 *lbs. prepared sweetbreads*
    4 *medium eating apples*
    4 *small, very ripe bananas*
    8 *tablespoons [1 stick] butter*
    ½–1 *cup sweetbread cooking liquor*
    1 *tablespoon cognac*
    ¼ *cup heavy cream*
    lemon juice, salt, pepper

optional: sugar

Slice the sweetbreads into pieces about ½ inch thick. Cut up the apples and stew them in 2 tablespoons of butter in a covered pan; strain them and throw away remains of peel and core. Mash the bananas thoroughly and mix them with the apple purée. Sweeten if necessary, and add a little lemon juice—very good apples and scented bananas will need hardly any additions. Keep this purée warm. Brown the sweetbreads in the rest of the butter; pour in about ½ to 1 cup of their cooking liquor little by little, so that it reduces to a rich glaze on the sweetbreads (see preceding recipe). Arrange the sweetbreads on the fruit purée, swill the pan juices round with the cognac and scrape all the nice brown bits into the sauce as it bubbles. Stir in the cream and cook gently for a few moments. Season this smooth rich mixture with salt, pepper and lemon juice to taste, pour over the sweetbreads and serve immediately. Boiled rice is a good accompaniment.

Sweetbread pie or pâté   (for 6 to 8)

On a recent trip into Burgundy, we visited the town of Avallon, not far from Vézelay. After looking at the carved portal of the church, we wandered down the small main street in search of picnic food. As we waited to be served in the charcuterie, we gazed at the wonderful display, at the puff pastry pies slashed and shaped like an Elizabethan hat, at the hunks of farm-made butter, at the many sausages and hams—and then, with astonishment, at the pâtés. The cheapest was 22 francs the kilo, and the most expensive—a sweetbread pâté—bore a ticket marked 44 francs (in American terms, about $6 a pound). How, I wondered, could the burghers of this small town of about 7,000 inhabitants pay such prices? Even if some of them do happen to be prosperous biscuit manufacturers? The pâté didn't look at all as if it was made once a year, and dusted off daily, for show only. I still haven't worked out the answer, and we bought brawn (headcheese). But I've a new respect for this recipe:

shortcrust pastry: 3 cups flour
         12 tablespoons butter and lard mixed

1 rounded tablespoon confectioners' sugar
water to bind

for glaze: egg yolk or cream

filling: 1 lb. prepared sweetbreads
¾ lb. lean pork, or veal & pork mixed
½ lb. hard back pork fat [fatback]
2 rashers green back bacon [see footnote, p. 33]
2 large eggs, beaten
1½ tablespoons flour
¼ cup cream, heavy or light
¼ lb. mushrooms, roughly chopped
2½ tablespoons finely chopped onion
1 clove garlic, crushed
6 tablespoons butter
salt, pepper, thyme

Make the pastry in the usual way. Separate the sweetbreads into neat, even-sized pieces. Make a forcemeat by grinding the pork and bacon, first coarsely, then finely. Add beaten eggs, flour and cream. Cook mushrooms, onion and garlic in the butter slowly for 15 minutes. Mix into meat and season well.

Line a 1-quart-capacity loaf tin with the pastry, keeping aside enough for the lid. Lay in about a third of the forcemeat; arrange half the sweetbreads on top in two parallel rows. Use another third of the forcemeat to tuck round and over the sweetbreads. Arrange the rest of the sweetbreads on top in the same way, and cover them with the last of the forcemeat. Mound it up nicely above the height of the loaf tin, to support the pastry lid. Moisten the pastry rim, lay on the lid and finish in the usual way, brushing finally with a glaze of egg yolk and water, or with light cream. Decorate with pastry leaves, roses, etc. Bake for an hour and a half in a moderately hot oven, 350°–375° (protect the lid with thick paper, when it gets brown). Eat warm.

If you decide to make a pâté without a pastry crust, cover the pâté with a double layer of foil, removing it for the last 20 minutes of cooking time to brown the top. Cool under a light weight overnight.

Bouchées à la reine   *(for 6)*

If you have to stretch a few sweetbreads (or use some left over from another meal), make these *bouchées à la reine*, which have no hint of frugality about them. Cold chicken is the meat often used, but I've noticed that sweetbreads are usually included. Sometimes they're the only meat used. These *bouchées*, these queenly mouthfuls, were named for Maria Leszczyńska, gourmet daughter of Stanislas Leszczyński, king of Poland, and wife of Louis XV of France.

Should you feel disinclined to make puff pastry, bake shortcrust tartlets instead, or one large pastry case. Alternatively, 2-inch-thick slices of bread can be deep-fried (cut the crusts off, and hollow out the middle part to contain the sweetbreads first). The filling can be put into scallop shells or small pots, covered with buttered crumbs and set in a hot oven, or under the broiler, until browned and bubbling. None of these will be *bouchées à la reine*, but they'll be appetising all the same.

> 12 baked vol-au-vent cases
>   *or* 1 large baked puff pastry case
> 10 oz. diced, prepared sweetbreads,
>   *or* mixed sweetbreads & chicken
> 2 tablespoons butter
> 1½ tablespoons flour
> 1 cup hot sweetbread cooking liquor
> ½ cup hot milk
> ¾ lb. mushrooms, sliced thinly
> ½ cup heavy cream
> salt, pepper, lemon juice

Melt butter, stir in flour and cook for 2 minutes. Gradually incorporate sweetbread liquor and milk. Simmer this sauce until it is reduced to a thick consistency. Add the mushrooms, and cook for another 10 minutes, then add the cream. Simmer again until the sauce is thick without being gluey. Season well with salt, pepper and lemon juice. Reheat the sweetbreads, or sweetbreads and chicken, in the sauce carefully so that they don't disintegrate. Be sure to bring it to the boil, then simmer for 5 minutes.

Meanwhile put the vol-au-vent cases (or puff pastry) into the oven to heat up. Arrange them on a serving dish and pour in the filling. Replace the lids and serve immediately.

Sweetbreads with oysters *(for 4)*

This American recipe is in the old European tradition of oysters with meat, from the days when oysters were a poor man's food and used as a seasoning.

> 1 *lb. prepared sweetbreads*
> 2½ *tablespoons flour*
> ½ *teaspoon paprika*
> 2 *tablespoons butter*
> ½ *cup heavy cream*
> 2–3 *dozen oysters with their liquor*
> *salt and mace to taste*
> ⅓ *cup dry sherry*

Divide the sweetbreads into small pieces. Roll them in the flour and paprika mixed together, then fry them in the butter until they are a nice golden brown. Pour in the cream and make a sauce by stirring it well into the pan juices. Add the oysters and their liquor; when the edges begin to curl up the dish is ready. Season with salt, mace and sherry to taste.

Serve with triangles of bread fried in butter.

RABBIT & HARE

Rabbit, or at any rate wild rabbit, needn't be so much undervalued as a poor relation of the hare. Rabbit was introduced late in the twelfth century from Norman France as rather a lordly meat, raised not in hutches in the modern backyard style, but in long artificial mounded burrows, or conygers, which, like the dovecote, formed part of the perquisites of the lord of the manor. The rabbits flourished and escaped to provide, in due time, some of the only meat regularly eaten by the poor. This abundant source of protein came to an end in 1953 with the introduction of myxomatosis, a virus disease, and in effect a rabbit plague, from France. Before the disease rabbits were seen by the hundred; now it's quite an event to see a white tail flying from one's feet across the fields.

The hare has always been game, not an adjunct of feudal economy, and highly regarded as a richly flavoured food. That's really the difference—the hare rich and gamy in flavour, the rabbit (good wild rabbit) fresh and succulent. The hare makes one think of port, burgundy, red currant jelly, spices and cream; the rabbit needs onions, mustard, white wine, dry cider and thyme.

Every year wild rabbits increase in Great Britain, though there is little hope that they will ever again be sold at low pre-myxomatosis prices. But they are still cheap. And so is hare, which can provide two or three dishes for a family of four. In England, the poulterer hangs hare for at least three days (longer hanging time depends on taste, and humidity, ten days being in our climate the maximum). He will save its blood, to which a few drops of vinegar should be added to prevent it coagulating. The poulterer will also skin and joint both animals, and split the head.[1]

A number of recipes can be used interchangeably for both creatures. For instance, rabbit can be jugged or turned into a civet. Hare is delicious cooked in the sweet-sour style (recipes below). A point to notice is that extra fat usually needs to be added when cooking hare and rabbit, as they both have dry-textured meat. Cubes of fat bacon are often used, slices of pork belly, hard back fat tied round the joints jacket-fashion or introduced into the meat as strips, with a larding needle.

Rabbit with mustard   (for 4)

This is one of the best meat dishes I know for piquant contrast of flavours. For four people, you need the saddle, cut in two, and the hindquarters. The forequarters and head can be used for soup, or a pâté. You will also need:

    1½ lbs. pork belly
    3 medium carrots, chopped
    ½–¾ lb. chopped onions
    1 large clove garlic, crushed
    1 tablespoon thyme, or wild thyme (½ if dry)
    1 bay leaf
    1 tablespoon chopped parsley

[1] The time the very first English hares arrived on this side of the Atlantic may have gone unrecorded, but by 1760 at least four brace were sent from Woodcote at the request of Maryland's governor. The North American hares, known variously as jack rabbits, or snowshoe rabbits, weigh as much as 10 to a record 13 pounds. Hunters in the South and the Plains states find them good eating. Frozen hare from Canada is sometimes available in U.S. meat markets. In supermarkets one usually finds domestic rabbit meat which can be substituted in any recipe for hare.

½ cup dry white wine
  or chicken stock plus scant tablespoon wine vinegar
¼ cup brandy
1 egg yolk
¼ cup heavy cream
1 tablespoon Dijon mustard
Extra parsley to garnish, salt, black pepper

for serving: plain boiled potatoes

Skin (but save the rind), bone and slice pork. Mix carrots, onion, garlic and herbs. Lay half the pork in a casserole, then half the vegetable mixture. Season well. Add the rabbit, then the rest of the vegetables, then the rest of the pork. Season. Lay the pork skin on top. Pour wine and brandy over, cover tightly and cook in a slow oven, 325°, for 2½–3 hours, until the rabbit is tender. Arrange meat and vegetables, well drained, on a serving dish, and keep them warm. Skim fat off the cooking juices. Beat yolk and cream together, add the skimmed juices and cook gently. Stir this sauce well, but don't let it boil. When it's thick, add the mustard, salt and pepper. Pour over the rabbit, etc., sprinkle with parsley, and serve with some plain boiled potatoes.

Young rabbit with chives

Although this French recipe is intended for domestic rabbit, it can be used most successfully with young wild rabbit. But be sure it's young. Older rabbits need the slow stewing of the recipe above.

1 rabbit, jointed [cut in pieces], or 3 lbs. rabbit joints
seasoned flour
4 tablespoons [½ stick] butter
1 tablespoon Calvados, or applejack brandy
16 small onions, peeled
½ cup chicken or veal stock
¾ cup cream
salt, black pepper, cayenne pepper
thick bunch chives, finely chopped

Cut the hind legs of the rabbit into two pieces. Turn all the rabbit pieces in seasoned flour, and fry to golden brown in butter. Use a large heavy frying pan; cast iron is best. Warm the Calvados or applejack brandy, set alight and pour over the rabbit, turning the pieces about in the flames. Add the onions, giving them a few moments to colour slightly in the pan juices. Stir in the stock, cover the pan (foil will do, if it has no lid) and simmer for 40 minutes or until the rabbit is cooked. Remove meat and onions to a warm serving dish. Reduce the liquid in the pan by boiling it down, then stir in the cream. After a few moments' bubbling, the sauce will have thickened nicely. Add salt and pepper if required; then a pinch of cayenne pepper and the chives. Pour the boiling sauce over the rabbit and onions and serve.

NOTE: Chicken can be substituted for rabbit, and tarragon for the chives. Add a teaspoon of fresh (or ½ teaspoon dried) tarragon to the pan with the stock.

Rabbit with mushrooms *(for 4-6)*

Wild rabbit and wild mushrooms—cepes, horns of plenty or field mushrooms—make a fine combination in this Breton dish. It's worth making the effort to find out where funguses grow in your area, as they are often allowed to rot by the thousand in English woods.[2] All those wonderful flavours entirely wasted (see p. 193).

1 rabbit, jointed [cut in pieces]
1–2 lbs. wild mushrooms
 or 1 lb. cultivated mushrooms
2 tablespoons olive oil
½ lb. streaky bacon, cubed [see footnote, p. 33]
seasoned flour
½ lb. chopped onions
6 tablespoons butter

[2] Unless you are an expert, consult the Department of Agriculture Circular #143, "Some Common Mushrooms and How to Know Them," by Vera K. Charles, obtainable from Superintendent of Documents, Washington, D.C., for 35¢.

bouquet garni
½ cup dry white wine, or cider
1 large garlic clove, crushed
beef stock
parsley to garnish
triangles of toast or fried bread

To prepare mushrooms: cut off the earthy parts, then rinse them quickly under the cold tap. With cepes, remove the spongy underlayer of tubes from the cap, unless they are very young, and cut out the wormy bits. Slice all mushrooms except horns of plenty. If you wish to use dried cepes, follow the soaking instructions on the packet—i.e., about 20 minutes in plenty of hot water.

Brown bacon, rabbit rolled in seasoned flour, and onions in the oil and butter. Transfer to casserole with mushrooms, bouquet garni, wine and garlic. Pour 1 cup stock into the frying pan, and bring to the boil, scraping in all the little brown bits. Pour over rabbit. Add more stock to cover, if necessary. Simmer gently at 300°, for 2½–3 hours. Strain off liquid, and reduce by boiling until the taste is well concentrated. Pour over rabbit and mushrooms, sprinkle with chopped parsley and serve with toast or fried bread.

NOTE: Domestic rabbit will take about 1 hour to cook.

Rabbit rillettes

This light-textured form of potted meat will keep for months in a cool place. Serve it as an hors d'oeuvre, accompanied by good bread and sea salt, or as a teatime snack for children. The true basis of rillettes is pork, but rabbit, goose, pigeon, duck or turkey is often added for variety.

2 lbs. rabbit joints [pieces]
1½ lbs. pork belly
¼ lb. hard back fat [fatback]
good-sized sprig of thyme (or ½ teaspoon dried)
nutmeg, cinnamon, black pepper, salt
lard

Cut pork and pork fat into 1½-inch cubes. Put into a heavy-bottomed pan with the rabbit and thyme, and a ladle of water. Cook, covered, over a low heat or in a low oven, 275°, for four hours, or until the meat falls off the bones. Pour contents of the pan into a large strainer set over a bowl. Remove bones, pork skin and thyme stalks. Crush the meat with a pestle, then tear it into shreds with a couple of forks. This demands a little patience. One shortcut is to drop the meat onto the whirling blades of a blender, but it must not be pulverized to sludge. (Whatever you do, *don't put it through the grinder*.) The final result should be unctuous and thready. Season the meat generously with spices, add some of the strained fat and juices, but be discreet or the rillettes will congeal too solidly as they cool. Reheat to boiling point, add salt to taste, and pack into sterilized bottling jars or stoneware rillettes mugs (from Elizabeth David Ltd, 46 Bourne Street, London S.W.1., and branches of Habitat or for U.S. sources, see p. 367). Cool. Cover with ½ inch melted lard, then with jam pot covers or cooking film. Keep in a refrigerator if possible.

Hannah Glasse's rabbit casserole with orange (for 4-6)

A good recipe to try when Seville oranges[3] come into the shops after Christmas. The bitter-sweet flavour goes well with wild rabbit.

> 1 rabbit, jointed [cut in pieces]
> seasoned flour
> 6 tablespoons butter or lard
> ½ cup dry white wine
> beef stock
> pepper, salt
> bouquet garni
> 1¼ tablespoon flour
> 2 tablespoons butter
> juice of 1 Seville orange
> 2 Seville oranges

[3] Unfortunately Seville oranges are almost impossible to obtain in the U.S.

If the rabbit is on the mature side, it's prudent to lard it (see hare with cream in the German style, p. 101). Turn the pieces in seasoned flour and brown lightly in the butter or lard. Put into a casserole (Hannah Glasse advises an "earthenware Pipkin"), and add the wine and enough stock just to cover the meat. Season with pepper and salt. Put in the bouquet garni. Cover and simmer until the rabbit is cooked. Meanwhile mash the flour into the butter, and divide it into a number of small knobs. Strain off the sauce into a small pan, reduce it to a good flavour by boiling, then keep it under boiling point and whisk in the knobs of flour and butter. This makes the sauce thick and slightly shiny. Cook for about five minutes, flavouring the sauce to taste with orange juice.

Cut the two oranges into thin slices, and notch the peel all round, cutting out tiny triangles which should be carefully kept. Put the rabbit pieces on a warm serving dish, pour the sauce over them and scatter the little bits of peel on top. The slices of orange should go round the edge of the dish.

Sweet-sour rabbit (or hare)
Italian style, with chocolate

It may need an act of faith to include the chocolate, but please don't leave it out. And make sure it's the bitter kind. Pine nuts can be bought at delicatessen or health food shops.

> 1 rabbit (or 1 young hare), jointed [cut in pieces]
> seasoned flour

marinade: 1½ cups red wine
   3 tablespoons chopped onion
   3 tablespoons chopped carrots
   1 tablespoon parsley
   1 tablespoon thyme
   1 bay leaf
   3 cloves
   plenty of black pepper
   ½ teaspoon salt

sauce: 2½ tablespoons lard
 2 oz. fat bacon, diced [see footnote, p. 33]
 ½ cup chopped onions
 beef stock
 1½ tablespoons sugar
 3½ tablespoons wine vinegar
 ¼ cup sultana raisins [yellow raisins]
 2½ tablespoons pine nuts
 2 oz. candied peel, cut in strips
 3 oz. bitter chocolate, grated [3 squares]
 salt, pepper, lemon juice

Soak the rabbit or hare in the marinade ingredients for at least 4 hours. Drain and dry the meat, roll in seasoned flour and brown in the lard, together with bacon and onions. Put into a casserole. Strain the marinade liquid over the rabbit and add enough beef stock to cover it. Season well and simmer for 1½ hours, or until the meat is cooked. Melt sugar in a thick saucepan until it turns pale brown, add vinegar, stirring vigorously—the mixture will become a brown syrup. Pour into the casserole, and add the raisins, pine nuts, candied peel and chocolate. Simmer 5 minutes. Correct the seasoning with salt, pepper and lemon juice. No accompanying vegetables are needed.

Hare with cream in the German style

Only the saddle is needed for this recipe; the rest can be used up in a civet (p. 103). Be careful to remove the pearly skin. The saddle should be larded to keep it moist during the cooking. This is not at all difficult to do—buy a fat end of bacon, or a piece of hard back pork fat [fatback], and chill it well. Cut into strips about 2 inches long and ¼ inch wide. Thread the first strip into the open end of a larding needle, and take a stitch into the meat, parallel to the backbone, as if you were sewing. The ends of fat will protrude. With a little practice, one can do this quite elegantly so that the slices of meat are neatly patterned with the bits of fat. This excellent and decorative way of making dry meats such as pigeon, fillet steak, venison and hare more succulent certainly justifies the 3/–spent on a larding needle.[4]

> saddle of hare, larded
> 4 tablespoons chopped mild onion
> 4 tablespoons chopped carrot
> 1 cup heavy cream
> ½ cup sour cream
> 2½ teaspoons wine vinegar
> red currant jelly
> ¼–½ cup red wine or port

Choose an ovenproof cooking pot that just accommodates the hare. First put in the vegetables, then lay the saddle on top. Pour cream and vinegar over, which should ideally come well up the saddle of hare. Roast in a moderate oven, 350°, for about 45 minutes or until the hare is cooked. Baste frequently with the juices. Remove hare to serving dish and keep warm. Strain cooking liquid into a heavy pan. Boil gently, adding jelly and wine to taste. This is usually served with chestnut purée, but I prefer whole boiled chestnuts mixed with Brussels sprouts.

Jugged hare (or rabbit) with forcemeat balls

We've been eating stewed hare for hundreds of years, but we've only been calling it "jugged" hare (which sounds so traditional) for a couple of centuries. "Jugged" means, precisely, cooked in a jug. You could use one of the brown stoneware half-gallon milk jugs, sold by London's Elizabeth David or any good cookery equipment shop in the U.S. (see p. 366), but an ordinary casserole does perfectly well.

> 1 hare, jointed [cut in pieces]
> seasoned flour
> ½ lb. streaky bacon, cubed [see footnote, p. 33]

---

[4] About 70 cents in the U.S.

½ lb. chopped or pickling [small whole] onions
6 tablespoons lard
1½ teaspoons dried thyme
1½ tablespoons chopped parsley
bay leaf
beef stock
½ cup port
red currant jelly

optional: hare's brain, liver, blood

Roll hare pieces in seasoned flour, then brown with bacon and onions in lard. Pour off surplus fat, add herbs, cover with stock and bring to boil. Transfer to a jug, cover with foil, and stand in a large saucepan of hot water. Put into a slow oven, 300–325°, until the meat parts easily from the bone. Mash brain and liver, pour on some of the hot liquid and cook in a little pan for five minutes, stirring. Add blood, off the heat, and stir the whole thing into the jug of hare. Keep it just under boiling point for five minutes. Stir in port and red currant jelly to taste. Serve with forcemeat balls:

¼ cup fresh white bread crumbs
¼ cup chopped suet or melted butter
about 1 teaspoon dried thyme
about 1 tablespoon chopped parsley
grated rind of half a lemon
1 beaten egg

Mix together, form into balls, and fry in lard until golden brown.

Civet of hare or rabbit

Civet is really just another word for stew, a French word which has been naturalized in England since the Middle Ages. It's said to derive from cive, chive, indicating that essential flavouring of most stews—onion. More recently, a civet has been used to describe a stew thickened with the blood of the animal being cooked.

hare, or rabbit, jointed [cut in pieces]
2 cups dry white wine
nutmeg, cinnamon, black pepper
1 teaspoon dried thyme
seasoned flour
½ lb. bacon, cubed [see footnote, p. 33]
½ lb. onion, chopped
6 tablespoons lard
3 tablespoons brandy
beef stock
20 small whole mushrooms (½ lb.)
20 pickling [small whole] onions
4 tablespoons butter
1¼ tablespoons sugar
hare's brains, liver, blood
¼ cup cream
about 1 tablespoon red currant jelly
pieces of fried bread
parsley to garnish

Marinate the hare pieces for 48 hours in wine, well seasoned with spices. Drain and dry them well, roll in seasoned flour. Brown with bacon and chopped onion in the lard. Heat the brandy, set it alight and pour into the frying pan—turn the pieces of hare over in the flames. Transfer to a casserole, pour in the marinade with enough beef stock just to cover the meat. Wedge the lid firmly on to the pot with foil. Simmer, either on top of the stove or in the oven, for an hour, then add mushrooms. In another pan brown the pickling onions in butter, add the sugar and shake the onions about until they are caramelized. Add them to the pot and complete the cooking; the onions will need at least 20 minutes, but can have longer. Mash brains and liver, mix blood with cream; incorporate them with the stew following the preceding jugged hare recipe. Season with red currant jelly, black pepper and more salt if necessary. Serve with fried bread and a garnish of chopped parsley.

PIGEON

One of the pleasures of the English autumn is the arrival of wood pigeons[1] at the poulterer's. They taste delicious—and even better when the winter is over, if the spring is mild enough to allow them to grow fat on young corn. Also they can cost as little as 2s apiece, if you are prepared to pluck and dress them yourself. This is not so trying as it sounds. But remember to dampen the feathers before you start, to prevent their flying all over the kitchen. As an extra precaution, it's wise to pluck them inside a paper sack, with a bowl of water alongside to rinse your cluttered hands in from time to time.

The wood pigeon's gamy flavour makes it suitable, along with wild

---

[1] European ringdoves (Columba palumbus). One of the most popular game birds in the U.S. is the mourning dove, although the hunting of doves is banned in 19 states. In several southwestern states, the ban-tail and white-wing pigeons, both similar to the mourning dove, are also hunted. But there is no wild pigeon available commercially. Only squabs, the young of the domestic pigeon (rockdove), can be purchased; they are frequently found in fine meat and poultry markets in major cities. If you use poultry-farm squabs, the cooking time in all of these recipes will be much shorter (no more than an hour) and the amount of liquid should be less.

rabbits and with hares and the more expensive game, for cold game pâtés and pies. Patience is needed, rather than any special skill, and nerve enough to suppress any feeling that only London's famous Fortnum and Mason food store or the kitchens in that grandiose edifice called Castle Howard in Yorkshire designed by Sir John Vanbrugh can cope with such lordly specialities.

Lark is another fat, gamy-flavoured, autumnally eaten bird, but to enjoy lark in pâtés—since Shelley and ornithology—you have to go to Chartres, Orléans or Pithiviers, on the edge of the Beauce, the great farm plain of northern France.

Incidentally, from March to September, American squabs bred in Kent can be bought from Harrod's poultry counter, or from John Baily & Son in London (for U.S. sources, see p. 367). They're similar to the pigeons which cooed in the dovecotes of medieval lords of the manor, or to modern French *pigeonneaux*, or for that matter, to the pigeons which were given nesting boxes by early Mesopotamian farmers 6,000 years ago. They are bland and tender, take less time to cook than wild pigeons, and can be roasted without larding—but they are not cheap. (It follows that if you adapt American or French pigeon recipes to wood pigeons, you must increase cooking time.) I believe that there is only one breeder of these American squabs in Britain, which seems ridiculous. Like venison, these delicious birds could add a welcome variety to our meat dishes, if they were produced in greater quantity for the home market.

As a feudal perquisite of big houses, dovecote pigeons were a source of meat in the days when cattle could not be fed through the winter. Turnip culture—introduced in the eighteenth century—saved the cattle and made winter steaks and sirloin possible. And it had long been thought intolerable that privileged pigeons should fatten on other people's fields and gardens. So exit the squab.

Wood pigeons are just as much of a nuisance, an enormously successful species. All the same it isn't impossible that wood pigeons as well will disappear from the kitchen. Farmers say it won't be economical to shoot them much longer, with the present high price of cartridges. Recently, though, pigeon shoots have been organized on a large scale, as a way of combining pleasurable sport and pest control. The birds are dressed and supplied to butchers on a commercial scale. Some are frozen. If the shoots are seen to be an efficient way of controlling the farmer's enemy, we may soon be able to buy woodpigeons regularly and reliably from the poultry counter—even from the deep freeze.

Pigeons with grapes (for 4)

This dish comes from the Bas-Vendômois, where pigeons in autumn are fat with maize, and grapes ripen on house walls and south-facing hills.

4 pigeons (see note, p. 105; if using commercially
    produced squab)
¼ cup chopped mild onion
6 tablespoons butter
1½–2 lbs. white or black grapes
3½–4 tablespoons marc or brandy

for serving: boiled rice

Soften onion for 10 minutes in half the butter. Put into the casserole (which should be just large enough to hold the pigeons) with a layer of grapes. Brown the pigeons in the rest of the butter; warm the marc, set it alight and pour over the pigeons, turning them about in the flames. Tuck them breast down into the casserole, filling the gaps with grapes. Keep a few back for garnishing. Season lightly and cover. Cook in a hot oven (450–475°) for 10 or 15 minutes, then lower the heat to 350°, or even less, to keep the pigeons at a gentle simmer. Cook for 1½–2½ hours according to the age of the pigeons; remove them as their flesh begins to part from the breastbone.

Strain the sauce into a clean pan. Boil down to about 1½ cups. Adjust seasoning and skim off the fat. Carve pigeons (keep carcasses for soup, see p. 118), arrange with the reserved grapes on a bed of boiled rice, and pour some of the sauce over them. Serve the rest of the sauce in a separate bowl.

Pigeons boiled with rice (for 4)

It's not unusual to eat pigeons with rice, quite the contrary. For a change, though, try this eighteenth-century way of preparing the rice with milk, cream and egg yolks—it makes a good background to pigeon meat with its tendency to dryness. The recipe occurs in one or two cookery books of the time, most notably in John Farley's *The London Art of Cookery*. He ran the London Tavern, and this dish is an example of the kind of good meat cookery England was famous for at that time.

Lamb or mutton stock was often used for boiling pigeons. The two flavours do go well together, especially if there's no wine in the recipe.

stock: about 2 lbs. mutton or lamb bones
water
bouquet garni
1 medium carrot, sliced
1 medium onion, sliced
salt, black pepper

pigeons: 4 pigeons (see note, p. 105 if using commercially
produced squab)
4 small bunches thyme, parsley, marjoram (if using dried
use a teaspoon of thyme & marjoram for each bird)
4 tablespoons butter
1 tablespoon oil

rice: 1 cup rice
2½ cups milk (or water)
2 large egg yolks
3 tablespoons heavy cream
salt
a very little nutmeg
juice of 1 lemon

garnish: 4 hard-boiled eggs, quartered

Put the bones into a large pan. Cover them with water, and add the rest of the stock ingredients, but don't add much seasoning. Simmer for 3–4 hours. Strain and reduce by boiling to 3 cups. Taste and add more salt and pepper if required.

Tuck the herbs into the pigeon cavities. Then brown the birds in butter and oil. Place them closely together in a casserole, breast down, and pour on the boiling stock, which should just cover them. Put the lid on the pot. Simmer until the pigeons are cooked, either on top of the stove or in the oven.

When the pigeon meat parts from the breastbones, start cooking the rice. Wash it first, then add to 2 cups of milk, which should be simmering in a large pan. Season lightly with salt, cover and leave to cook gently. Break the rice up from time to time with a fork, and add more milk if necessary.

Meanwhile divide the pigeons in two, discarding the main part of the carcass. Keep the pieces warm in a covered dish while the stock in which the birds were cooked boils down to a strongly flavoured sauce. Skim it well.

Immediately before serving drain the rice of any surplus liquid and beat the egg yolks and cream into it. Season with nutmeg and more salt if required. Using about two-thirds of the rice, make a bed of it on a warm serving plate and lay the pigeon halves on top. Arrange the rest of the rice over them, so that they are smothered but visible. Pour lemon juice over the dish and garnish with egg quarters. Once the egg yolks are added to the rice, they will begin to cook slightly, so don't keep the dish hanging around or the yolks will harden and cause the rice to turn unappetisingly solid.

Pigeon with cabbage (for 4)

Cabbage growing is a British national sport as well as an industry. Yet we cook it appallingly. (How often do you meet anyone who really likes cabbage?) We ignore its wonderful quality of absorbing meat flavours while retaining an agreeable crispness and bite, as in this recipe.

> 4 pigeons (see note, p. 105, if using commercially
>   produced squab)
> ½ lb. fat bacon, diced [see footnote, p. 33]
> 1 tablespoon butter
> 20 small onions (about ¾ lb.)
> ½ cup dry white wine
> 1 cup beef stock
> 1 head savoy cabbage

Fry bacon gently in butter until its fat flows. Add pigeons and onions, and brown them. Transfer to casserole, pigeons breast down. Pour off remaining fat. Bring wine and stock to the boil in the frying pan, scraping in all the brown bits, then pour over the pigeons (wood pigeons should be almost covered, so you may need to add more hot stock). Put on the lid. Simmer gently. Meanwhile plunge the cabbage into a pan of boiling salted water for 10 minutes. Drain and open out into a nest shape. Half an hour before the pigeons are likely to be cooked, remove them from the casserole, place them breast down in the cabbage, and return the whole thing to the casserole. When cooked, arrange pigeons, cabbage, onions and bacon on a serving dish. Skim fat off the sauce and reduce to a concentrated flavour. Pour over the pigeons, etc., and serve.

NOTE: Some recipes put the blanched cabbage into the casserole with the pigeons immediately after the browning stage. But the above method leaves the cabbage crisper. It also has the advantage, particularly with wood pigeons, that most of the cooking can be done in advance without spoiling the fresh flavour added by cabbage when it is more lightly cooked.

Pigeon pie   (for 4)

Wood pigeons can quite well be used for this very English pie, which was originally intended for dovecote pigeons.

> shortcrust or puff pastry (using 1½ cups flour,
>   other ingredients in proportion)
> 1 egg, beaten
>
> filling: 4 pigeons
>   4 tablespoons butter
>   beef stock
>   6-oz. piece rump steak
>   4 hard-boiled egg yolks
>   1 tablespoon finely chopped mild onion
>   ½ lb. mushrooms, sliced
>   parsley, salt, pepper

Brown pigeons in butter, and then, if they are wood pigeons, simmer them for 1¼ hours, covered in beef stock. Halve the pigeons along breastbone. Lay steak on the bottom of a buttered pie dish, season, and lay pigeon halves on top. Season again and fill the gaps with hard-boiled egg yolk, crumbled. Add onion, mushrooms, plenty of parsley and stock to cover the meat. Put a band of pastry round the rim of the dish, moisten it, then cover with a lid of pastry. Knock up the edges,[2] decorate and brush with beaten egg. Put into a good hot oven to start with (for puff pastry, 450°; shortcrust, 425°) for 10 minutes, then reduce the heat to 375°. When pastry begins to look nicely browned, protect it with thick paper or several layers of greaseproof paper. Total cooking time for the pie 1½ hours.

Spanish pigeons with chocolate sauce (for 4)

Chocolate makes an excellent seasoning for game sauces. Italian dishes of hare with chocolate and pine nut sauce are famous; here's a Spanish recipe of a similar but lighter kind. Don't be nervous of the chocolate if you've not come across this kind of recipe before: so little is used that it is unidentifiable, yet the difference it makes in richness of flavour is surprising. Another important point of the dish is the glazed onions. Their moist sweetness goes well with dark close pigeon meat. In Spain plump squabs would be used, so I've had to adapt the recipe to our tougher wild birds.

4 pigeons, larded (see note, p. 105, if using commercially
    produced squab and adjust timing of steps accordingly)
1 large onion, sliced
4 tablespoons olive oil
½ cup dry white wine
about 3 cups chicken stock, lightly seasoned
12–16 pickling [small white] onions
2 teaspoons sugar
7 tablespoons butter
1½ tablespoons flour
1½–2 teaspoons grated Bournville [semi-sweet or
    German type] chocolate
1 lemon, cut down into wedges

[2] See footnote, p. 51.

Brown the pigeons and sliced onion in the oil. Fit them into a casserole, the pigeons breast down. Pour in the white wine, then enough chicken stock to cover the birds. Bring to the boil and simmer for 1½-2 hours until the pigeons are cooked.

One hour before the pigeons are cooked, prepare the small onions: prepare enough to make a single layer in a large heavy saucepan. Cover with water. Add the sugar and 4 tablespoons of the butter. Boil hard so that the liquid evaporates to a golden brown glaze. Keep a careful eye on the onions towards the end of the cooking, as they must not burn. Shake the pan gently so that they're coated in the caramel.

When the birds are almost done, i.e., when the legs move loosely and the meat begins to part from the breastbone, remove 2 cups of stock from the casserole. Reduce it by boiling to just over a cup (this concentrates the flavour, which is why you must start with lightly seasoned chicken stock). Skim off fat and foam as it rises. Mash the remaining butter with the flour (beurre manié), and add it in small knobs to the reduced stock, which should now be kept at simmering point. When the sauce has thickened, correct the seasoning and stir in the chocolate gradually to taste.

Arrange the cooked pigeons on a warm serving dish, with the glazed onions round them. Pour a little of the sauce over the birds, and put the rest into a sauceboat. Arrange the lemon wedges among the onions.

Pigeons au soleil (for 4)

"Pigeons in the sun" were very popular in England and France in the eighteenth century. The recipe occurs in most of the cookery books of the time. And I'm not surprised. It's worth taking trouble to lard the pigeons—particularly when, as in this recipe, they are being served without a sauce. Fried parsley is not much used these days, but its agreeable sandiness goes well with the pigeons in their sunburnt coating of crisp batter.

> batter: ½ cup plain [all-purpose] flour
> pinch salt
> 1 tablespoon olive oil

½ cup lukewarm water or beer
1 large egg white

4 pigeons (see note, p. 105, if using commercially
    produced squab)
½–lb. piece of fat bacon, chilled [see footnote, p. 33]
1 large onion, sliced
1 large carrot, sliced
bouquet garni
3–4 cups chicken or veal stock
salt, black pepper
oil or lard for frying
2 bunches parsley

garnish: 1 lemon, cut into wedges

First of all make the batter, so that it has time to stand. Mix flour and
salt with the oil and water or beer, beating the ingredients well together.
Cover and leave in the kitchen, not in the refrigerator or other cold place.
The egg white is not added until the batter is required.

Cut the chilled bacon into 2-inch strips, and lard the pigeons (larding
needles are obtainable for two or three shillings at good kitchen suppliers
—for U.S. sources, see p. 367). This is done by taking a stitch about 1½
inches long. As the needle is pulled through, the fat stays behind. It's
a pleasant job. Neat-fingered people will soon be able to arrange the
lardoons in tidy symmetry.

Put a thin layer of oil or melted lard into a heavy frying pan, and
brown the birds and the vegetables in it. Transfer them to a casserole
(pigeons breast down). Add the bouquet garni and enough stock to cover
the birds. Season well, as this stock will not be reduced to make a sauce.
Simmer for 1½–2 hours, until the birds are cooked. Remove the large
breast fillets—carcasses and remaining meat on the legs, etc., can be used
with the cooking stock to make pigeon soup for another meal.

Whisk the egg white until stiff, fold into the batter. Coat the pigeon
fillets (it doesn't make any difference if they're still warm) and fry in
olive oil or lard, which should be about ¼ inch deep in the frying pan.
When they're golden brown on both sides, and crisp, put them onto a
warm serving dish. Fry the parsley until dark green, drain and arrange
round the pigeons with the lemon quarters. Serve immediately.

NOTE: 1 cup white wine may be added to the cooking liquor (reduce the amount of stock). Wine always has a good effect on meat which is likely to be dry or tough, and the flavour of your pigeon soup will be improved. In this case, use water for the batter, not beer.

Pigeon with olives   (for 4)

We could, I think, make more use than we do of olives in cookery. They're in every grocer's shop and delicatessen—black olives, green olives and stuffed olives, large olives, small olives, olives in bottles and olives in barrels—yet how rarely they appear once the apéritifs are finished. This is a pity. In stuffings and sauces, they add a light sharpness to meat, their firm flesh gives bite and richness.

The kind of olives chosen for a dish will depend on personal taste (and, in some places, on what happens to be available). I've a preference for small black shiny olives, though my eye is often seduced by the green ones stuffed with red pimiento. Many varieties are grown in Mediterranean countries, but the main division is a matter of ripeness—green olives are picked when fully grown but unripe, black olives have been left on the tree to darken in the sun. This obviously makes for difference in texture as well as in flavour. Very occasionally one may buy olives which taste unpleasantly of brine: the remedy is to pour boiling water over them, and to leave them for 5 minutes before draining.

4 pigeons, larded (see note, p. 105, if using
   commercially produced squab)
1 large carrot, sliced
1 large onion, sliced
8 tablespoons [1 stick] butter
1 cup white wine
bouquet garni
chicken or veal stock, lightly seasoned
1½ tablespoons flour
½–¾ cup olives

for serving: boiled rice or egg noodles

Brown pigeons and vegetables in 4 tablespoons of butter. Transfer to a casserole. Add wine, bouquet garni and enough stock to cover the birds. Simmer for 1½–2 hours, until they are cooked.

About half an hour before the end of cooking time, remove 2½ cups of liquid from the casserole. Reduce it by hard boiling to just over 1¼ cups—let flavour be your guide, remembering that the olives will add sharpness to the final result. In a small heavy saucepan, melt the remaining butter, stir in the flour and cook for two or three minutes. Add the reduced stock bit by bit until you have a sauce the consistency of heavy cream. When the pigeons are cooked, add the olives to the simmering sauce and correct the seasoning (give the olives a chance to heat through before you do this). Pour a little of the sauce over the birds, and serve the rest in a sauceboat.

Choose boiled rice or egg noodles to go with this dish, rather than potatoes.

Matelote of pigeon *(for 4)*

The red wine dishes of France, or to be precise of Burgundy, have the most comforting effect in winter—eggs en meurette, matelote of fish, beef à la bourguignonne. Pigeons cooked in the same way are delicious. Apart from the wine, the little pieces of fat pork, the button mushrooms and tiny glazed onions make this stew into a special dish for Sunday lunch, or dinner on a cold night.

> *4 pigeons, preferably larded (see note, p. 105,*
> *if using commercially produced squab)*
> *¾ lb. belly of pork*
> *1 large carrot, chopped small*
> *1 large onion, chopped small*
> *4 tablespoons butter*
> *2 cloves garlic, crushed*

1½ tablespoons flour
1–1½ cups red wine
chicken or veal stock
salt, black pepper
nutmeg, ginger, ground cloves
½ lb. button mushrooms
16–24 pickling [small white] onions
2–3 lumps of sugar
dash of wine vinegar
2 tablespoons chopped parsley

for serving: either 12 triangles of bread, fried
in butter, or boiled potatoes

Remove skin and any bones from the belly of pork, then cut it into small strips, about 1½ inches long and ¼ inch wide and thick. Brown pigeons, pork, carrot and onion in the butter with the garlic: do this at a moderate heat, so as not to burn the butter. Put into a casserole (pigeons breast down). Stir the flour into the remaining fat. Cook for 2 or 3 minutes, then add the red wine and about 1 cup of stock. Pour into the casserole, adding more stock if necessary to cover the pigeons. Season with salt and pepper. Add a grating of nutmeg, and a good pinch of ginger and powdered cloves. Simmer for 1½ hours.

Now put the mushrooms into the pot, pushing them down below the simmering liquid. The onions can be added at the same time—or else they can be cooked and glazed separately (see Spanish pigeons with chocolate sauce, p. 111), which gives more flavour to the dish as well as improving its final appearance.

After a further ½ hour pigeons and mushrooms, etc., should all be cooked. Strain off the sauce into a clean pan, skim and reduce it by boiling if necessary. Use the sugar, wine vinegar and additional spices, if necessary, to improve the flavour.

Arrange the pigeons and vegetables in a large round serving dish. Pour the sauce over, sprinkle with parsley and put triangles of fried bread or boiled potatoes in a ring round the edge of the dish.

NOTE: This delicious way of cooking pigeons may be further improved by flaming the birds with a glass of brandy, after they've been browned and before they're put into the casserole.

Pigeon or game pâté

6–8 oz. boned pigeon, rabbit, hare or venison
liver of pigeon, rabbit or hare
3 oz. hard back pork fat [fatback]
½ lb. belly of pork
2 rashers bacon [see footnote, p. 33]
2 oz. veal or rump steak
½-inch slice of bread, crumbled
parsley and thyme
⅓ cup chopped onion
1 large clove garlic, crushed
4 tablespoons butter
1 egg, beaten
1½ tablespoons cognac,
   or ⅛ cup sherry or port
salt, pepper

Dice hard fat, liver and half the game. Finely mince the rest of the game, plus the pork belly, bacon and veal or steak (more game may be used; it depends how strong a flavour you like). Add bread crumbs, herbs. Simmer onion and garlic in the butter, without browning them, until soft and golden. Add to the pâté mixture with the beaten egg and cognac or wine. Season well with salt and pepper. Mix everything thoroughly with your hands. If you aren't sure about the seasoning, fry a little knob of the mixture and taste it.

Pack into a 2½-cup terrine, or 2 small ones—which is more practical, as the second pâté when cooked may be stored in the freezer. Cover with a double layer of foil, stand in a pan of hot water and bake for 1–1½ hours (time depends on the *depth* of the pâté, rather than its extent) at 325°; remove the foil about 10 minutes before the end of cooking time for the pâté to brown. It is done when it swims in fat, clear of the terrine; or when a steel knitting needle is pushed in and comes out clean. Leave to cool under a light weight, until next day at least. It takes 2 days for the full flavour to develop.

Game pie

The pâté mixture above can be turned into a delicious game pie, if it's baked in shortcrust or hot-water crust pastry. Allow some extra pieces of game, nicely cut into strips, to be layered in with it.

For recipes, see pages 49–66.

Pigeon or game soup   (for 4)

This excellent but simple soup is a good way of using up small amounts of game and the carcass.

> legs & carcasses of 4 or more pigeons
>> or head & forequarters of rabbit or hare
>> or mixture of game
> 1 medium carrot, sliced
> 1 medium onion, sliced
> bouquet garni
> about 1 quart beef stock
> port
> lemon juice
> salt, pepper

optional: red currant jelly

for serving: forcemeat balls (p. 102) or small croutons of fried bread

Simmer game, carrot, onion, bouquet garni and stock until meat begins to fall off the bones. Pour through a sieve into a clean pan. Remove the pieces of meat from the sieve—or as many as you can without too much trouble—and blend with about 3 cups of the strained stock (discard the vegetables, herbs and bones: they've done their work). Season with port wine, lemon juice, pepper and salt. The lemon juice is particularly important if you have no port. Red currant jelly may also be used as a seasoning.

Serve with tiny forcemeat balls, or with croutons.

NOTE: For a clear soup, add ½ lb. shin of beef and 1 pig's trotter [*foot*] to the game, and omit pureeing in the blender. Strain through layers of cheesecloth or a muslin-lined sieve, and skim well.

VENISON

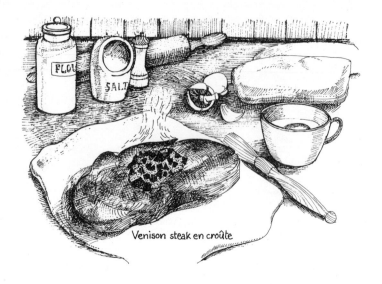

Venison steak en croûte

In the past noble lords and rich men—when they could get a license from the Crown—built themselves a living larder in the shape of a deer park with high fences and walls. They went out and formally hunted the deer inside, and then, to mix metaphors, made pigs of themselves on the venison. Now some of them are glad to sell their venison to the people, you and me, who used to poach it—if we could. Most of the English venison comes from fallow deer, the kind that drop their horns in April and May in the royal park at Richmond in Surrey—these are the traditional inhabitants of deer parks.[1] At Richmond, too, one may see red deer, which also provide venison, though more particularly in Scotland than in England.

French chefs have often complained that they could get nothing but

[1] Colonel William Byrd, 1674–1744, who had spent much time in England on business and otherwise, and who was the founder of Richmond, Virginia, made this comparison in 1728: "We had a haunch of venison for dinner, as fat and well tasted as if it had come out of Richmond park. . . . I believe the buck which gave us so good a dinner had eaten out his value in peas, which will make deer exceedingly fat."

the venison of roe deer to cook with. The flesh, said Escoffier, was "very often mediocre in quality," and he thought that the small, white-spotted fallow deer from an English park "has no equal as far as delicacy and tenderness are concerned." Those chefs devised very good recipes all the same.

When you eat venison, reflect that it was an integral part of living it up in the Middle Ages. The menu survives of a feast given in 1443, at the installation of John Stafford, archbishop of Canterbury. The game—strange list—included pheasant, swan, heron, crane, curlew, partridge, plover, rails and quails, and no less than three different dishes of venison.

They knew, the cooks of those days, that venison is a rich and gamy meat which needs tempering a little. They served it with saffron-flavoured frumenty pudding (p. 132), the wet ancestor of the modern cooked breakfast cereal, and with an early version of poivrade sauce (p. 130). Sometimes it was enclosed in pastry. Venison cooking by the Victorian age had multiplied accompaniments of fruit and berries—pears, apples, oranges, cherries, juniper berries, even bananas. In the United Kingdom port wine was as essential as red currant jelly, the two being combined in Francatelli's deliciously simple sauce for venison (p. 129), and in the better-known Cumberland sauce for cold venison (p. 131).

Venison is easy to cook. No problem there. The trouble may be to buy it. In England certain chain stores will take an order for venison; so will butchers specializing in game. People in the London area can have venison delivered from Groom & Sainthill, 3 Halkin Arcade. If they have a freezer, they can write to Game and Meat Products Ltd., Southampton, for the current price list: orders of a reasonable size are delivered to any part of the United Kingdom.[2]

Only persist. The venison is there on the hoof. The sad thing is that three-fourths of it goes abroad (like our best scallops, pigs, horsemeat and lobsters), mainly to Germany. It seems, though, that our producers are

[2] *In the U.S. try Hammacher Schlemmer, 147 E. 57th St., New York 10022; Maryland Market, 412 Amsterdam Ave., New York 10024; Czimer Foods Co., 953 W. 63 St., Chicago, Ill.; also for buffalo and elk write to Custer State Park, Hermosa, South Dakota. Hunting regulations vary from state to state and sometimes from year to year; such regulations stipulate conditions under which game can be sold in markets in the U.S. and purchases from reputable dealers are therefore assumed to be reliable. Protection of deer began in the Colonial period with Massachusetts enacting the first such legislation in 1694. The result is bountiful, though restricted, hunting: in one recent year, for instance, 114,529 deer were killed by 128,000 hunters in Colorado alone. Still, the bounty does not necessarily laden tables with good eating, for too many American cooks lack the confidence to cook venison as deliciously as it can and should be prepared.*

CUTS OF VENISON

Neck

Shank

Chuck

Brisket

Rib

Plate

Short loin

Flank

Loin end

Rump

Round

Hind Shank

Rolled neck
Boneless neck
Stew or loaf
Hamburger
Mincemeat
Meat balls

Chuck pot roast
Triangle pot roast
English cut
Arm pot roast
Arm steak
Blade pot roast
Blade steak
Venison brisket
Spare ribs
Hamburger

Knuckle soup bone

Cross cut for shank soup

Standing rib roasts
Rib steaks
Rib chops
Rolled rib roasts

Short ribs
Hamburger
Plate boiling venison
Rolled plate

Club steak
T-bone steak
Porterhouse steak

Rolled flank
Flank stew
Flank steak
Flank steak fillets

Tenderloin, Filet mignon
Sirloin steaks

Rolled rump
Rump roasts
Rump steaks

Sirloin tip
Top round
Bottom round
Round roasts
Round steaks

Heel of round

Stew or Hamburger

beginning to meet tough competition from Russia and New Zealand, and may have to consider new markets. They might, who knows, consider us, their fellow countrymen. With intelligent and patient publicity (think of the avocado pear and chicory campaigns) venison could soon become part of our normal choice of meat. It's not, after all, an exotic, but a familiar item of our traditional food and folklore.

Venison soup (for 6)

A good nineteenth-century soup, using the cheapest parts of venison, and the bones. It's a recipe that can be easily adapted to other game, hare, pigeon, etc.

> 1 lb. stewing venison, plus bones
> 1 thin slice gammon [or Canadian bacon]
> 1 stalk celery, cut into 3 pieces
> 1 medium onion, quartered
> 4-oz. piece carrot [1 carrot about 6 inches long]
> bouquet garni
> scant teaspoon mace
> 6 cups water
> 1 tablespoon butter
> 1 tablespoon flour
> ½ cup port
> salt, black pepper

optional: red currant jelly

Put everything, except butter, flour, port and jelly, into a large pan. Simmer for about 2 hours until the venison is cooked (the time depends on the age of the venison). Skim and strain the soup. Pick a few nice pieces of meat out of the strainer and keep them warm; put the rest of the meat, without skin, bones, etc., back into the soup and mash in blender or push through the food mill. Bring back to the boil, turn the heat down a little and add the butter and flour, which should be mashed together, in little knobs. Keep stirring as you do this, and the soup will thicken smoothly after about 4 or 5 minutes: it should not boil hard, but simmer. Add the port wine and the pieces of venison. Correct the seasoning with salt and pepper, adding a little red currant jelly if you like. As with all venison dishes, this soup should be served very hot, with very hot soup plates.

Venison cutlets in the Ardennes style   *(for 4)*

If you've never cooked venison before, try this recipe from Elizabeth David's *French Provincial Cooking*. For one thing it's an introduction to the fine combination of venison and juniper berries; for another, the method of baking the cutlets or chops gives one plenty of chance to make sure that all is well. The worst of trying some new things—a soufflé for example or a steak and kidney pudding—is that there's no way of knowing whether you've succeeded or flopped until everyone starts eating. So build up confidence with this exceptionally delicious recipe before committing yourself to the grander enterprise of a whole roast of venison.

8 cutlets or 4 thick loin chops of venison
12 crushed juniper berries
dried marjoram or thyme
salt, freshly ground black pepper
lemon juice
4 tablespoons butter
1 small onion, chopped
3 carrots, diced
½ cup white wine or vermouth
½ cup water
about 4 tablespoons chopped cooked ham
⅓ cup bread crumbs
¼ cup chopped parsley
extra butter
2–3 teaspoons red currant jelly
juice of half a bitter orange

for serving: boiled potatoes

Mash juniper berries with some dried marjoram or thyme, salt and pepper. Squeeze lemon juice over the meat and rub the pieces with the juniper mixture. It's a good idea to do this an hour or two before you start the cooking. Melt 4 tablespoons butter in a shallow pan, add onion and carrots. When they are light brown, put in the meat and brown it on both sides too. Pour in wine or vermouth, and boil steadily to reduce it a little. Add the water. Put some chopped ham on top of each cutlet or chop (transfer them, if more convenient, to a shallow ovenproof serving dish), then some bread crumbs mixed with the chopped parsley. Dab a little butter on top of the bread crumbs. Bake in a low oven, 300–325°, uncovered. The time required will depend on the condition of the venison, varying from 1 to 2 hours. After about 45 minutes, pierce one of the chops gently with a larding needle or skewer to see if it's nearly ready.

When the meat is tender, pour off the juices into a wide pan (keep the meat warm in the oven, at a reduced temperature) and boil the juices down until the flavour is well concentrated. Stir in the red currant jelly and bitter orange juice (use a little dark marmalade when Seville oranges are not in season and less jelly). Pour over the cutlets. Serve very hot, with a few boiled potatoes.

Venison in the Villeneuve style (for 4)

We do not seem to have much of a habit in Great Britain of wrapping chopped meat and seasonings into small delicious bundles, enclosed—and perpetually basted as they cook—by the web of fat known as the caul. Faggots, those good but hefty West Country meatball specialities, are the only example I can think of. They are really a rough pâté, eaten hot, and made most usefully from the liver and lights of freshly killed pigs. The recipe I give here is a much finer affair (and much simpler to make) from Escoffier. He served these venison packages with chasseur sauce and a purée of celery. You could try them without a sauce, accompanied by bananas, split and fried in butter. Or with a potato and celeriac purée.

The finest meat from loin or haunch may be used; or the less noble parts, as long as they are well trimmed of fat, skin and gristly bits.

¾ lb. lean trimmed venison
milk
½ cup white bread crumbs
¼ cup heavy cream
8 tablespoons melted but cool butter
salt, pepper
piece of caul fat
butter for frying

Chop or grind the meat. Add a very little milk to the bread crumbs and squeeze them out, so that the bread forms a thick paste. Mix meat, bread, cream and butter. Season well. Divide the mixture into 8 or 12 knobs. Soften and stretch the caul fat in warm water. Cut it into 8 or 12 squares and wrap up the venison knobs neatly, flattening them into ovals about ½ inch thick. Fry in butter on both sides until golden brown, about 15 minutes in all.

Venison en croûte (for 4)

Venison steaks may be encased in puff or short pastry, in the same way as fillet of beef.

¾ lb. short or puff pastry
4 loin or rump steaks of venison (without bones)
¼ lb. mushrooms, chopped
1 large clove garlic, crushed
6 tablespoons butter
about ¼–½ cup bread crumbs
1 egg yolk
salt, black pepper

Roll out the pastry and cut into four oblong pieces large enough to enclose the steaks. Cook mushrooms and garlic in butter, then add enough bread crumbs to make a moist stuffing. Season well with salt and pepper. Sear the steaks quickly on both sides in a heavy pan which has been rubbed over with lard. Put some stuffing into the centre of each piece of pastry, lay the steaks on top, then the rest of the stuffing. Brush the pastry edges with egg yolk and bring them together to form turnovers. Brush the tops with egg yolk, and bake for 20 minutes at 425°.

Civet of venison (for 8)

A dish for a banquet, or at least for a meal of celebration.

3 lbs. stewing venison, diced and trimmed

marinade: ½ bottle red wine
1 medium onion, sliced
⅓ cup brandy
⅓ cup olive oil
salt, black pepper

sauce: ½ lb. streaky bacon in a piece [see footnote, p. 33]
4 tablespoons butter
2 large onions, chopped
1 large carrot, diced
large clove garlic, crushed
4 tablespoons flour
beef or venison stock
bouquet garni
¼ lb. mushrooms, sliced

garnish: 8 tablespoons [1 stick] butter
2 teaspoons sugar
24 small onions (pickling size)
beef or venison stock
24 small mushrooms
salt, pepper
8 slices bread
chopped parsley

Mix the marinade ingredients together, seasoning them well, and soak the venison in marinade overnight. Next day, make the sauce. Cut bacon into strips about 1 inch long and ¼ inch wide and thick. Melt butter in a heavy pan, and in it brown the bacon. Drain the venison, reserving marinade. When the fat runs from the bacon, put onions and carrot and garlic into the pan to be browned lightly, then the well-drained venison. Stir the flour into the pan to take up the fat, and make a sauce by adding the strained marinade, plus enough stock to cover the ingredients (everything can be transferred to a deep casserole if this is more convenient). Add the sliced mushrooms and bouquet garni, simmer until the venison is cooked—about 1½ to 2 hours. Skim off any surplus fat. (The cooking up to this point may be done the day before the venison is to be eaten.)

Half an hour before the meal, prepare the garnish (and reheat the civet if necessary). Melt 2 tablespoons of butter with the sugar in a heavy pan. Turn the small onions in this until they are well coated. Add just enough stock to cover them, and cook at a galloping boil. This will reduce the liquid to a spoonful or two of caramel. Be careful it doesn't burn, and keep shaking the onions about in it so that they are nicely glazed. Cook the mushrooms whole in 2 tablespoons of butter, with salt and pepper. Cut the bread into triangles, and fry in the last 4 tablespoons of butter.

Arrange the civet on a large hot serving dish, put the mushrooms and onions on top, pushing them down a little so that they look naturally part of the dish (but not too far so that they disappear). The croutons go round the edge. Sprinkle with parsley and serve very hot.

Venison chops grilled   *(for 4)*

A simple recipe which shows off very well the flavour of venison.

4 venison loin chops, thick ones
piece of caul fat
¾ lb. mushrooms, or 20 juniper berries
6 tablespoons butter
salt, freshly ground black pepper

Season the chops with salt and plenty of pepper. Soften the caul fat in tepid water, cut it into four pieces and wrap up the chops (trim off the surplus—the meat should not be swaddled). Broil for 20 minutes, turning once, keeping the heat high for 5 minutes, then turning it down to medium. Stew the mushrooms or crushed juniper berries in the butter. Season and pour over the chops just before serving them.

Roast venison

It's not necessary to marinate roasting joints of venison (should you wish to do so, use the marinade given with the civet recipe, p. 104), but they should be larded. Which is a reasonable precaution to take with any piece of very lean meat—hare, beef steaks, pigeons, etc., as well as venison. Buy a piece of fat end of bacon. Chill it firm, and cut it into strips 2 inches long and just over one-eighth of an inch wide and thick. Push a piece into the open end of a larding needle and take a stitch in the joint as if you were sewing, leaving the fat bacon behind. Repeat until the whole joint is nicely studded with fat.

To roast the venison, tie a jacket of pork back fat (or a fatty piece of pork or bacon skin) round it and cook at 350°. Venison should be slightly rare: the time required for a small roast is about 20 minutes per pound, plus 20 minutes. When roasts are larger, above 4 pounds, reduce the time per pound to 15 minutes. Should you ever have the good fortune to be presented with a haunch of venison, i.e., a leg plus half the saddle in one magnificent piece, it will require 3 to 4 hours of cooking.

Serve roast venison with one of the following sauces:

Francatelli's venison sauce

Of all the sauces for venison, I think that this one, invented by Queen Victoria's chef, Francatelli, is the best. It happens to be easy to make as well.

> 2½ tablespoons port wine
> 1 cup red currant jelly
> small stick of cinnamon, bruised
> thinly pared rind of a lemon

Simmer together for 5 minutes, stirring. Strain into a hot sauceboat.

Poivrade sauce (pepper sauce)

Poivrade sauce started out in the Middle Ages as a kind of bread sauce, with stock and wine or vinegar replacing the milk. The seasoning was, of course, pepper. It was still popular with people of old-fashioned tastes in 1846. But by that time this much more complex sauce had been developed by the great chefs. The quantities sound enormous, but as it forms the basis of several sauces to go not only with venison but also with lamb and hare, it's worth making the full amount and storing the surplus in the freezing compartment of a refrigerator.

1 carrot, diced
1 onion, diced
5 tablespoons corn oil
⅓ cup flour
3 cups beef stock
1½ tablespoons tomato paste
bouquet garni
venison bones, if possible
½ cup vinegar
½ cup marinade (see civet recipe, p. 127)
8 crushed peppercorns
½ cup red wine

Brown carrot and onion in the oil. Add flour, and when it's browned, stir in stock and tomato paste. Put the bouquet garni and bones, if used, into the pan, and simmer for 2 hours, covered. Skim off the fat. Meanwhile reduce vinegar and marinade in a small pan with the peppercorns. When it measures about ¾ cup, put it into a larger pan and add the strained brown sauce. Simmer for a further half hour and then add the red wine.

Venison sauce: 1½ cups poivrade sauce and 1 teaspoon sugar boiled down to just over 1 cup. Remove from the heat, and stir in 4 tablespoons butter in small pieces. Added at the last moment like this, without being too much heated or cooked, the butter gives a wonderful flavour and sheen to the sauce.

Cherry sauce: Heat 1 cup each poivrade sauce and red currant jelly together. Stir in ¼ cup drained black pitted cherries (Swiss canned ones are very good). An excellent sauce, too, for duck.

Cream sauce: Pour fat from the roasting pan, leaving the juices behind. Warm about 2 ounces of brandy or gin or other spirits, set alight and pour into the pan, scraping in all the delicious brown bits. (If you've used gin, add 2 or 3 crushed juniper berries as well.) Pour in ½ cup heavy cream and a generous tablespoon of poivrade sauce. Correct the seasoning.

If you've no alcohol, season the sauce with lemon juice and a little sugar at the end.

Cumberland sauce for cold venison

Melt 1 cup red currant jelly with the juice of two oranges and 1 lemon, a teaspoonful of prepared mustard, a dash of cayenne pepper and a dash of ginger. Meanwhile cut finely into shreds the peel of 1 orange and 1 lemon (no pith) and simmer them in boiling water for 5 minutes. Drain and add to the jelly, with 2 or 3 tablespoons of port. Sometimes some glacé cherries are added, but they should be well washed first under the hot tap to remove the sticky syrup which coats them: not, I feel, a good embellishment.

ACCOMPANIMENTS TO VENISON

French beans, dressed with plenty of butter, are usually served with venison in Britain.

Chestnuts or lentils, cooked whole, or served as a purée.

Celery or celeriac, the latter usually made into a purée with potatoes (see p. 161).

The edible funguses, from cepes and girolles through to cultivated mushrooms—and truffles.

Pears—the Baden-Baden style of presenting venison includes pears, cored and quartered, stewed with lemon rind and cinnamon in water, *without sugar* (though a little red currant jelly added towards the end of cooking time is an advantage).

Apples, sliced and fried in butter, or stewed with cloves.

Bitter oranges sliced, and *sauce bigarade.* Melt 2 tablespoons butter and stir in 2 tablespoons flour. Cook until pale brownish colour. Stir in 2 cups of hot venison or beef stock. Peel two Seville oranges thinly, cut peel into strips, and simmer in water for 5 minutes. Drain and add to the sauce with seasoning. Cook slowly for 5 minutes. Put in the juice of the two oranges and 3 or 4 teaspoons of sugar and the meat juices from the roasted venison.

Frumenty flavoured and coloured with saffron was, as I've said, a favourite accompaniment to venison in the Middle Ages, especially to salted venison. This recipe comes from a fifteenth-century manuscript in the British Museum: "Take wheat and pick it clean. Put it into a mortar with a little water and pound it with a pestle to loosen the husks. Then fan away the husks and put it in a pot and let it simmer until it bursts. Drain it well, add some sweet milk, and simmer it again, stirring. When it's cooked colour it with saffron, and season it with salt." Other recipes enrich the frumenty with beaten egg yolks.

Vegetables

ASPARAGUS

How would you describe the best asparagus? Thick, certainly. Fresh certainly, as, whatever kind is grown, its flavour will deteriorate with delay. No argument here.

But after that, would you prefer it to be blanched white? Or white with a yellowish head? Or green and white streaked with pinkish purple? Or as green as possible?

The answer will tell me more about you than about absolute standards of asparagus perfection. Italians like white asparagus with a yellowish head (the fattest and most delicious asparagus I've ever eaten was in a restaurant at Bassano del Grappa—a rich little Italian town with a famous bridge, famous painters, famous brandy and famous asparagus). The French like their violet and green and white spears. And the English and Americans[1] like unblanched, tender greenness. In our favour, I will

---

[1] European types of asparagus are seldom obtainable in the U.S., but fresh, spring-green, slender spears come from California and especially the Sacramento Valley; don't buy thick stalks without certainty that they represent an imported European variety.

modestly add that European chefs working in England have said, do still say, that our fresh asparagus beats all for flavour.

That's the theory anyway. In practice, your answer would more likely have been curt, rather than considered: "The best asparagus is the asparagus I can afford—when I can find it."

There is an aura of aristocracy, a mystique of asparagus which seems to stop gardeners growing it. And English housewives buying it. Asparagus is not for us. Its past is long, cherished and peppered with great names. Pliny described asparagus spears weighing 4 ounces (Super Extra Selected Roman style). Louis XIV ate asparagus in January—did it, I wonder, have any flavour at all?—forced in his gardens at Versailles. Pepys bought "sparrowgrass" (it's still called "grass" in the trade) in 1667 in Fenchurch Street, a hundred spears for 1s.6d. Proust's eye was caught by the rainbow asparagus lying on his aunt's kitchen table at Illiers.

I remember as a child being told by an elderly gardener in Gloucester that the huge bed we were contemplating had taken seven—or was it ten? —years to establish. I forget his exact figure, but recall that it exceeded the number of years it had taken to establish me in the same world. He was choosing the finest asparagus for a luncheon party during the Three Choirs Festival. Severn salmon and strawberries were to complete the meal. It all sounded very grand.

In fact the old man was quite wrong with his figures. With modern methods, planting one-year-old crowns, English kitchen gardeners can pick a little asparagus the first season, more the second, and as much as one likes the third. This is because nowadays asparagus growing is better understood, thanks to Mr. Kidner of Suffolk. He discovered that to be sure of asparagus producing a high proportion of fine fat heads (as opposed to the thin "sprue"), he had to select and breed it like cattle. He was one of a family of stock breeders, and had first applied their methods to asparagus in 1908 in his own kitchen garden. It was not until 1931 that he turned wholly to asparagus farming. Much work is still being done to produce more and more reliable asparagus: growers like Mr. Paske of Regal Lodge, Kentford, Suffolk, import Dutch and French strains to improve their own stock. (He will supply both crowns and bunches of asparagus by post.)[2]

Given all this hard work and intelligence, it seems ridiculous that in our country of cheap food we can't buy good cheap asparagus. It makes

[2] One-year-old *Mary Washington* or *Waltham Washington* plants are recommended for Americans by Angelo M. Pellegrini in his *The Food-Lover's Garden*.

me angry that we haven't encouraged growers to grow more. We have 1,000 acres of asparagus in England, commercial acres, and little or none in Scotland, Ireland and Wales. Holland has twenty times as much. I wonder why this is? Are we of all the people in Europe so cowed by past grandeur that we cling to cabbages and to giant, stringy scarlet runners and Olympian marrows? What a waste of ground.

I have this image of early summer, May and June. We walk home slowly up the village street, which runs across the cliff at a kindly slope. The midday Angelus rings from the church tower above us. Children scream out of school, and flow politely past our slower feet into open cottage doors. The air pulses with the warm smell of lilac, but as we pass each door, the lilac dominance is subdued by heady wafts of asparagus cooking.

This is not Utopia. It's a poorish village, less than 300 miles south of London. The inhabitants have the sense to grow asparagus, that's all. If they haven't a garden patch across the river, they can buy asparagus at 7/– the two-pound bunch in the village shop. No aristocratic aura. Not even a whiff of bourgeois privilege, just a universal smell of asparagus.

Yet in spite of this abundance, in spite of this daily luxury, it's from village neighbours that I've learned:

How to make the most of asparagus
(for 4 to 6)

2-lb. bunch of asparagus
1½ lbs. new potatoes
4–6 hard-boiled or coddled eggs

Scrape the new potatoes and leave them in water until required. Peel the hard part from the asparagus stems, then trim 2–3 inches from the bottom —this is the part usually left on the side of the plate. Tie the asparagus into bunches.

Take a large saucepan. Put 2 inches of water into it with a teaspoon of salt, and bring to the boil. Stand the bunches of asparagus upright in the pan, put the stem trimmings round them, and the new potatoes on top of trimmings. Put the lid on the pan, or arrange a domed cover of foil on it if the asparagus heads come above the rim. They will cook in the steam and be tender by the time the lower part of the stalks is done. Allow 20–40 minutes according to thickness and type.

Special pans with an internal strainer can be bought, in France, for cooking asparagus. One or two shops in London or in various U.S. metropolises may be able to supply them, but usually one has to improvise with pan and foil. Unless you grow asparagus, the cost of a special pan is hardly justified.

Remove the asparagus, when cooked, to a colander to drain (but save the cooking water—see next recipe), or arrange the stalks on an old-fashioned meat dish with a removable strainer. Put the potatoes, which will be delicately flavoured with asparagus, round the edge of the dish, together with the eggs cut in half. Serve hot, warm or cold, with one of the sauces given on pages 139–41.

This dish makes an excellent main course for a summer lunch, but if you want to make it a little more substantial, wrap thin slices of Bayonne, Westphalian or Parma ham round the bundles of asparagus. In Switzerland, air-dried beef from the Grisons is eaten with asparagus in this way.

You are left with the asparagus water and stalk trimmings, enough to transform the evening's soup into something unusually good:

> ½ lb. potatoes, peeled & cubed
> ½ cup chopped onion
> 1–2 cloves garlic, chopped
> 4 tablespoons butter
> 2 teaspoons flour*
> asparagus water & trimmings
> milk or chicken stock
> cream or butter
> chopped parsley & chervil,
>   or a head or two of asparagus saved from lunch

Sauté potatoes, onion and garlic gently in the butter, without browning them. If you intend to put the soup through a strainer or food mill, stir in the flour; if you're going to liquidize it, the flour* is unnecessary. Pour in the asparagus water and simmer until the potatoes are just cooked. Add the asparagus trimmings, and when they are heated through, sieve or liquidize the soup in a vegetable juicer, or a blender.

Return it to a clean pan, and bring it to the right consistency by adding milk or stock. Reheat to just below boiling point, and finish the soup with a spoonful of cream per person, or a knob of butter. Sprinkle with the chopped herbs, or with the asparagus cut into pieces the size of peas.

HOT SAUCES FOR ASPARAGUS

Flemish sauce

Serve each person with a hard-boiled or coddled egg (exactly 6 minutes in boiling water for a large one, leaving the yolk slightly liquid), and have a sauceboat of melted butter on the table (allow 2 tablespoons per person). The eggs should be crushed with a fork, seasoned, and then moistened with melted butter. The asparagus is dipped into this mixture before being eaten in the usual way.[3]

A French version of this method serves each person with a boiled egg and a little pot of melted butter. First dip the asparagus into the butter, then into the runny egg yolk, as if it were a child's bread "soldier."[4]

Maltese sauce

If Flemish sauce is the simplest, Maltese sauce is the best to serve with asparagus. It is really a variation of hollandaise sauce.

>   3½ *tablespoons white wine vinegar*
>   2½ *tablespoons water*
>   10 *white peppercorns*
>   3 *large egg yolks*
>   12 *tablespoons* [1½ *sticks*] *unsalted butter, cut into 12 pieces*
>   *juice & grated rind of an orange, preferably a blood orange*
>   *salt & lemon juice to taste*

[3] *With fingers, of course. In Europe it's fair to say that using a knife and fork would be regarded as vulgar—a kind of super-genteel vulgarity.*

[4] *When children have boiled eggs in England a slice of buttered bread is cut into fingers (sometimes called bread soldiers) to be used to sop up the runny yolk.*

Boil vinegar, water and peppercorns in a small pan until they're reduced to 1 tablespoon of liquid. Strain it into a large bowl or the top of a double boiler, and leave to cool. Beat in the egg yolks with a wooden spoon, then set the basin over a pan of simmering water on a low heat. Add the butter knob by knob, stirring all the time. Remember that you are really making hot mayonnaise, so don't add more butter until the previous piece is absorbed. If the sauce curdles, the remedy is the same as for mayonnaise: put another yolk into a clean basin, and start again, adding the curdled mixture slowly. The sauce is finished and ready for its final seasoning when it coats the back of the spoon like a custard. Finish with the rind and juice of the orange, some salt and a little lemon juice if extra sharpness is needed.

The consistency of the sauce may be varied by using less butter, say ¼ pound to 3 yolks; Escoffier used ½ pound of butter to 2 yolks.

This sauce is not difficult: it needs concentration, and calm patience. See that the water keeps at a bare simmer; if it begins to boil hard the eggs are likely to scramble. I recommend the following timetable: (1) peel the asparagus; (2) make the sauce and stand it at the side of the stove, over hot but not simmering water, while you (3) cook the asparagus. The sauce will come to no harm, so long as you give it an occasional stir and make sure it doesn't get too hot.

Sauce hollandaise: the preceding recipe without the orange juice and rind. A basic sauce, for salmon, and other poached fish, eggs and vegetables to be served as a course on their own—true French beans, broccoli of all kinds, globe artichokes, sea kale, and of course asparagus.

Sauce mousseline: beat ⅓–½ cup heavy cream until thick, and fold it carefully into *sauce hollandaise* just before serving. Correct the seasoning.

COLD SAUCES FOR ASPARAGUS

Vinaigrette aux fines herbes

One tablespoon lemon juice or tarragon wine vinegar beaten up with salt, pepper, a teaspoon of sugar, and 5–6 tablespoons of olive oil.

Flavour with plenty of chopped parsley, tarragon, chervil, and chives or spring onion tops.

Mayonnaise Maltese style

Two egg yolks, salt, pepper, well beaten together with 1 teaspoon lemon juice or wine vinegar. Drop by drop, beat in ½ cup olive oil; then another ½ cup in a steady stream. Season with more lemon juice or vinegar, and the grated rind and juice of a blood orange.

Tarragon cream

This is a delicious, quickly made sauce from *Food for the Greedy*, by Nancy Shaw, published in 1936: "Season some thick cream with salt and pepper, and a dust of curry powder; and whip it until thick. Then flavour it by adding gradually a few drops of white tarragon vinegar and place it on ice for a short time before being served. To be sent up in a sauce boat for cold asparagus." Don't overdo the chilling: in the thirties, domestic refrigerators were the new kitchen toy, food was chilled whenever possible—not always a good thing for delicate flavours.

Dijon sauce

Crush the yolk of a hard-boiled egg with 3 *petit-suisse* cheeses to a smooth paste. Add 2 tablespoons Dijon mustard, then drop by drop ½ cup oil. Flavour with lemon juice. This sauce, which I've taken from a French periodical, is good with hard-boiled eggs on their own, and with other cold vegetables such as artichokes. It should be the consistency of mayonnaise.

Chicken, rabbit or lamb in
the Argenteuil style   (for 6)

I like the proud habit of calling a dish after the place where a main ingredient flourishes. Eggs Florentine (spinach), Crécy soup (carrots), *omelette Lyonnaise* (onions), *sauce Maltaise* (blood oranges). We could by the same token call this dish chicken Evesham style, or Battersea style, in memory of those acres and acres of early asparagus beds that lie now under rows of grey houses, a power station and a fun fair. Argenteuil, though, must be allowed, because it's unmistakably a French recipe and a good one. It also seems suitable that Argenteuil, where Monet set up his easel beside the Seine, should produce asparagus. Potatoes, carrots, onions have solid merits, I agree; one could not imagine life without them, but asparagus is a most Impressionist vegetable. Proust saw a pile of them lying on the kitchen table, "tinged with ultramarine and rosy pink which ran from their heads, finely stippled in mauve and azure, through a series of imperceptible changes to their white feet, still stained a little by the soil of their garden-bed."

> 2–3 lbs. asparagus
> 1 large chicken, or rabbit, jointed,
>   or 2 lbs. boned shoulder of lamb cut in 2-inch pieces
> 4 tablespoons butter
> 4 small onions, chopped
> 1½ tablespoons flour
> ½ cup cream
> lemon juice, salt, pepper to taste

Clean and cook the asparagus in the usual way. Save the cooking water, and put a quarter of the asparagus through a sieve or blender to make a purée. Meanwhile brown the meat and onions lightly in the butter. Stir in the flour, then about 1 cup of the asparagus water. Simmer until the meat is cooked, stirring it about every so often. Be careful that the liquid does not evaporate too quickly: if you cannot turn the heat down very low, it's a good idea to cover the pan with a lid or piece of foil, so that the liquid is conserved. More asparagus water can be added, but watch the saltiness.

When the meat is just cooked, stir the cream into the sauce and keep it boiling for three or four minutes until it begins to thicken nicely. Then add the asparagus purée and bring it back to the boil. Correct the seasoning with salt and pepper, and sharpen with a little lemon juice. The sauce should be well amalgamated and thick, without being heavy. It will also be a most beautiful green colour. There should not be too much of it (the English tend to souse meat in thin liquids).

Arrange the cooked asparagus on a hot serving dish, either in bunches or as a circle round the edge. Pour the meat and sauce into the centre. Serve immediately.

Out of season, this dish may be made successfully with frozen asparagus. Three packages are the minimum requirement, four are better. In either case, allow half a pound of cooked asparagus for the purée.

Asparagus and egg tart

This and the following recipe provide good ways of stretching a small quantity of asparagus (they both lend themselves to tactful adjustment according to the resources of the larder as well). Don't use the finest quality, thick asparagus, but the thinner kind with spears about one-fourth inch thick; out of season, frozen asparagus may be used.

> shortcrust pastry shell, 9 inches diameter
> ½–1 lb. asparagus
> 8 eggs
> 4 tablespoons butter
> 1 small clove garlic, crushed
> salt, pepper

> optional: 2½ tablespoons cream

Prebake the shortcrust pastry in the usual way until fully cooked; clean and boil and drain the asparagus, having first trimmed it to 4-inch lengths (use trimmings and asparagus water for soup, see p. 138). Beat the eggs just enough to amalgamate yolks and whites; melt the butter slowly in a heavy pan with the garlic, and add the eggs. Stir them with a wooden spoon over a very low heat until they start to look scrambled but are still rather liquid. Then remove the pan from the heat and add the cream if used (the eggs will continue to cook in their own heat). Season with salt and pepper.

While the eggs are cooking, reheat the pastry case in the oven, and the asparagus in a little of the cooking water. Turn the scrambled egg into the pastry case, and arrange the asparagus on top. Serve immediately.

If you wish to serve the tart cold, let all the ingredients cool, and assemble just before serving so that the pastry has no chance of becoming soggy.

Asparagus au gratin (for 4 to 6)

Vegetables au gratin—leeks, purple sprouting broccoli, sea kale, potatoes and so on—make a good supper dish, or a delicious first course for a dinner party. Vegetables and sauce can both be cooked and put together several hours before the meal, then reheated just before the meal begins.

1–2 *lbs. asparagus*
2 *generous tablespoons butter*
2 *heaping tablespoons flour*
1 *cup hot milk*
1 *cup asparagus water*
¼ *cup cream*
nutmeg, salt, pepper to taste
4–6 *hard-boiled eggs, sliced*
¼ *cup grated cheese (preferably Gruyère)*
1 *heaping tablespoon bread crumbs*
2 *tablespoons melted butter*

optional: 2 *slices cooked ham*

Cook and drain the asparagus in the usual way. Melt the butter in a heavy pan, stir in the flour and leave to bubble for a moment or two. Add the milk and asparagus water gradually to make a smooth sauce. Simmer for 15 minutes or more, until the sauce is thick. Chop the ham, if it's to be used, and add to the sauce with the cream. Season with salt, pepper and nutmeg.

Arrange the asparagus in an oval gratin dish, with the sliced hard-boiled eggs on top. Pour the sauce over them, leaving a clear quarter-inch at the top of the dish or the sauce will boil over and make a mess. Mix cheese and bread crumbs and scatter them on top of the sauce. Dribble the melted butter evenly over them, and put into a hot oven, 425°, for about 20 minutes until the dish is bubbling and brown (the final browning can also be done under the broiler).

CARROTS

Carrots are sweet. And carrots are a beautiful colour. And they are cheap.

It's impossible to imagine cooking without them; they've become a basic potherb of European kitchens. English, Irish, Scottish, American, French, German and Italian soups and stews demand carrots. So do Italian tomato and beef sauces for pasta (carrots were first cultivated in the Mediterranean gardens of Greece and Rome).

We rely on these fashionably coloured roots without a thought. Except perhaps for a moment's gratitude when children nibble them raw, rather than sweets, even if they don't make their hair curl. Or when they arrive at the greengrocer's in late spring, yellow-orange bunches with plumed green leaves—and a higher price than we've been paying for carrots all winter.

They're worth more attention. I'm not suggesting carrots at every meal, as in our house when I was preparing this chapter; and as in nineteenth-century Vichy, where smart doctors still seemed to agree with Galen, the great second-century Graeco-Roman physician to Marcus Aurelius, that carrots help to break wind and scour the digestion. It's their gayer virtues that need exploiting. For instance, carrots make vivid apricot-coloured jam, and good puddings like the angels' hair charlotte on page 153, or Hannah Glasse's carrot pudding on page 154. It's sad that we've given up making such things, though a hint of them did come back during the last war. In those days anything sweet was welcomed and exploited. There was a popular Christmas pudding recipe containing grated carrot. And I remember a high spot of school catering, a carrot flan, the bright orange disks, boiled with some sugar first, set in lemon jelly discreetly flavoured with ginger. The strange pudding looked beautiful. After a moment or two of schoolgirl priggery, hunger overcame dislike of the unknown, and we found the flan delicious. Now I try all the sweet carrot recipes I can find. It's the combination of flavour, colour and agreeable chewiness that makes the carrot so successful a pudding ingredient.

To start with, though, we put carrots into soups or salads; their freshness stimulates tired appetites at the start of an evening meal.

Carrot salad

Of all carrot recipes, this shows off the fresh sweetness and brilliant colour of the carrot to best advantage. I'm always surprised that it's not served more often in homes and restaurants. Children love it. It costs very litle. It's the easiest dish in the world to prepare, and, by changing the green herbs, the flavour can be varied quite simply.

Use old carrots for the richest, sweetest flavour, new carrots for the lightest. The best version of this salad I've ever eaten was seasoned with chopped new fennel leaves, and served on a bright pink oval dish.

> 1 lb. carrots
> about 2½ tablespoons chopped fennel, or parsley, or chives,
>   or chervil, or tarragon
> 5 tablespoons oil
> 1 tablespoon lemon juice
> salt & sugar

The carrots may be grated to extreme fineness, or to the thickness of matches. Mix in the other ingredients, adding sugar and salt to taste. Chill for at least an hour, and before serving, turn the mass of carrots over; drain it well. The salad should be moist, not swimming in liquid.

Crécy soup *(for 4)*

Two small towns dispute the title to carrot soups and purées in France—Crécy-en-Ponthieu, the site of the English victory in 1346, up near Abbeville on the Somme River, and Crécy-en-Brie, to the east of Paris, in the cheese and sugar beet district of the Marne. Both areas grow good root crops. I'm sure battle associations are not intended: the French—or any other nation—would never commemorate their own defeat, a notable defeat, with such a lasting monument as this excellent soup.

> ½ lb. carrots, sliced
> 1 medium onion, chopped
> 10 tablespoons [1¼ sticks] butter
> 2 tablespoons rice
> 2½ cups veal or chicken stock
> sprig of thyme
> 3 half-inch slices bread, cubed

Simmer carrots and onion in a covered pan with 4 tablespoons of the butter for about 10 minutes. Don't let them brown. Add rice, stock and thyme—which is most important to the flavour. Cook gently for 20–30 minutes. Remove thyme stalk, and strain soup or whirl it in a blender, adding more stock if necessary. Reheat. Stir in 2 tablespoons of butter just before serving. Meanwhile fry the bread dice in the last 4 tablespoons of butter. Serve with the soup.

Wonderful flavour apart, the muted orange of the carrots and the golden cubes of bread make this soup a beautiful start to an evening meal, however grand. If you use a good homemade stock, rather than a stock cube, the flavour will repay the extra trouble.

Carottes à la Vichy   (for 4)

The chilling reason for the title of this delicious recipe is that, "At Vichy" (according to a turn-of-the-century doctor), "where derangements of the liver and of the biliary digestion are particularly treated, carrots in one or another form are served at every meal. . . ." Yellow carrots for the yellow results of indigestion, according to earlier theories of medical treatment.

Some cookery books give the impression that it's the water from Vichy's illustrious springs that makes all the difference to this way of cooking carrots. In fact I've used Vichy water, the recommended substitute for which is tap water and bicarbonate of soda, and tap water on its own, and could taste no difference in the results. It's not water magic, but butter and sugar and concentration of flavour by reducing the cooking liquid that make Vichy carrots so much better than plain boiled ones. They could almost be eaten at every meal.

> 1 lb. carrots, old or new
> 1½–2 cups water
> 2 tablespoons sugar
> 4 tablespoons butter
> ½ teaspoon salt, or to taste
> chopped parsley, lemon juice

Scrape the carrots and slice them diagonally. Put with the water, sugar, butter and salt into a pan (the water should barely cover new carrots). Boil hard, without a lid on the pan, until the water is reduced to a spoonful or two of syrup, and the carrots are cooked. Old carrots may need another 5 or 10 minutes over low heat, with the lid on the pan to prevent total evaporation and burning. Finish with chopped parsley and lemon juice to taste.

NOTE: If a little sauce is required, put 3 tablespoons of cream into the pan at the end of the cooking time, and simmer for a few moments before adding parsley and lemon juice.

Boeuf à la mode   *(for 8 to 12)*

Marriages of beef and carrots are a commonplace of European cookery. Think of most tripe recipes, beef stews, beef stock, beef sauces and boiled beef, and of the finest partnership of them all, *boeuf à la mode*.

Flavour and texture apart, it's the ideal for a Sunday lunch party. Served cold, with no extra accompaniments, it feeds twelve economically and satisfyingly. Served hot, with bread or a few boiled potatoes, it is generous for eight, and much more panic-free to cook than a roast.

3–5 lbs. top beef round in one piece
¼ lb. fat bacon [see footnote, p. 33]
¾ cup chopped onion
a little oil
¼ cup brandy
1¼–2 cups red wine
4 pig's trotters [feet]
   or 1 calf's foot
2 cloves garlic, crushed
1–2 bay leaves, 2 large sprigs thyme, 2 large sprigs
   parsley, tied together in a bunch
3 lbs. carrots, sliced
well-seasoned beef stock
2 teaspoons sugar
chopped parsley

Chill bacon until firm, cut it into strips and lard the beef (see p. 129). This is not strictly necessary, but will improve the beef, counteracting any tendency to dryness.

Brown the beef in a little oil, with the onion. Transfer to a deep casserole or saucepan. Warm the brandy, set it alight and pour flaming over the beef. Add the wine when the flames have died down, then the trotters or calf's foot, garlic, herbs and about one-sixth of the carrots. Cover with beef stock; bring to the boil, or rather to a desultory simmer, fix the lid on tightly and cook for 4 hours. This can be done in the oven, but it's easier to listen to the simmering, and see that it doesn't develop into a rolling boil, if the pan stays on top of the stove (use an asbestos mat over gas). Test the beef with a larding needle—a 3-pound piece should be done after 4 hours.

Skim off as much fat as possible, and replace the lid if more cooking time is needed, as it may be for a 4- or 5-pound piece. Meanwhile, cook the rest of the carrots separately in beef stock, with 2 teaspoons sugar.

To serve hot: put the beef on a warm serving dish, arranging the separately cooked carrots around it. Sprinkle with chopped parsley. Strain and skim some of the cooking liquid and serve in a sauceboat (the rest can be used for soups and sauces, and to make brawn with the chopped meat from the trotters) [*this is just chopped cooked pig meat—head, feet, tail—mixed with a little jellied stock and left to set in a mould*].

To serve cold: let the beef cool in the cooking liquid for 4 hours. Remove to a deep, close-fitting dish. Fit the separately cooked carrots round the meat, sliding them down under it and up the sides of the dish. Pour in carefully some of the beef cooking liquid which should have been strained, skimmed and boiled down to a rich flavour. Leave to set in the refrigerator before turning out onto a serving dish.

Chicken fricassee in the Berry style

The Berry lying between Touraine and Burgundy, and partly enclosed by a great sweep of the Loire, is not so famous for food as its two illustrious neighbours. Which is unfair. The wide farmlands centred on Bourges produce fine unpretentious dishes like this one, or like the pork and egg pasty on page 59.

3–4-lb. chicken, jointed [cut in pieces]

stock: chicken giblets
  1 medium carrot
  1 leek
  1 medium onion
  bouquet garni
  2 cups water

sauce: 2 lbs. carrots, cut into 1½-inch strips
4 tablespoons butter
1 tablespoon chopped shallots or scallions
1 clove garlic, crushed
1 heaping tablespoon flour
½ cup heavy cream
1 tablespoon wine vinegar
2 egg yolks

Make the stock by simmering the stock ingredients together for 1 hour. Strain.

Blanch the carrots in boiling salted water for 5 minutes, pour them into a strainer and rinse under the cold tap. Drain them well. Melt the butter in a large heavy pan, cook the carrots in it until they're lightly browned. Remove them, and put in the chicken pieces and shallots or onion, and the garlic. When they are golden brown, stir in the flour, and then the strained stock. Bring to the boil, then add the carrots. Leave the chicken to simmer, uncovered, for about 45 minutes, or until it's cooked, removing the quicker-cooking breast pieces when they are done to a warm dish. Mix cream, vinegar and yolks together. Put the cooked chicken and carrots onto the serving dish with the breast. Pour a little boiling liquid into the cream and egg mixture, return to the pan and cook without boiling until thick. Pour over chicken and serve very hot.

Mrs. Beeton's carrot jam
to imitate apricot preserve

carrots
to every lb. of carrot pulp allow:
1 lb. granulated sugar
grated rind of 1 lemon
strained juice of 2 lemons
6 chopped bitter almonds
3 tablespoons brandy

"Select young carrots; wash and scrape them clean, cut them into round pieces, put them into a saucepan with sufficient water to cover them, and let them simmer until perfectly soft; then force them through a sieve. Weigh the pulp, and to every lb. allow the above ingredients. Put the pulp into a preserving-pan with the sugar, and let this boil for 5 minutes, stirring and skimming all the time. When cold, add the lemon-rind and juice, almonds and brandy; mix these well with the jam; then put it into pots, which must be well covered and kept in a dry place. The brandy may be omitted, but the preserve will then not keep: with the brandy it will remain good for months."

NOTE: A food mill can be used to pulp the carrots. And if you cannot get bitter almonds, use the ordinary ones rather than none at all. Blanch and split them.

Angels' hair charlotte   (for 8)

We are, as I've said, out of the habit of using carrots for sweet dishes. One has to search older cookery books for baked or steamed puddings, for rich carrot tarts, for sweet carrot pickles or carrot and orange marmalade—or for the best of them all, angels' hair charlotte. At first it was the name I liked, the gay image of copper-nobbed angels in a blue sky. Then the taste proved to be as delicious as the title.

The angels' hair can be made several days, even months, before the charlotte, as it's really a carrot preserve or jam and keeps well.

            1 lemon
angels' hair: 1 lb. old carrots, weighed when cleaned
            2 cups sugar
            ½ cup water

Cut the peel thinly from the lemon, and slice into thin shreds. Cut the carrots into matchstick strips (a *mandoline* or mouli-julienne saves time). Put carrots, lemon peel, lemon juice, sugar and water into a heavy pan. Boil until setting point is reached (220° on a sugar thermometer). Pour into sterilized jars and seal.

charlotte: ½ cup heavy cream
½ cup light cream
6–8 oz. angels' hair
2 oz. blanched, split & toasted almonds
32 boudoir biscuits [or ladyfingers]
juice of 1 large orange

Use a charlotte mould, a soufflé dish, or a straight-sided bowl of 4–6 cups capacity. Make a 2-foot strap, 1½ inches wide, of doubled aluminum foil; fit it down, across and up the inside of the mould, so that the two ends stick up. Line the mould completely with foil. (This is not as arduous as it sounds, and ensures a perfect turnout for the charlotte.)

To make the charlotte filling, whip the two creams together until light and firm, and fold in the angels' hair and almonds.

To assemble the charlotte, dip the smooth side of the ladyfingers, one by one, into the orange juice. Fit them immediately into the mould to make a lining, sugar side outwards. Do the sides first, then cut biscuits to fit the bottom. Make sure they don't become too soggy. Pile in the filling. Biscuits, and bits of biscuit left over, can be used for a top layer, if there's enough room.

Cover and chill for at least 4 hours. Just before the meal, remove the cover, and ease the charlotte gently by moving the ends of the foil strap. Now place the serving dish, upside down, on top of the mould, and turn the whole thing the right way up. Finally, lift up the mould carefully, and peel off the foil strap and lining.

Hannah Glasse's carrot pudding *(for 4)*

I've often wondered why the English seem to have excelled in puddings and cakes, why earlier cookery books come alive only at the sweet sections (French bourgeois cookeries sparkle from soup through to vegetables, flagging slightly at dessert). A grandmother's reminiscence gave me a possible explanation. She described the kitchen of a prewar English middle-class household as forbidden territory, a silent battleground. Most cooks did not care at all to work under the eye of the mistress. A tactful housewife who wished to keep her cook restrained her own efforts to the "frills" of the meal, to making an occasional pudding or cake. One imagines two centuries of frustrated feminine creativity bursting out into the wonderful puddings which followed overroasted beef and aqueous cabbage.

> 4 oz. sweet shortcrust pastry (¾ cup flour, 1 tablespoon
>   confectioners' sugar, 4 tablespoons butter, small egg)

filling: ¼ cup finely grated carrot
    ¼ cup bread crumbs
    2 egg yolks
    1 egg white
    ½ cup heavy cream
    4 tablespoons melted but cooled butter
    1½ tablespoons brandy
    1 tablespoon orange flower water
    4 tablespoons sugar
    about ¼ of a nutmeg, grated

Line an 8½- or 9½-inch tart tin, with a removable base, with the pastry (Hannah Glasse used puff pastry, but nowadays I think English taste prefers the crispness of sweet shortcrust for open tarts). Beat the filling ingredients together, adding sugar and nutmeg to taste. If you cannot find orange flower water at local pharmacies or grocers' shops, add a little extra cream and more nutmeg. Bake in a moderate oven, 350–375°, until the filling has risen a little and acquired a golden crust. Eat warm or cold. The filling is delicious, with the texture though not the flavour of grated coconut.

CELERY

The fine pleasure of buying celery in earthy heads, after the first improving frosts of winter, is gradually being eroded by the wash of enterprise and aviation. Almost the year round in England, cleaned and slightly flabby greenish celery, sometimes from America, is on sale at inviting prices. It's the wise cook who averts her eyes from this profuse and plastic display and waits until November. Then crispness and flavour in the domestic crop are at their peak, and celery can provide a perfect antidote to the heavy diet of dark months. Everyone feels better for something light, something simple. In any case, one of the greatest luxuries you can have in England today is simple food of the best quality (how often do people in towns eat good boiled eggs?).

In the twelve days of Christmas particularly, it's worth exploiting celery, which is then, for English cooks, in prime condition. "This herb Celery is for its high and grateful taste ever placed in the middle of the grand sallet at our great men's tables, and our proctor's feasts, as the grace of the whole board." That was John Evelyn writing in 1699, when the habit (introduced from Italy) of eating blanched celery as a salad had been common for 20 or 30 years. But the recipes I've chosen for celery—and for celeriac—are not for salad only.[1] It's the most versatile of winter vegetables. Against other Christmas expenditure, celery at 8p. or 10p. a head is negligible, which makes experiment possible without anxiety. And it's quick to prepare, with little waste.

Celeriac [celery knob or celery rave] is a turnip-rooted variety of the same species, much used in Germany and France. Commonly on sale in shops in Britain [and in some areas of the U.S.], it is interchangeable in some of the recipes that follow—though it has a salad or two of its own. Its turnip root makes it keep much longer than sticks of celery. This is an advantage, but for me its rather solid texture puts it second to celery. However, a purée of celeriac goes well with strong-flavoured game, venison, pheasant, hare and so on, where you need something bland but more interestingly flavoured than potato. Like chestnut purée, which is often served with game as well, celeriac purée needs to be well flavoured, to be firm without being stodgy, creamy without being sloppy.

Celery and sea salt

This is the best way of eating first-class celery, but care must be taken with butter and salt. In London, Marks and Spencer now stock the best, unsalted butter from Normandy (at half the price one pays in France). Unadulterated sea salt is harder to come by, but worth the trouble—and expense. Once you've tasted it, you won't want to return to the free-running varieties. Maldon or Tidman's sea salt can be bought at health food shops and good groceries [and many U.S. supermarkets stock kosher salt, which also comes from the sea].[2]

Put on the table two or three heads of celery, outside stalks removed (use these for soup, or in stews), and the inner stalks separated, washed and chilled. Have a dish of unsalted butter at spreading temperature, and some

---

[1] In 1874 Dutch farmers near Kalamazoo, Michigan, tempted railroad travelers with the first large-crop celery grown in the U.S., and soon train butchers were regularly hawking it on the Michigan Central. Now it is a big winter crop in Florida.

[2] Among U.S. suppliers of Maldon's table sea salt, imported from Essex, is Country Kitchen, 270 W. Merrick Road, Valley Stream, N.Y. 11582.

sea salt (a salt mill isn't necessary). Each person puts butter fairly thickly into the channel of his celery sticks, then sprinkles a thin line of sea salt along it. Simple and delicious. Avoid embellishments. A good way to start a meal.

Céleri-rémoulade   *(for 4)*

An excellent hors d'oeuvre, which should be assembled not too long before the meal. Making the mayonnaise a day or two ahead, and storing it in the refrigerator, reduces the final work.

mayonnaise: 2 egg yolks
    1 good teaspoon Dijon mustard
    1 cup olive oil or corn oil
    wine vinegar, salt, pepper

  plus: 1 celeriac
    5 tablespoons vinegar or lemon juice
    chopped parsley

For the mayonnaise, warm a sturdy bowl or mortar under the hot tap and dry. Put in the yolks and mustard and beat well with a wooden spoon. As the yolks begin to thicken, begin pouring in the oil *drop by drop* until you've used up about half. The oil should be at warm room temperature. Advance cautiously to a steady trickle of oil until it's used up and the mayonnaise is thick and firm. Flavour with vinegar, salt and pepper.

Trim, quarter and peel the celeriac. Grate rapidly, in matchstick shreds, into a bowl of water acidulated with 2 tablespoons of vinegar. (A *mandoline*-style vegetable shredder which can be set flat over the top of the bowl copes well with this.) Bring 3 cups of water to the boil with 3 tablespoons of vinegar, add the drained celeriac and bring rapidly to the boil. Drain the celeriac again, dry well in a clean cloth and mix with the mayonnaise. Sprinkle with chopped parsley; serve well chilled. The vinegar (or lemon juice) in the water prevents the celeriac from turning grey—which is harmless, but unsightly.

Celery soup (for 4)

This simple soup tastes exceptionally good when flavoured with dried dill weed. Or with chopped fresh fennel leaves.

½ pound celery, chopped (outside stalks or celeriac)
½ cup chopped onion
½ cup diced potato
6 tablespoons butter
4 cups turkey or chicken stock
½–1 cup milk (optional)
about 1 teaspoon dill weed [2 teaspoons for fresh dill]
2½ tablespoons cream

Stew celery, onion and potato gently in the butter in a covered pan for 10 minutes. Don't let the vegetables brown. Add stock or water and ½ teaspoon of dill weed. Simmer for 20 minutes if you have a blender, 40 minutes if you use a food mill. Blend or purée the soup. Pour through a strainer into a clean pan (to remove the last few threads of celery), adding a little milk if too thick. Bring slowly to just under the boil, seasoning with salt, pepper and more dill weed if required. Put the cream into the soup dish, and pour the soup in on top. Swirl round with the ladle before serving, to mix in the cream.

There will be enough soup for six, if the rest of the meal is fairly copious.

Two celery stuffings

With lemon and parsley. This light and fresh-flavoured stuffing complements the flavour of turkey better than heavier mixtures of chestnuts and sausage meat. It also goes well with chicken, and with large fish which are to be baked in the oven. Quantities given here are enough for a 10–12-lb. turkey:

½ lb. onions, chopped [about 1 cup]
½ lb. celery, chopped [about 1 cup]
8 tablespoons butter [1 stick]
4½ cups fresh white bread crumbs
rind & juice of 1 large lemon
¼ cup chopped parsley
2 small eggs
salt & pepper

Soften onion and celery in the butter over a low heat, covered, for about 20 minutes. The vegetables should not brown. Remove pan from the heat and mix with the rest of the ingredients in a large bowl, seasoning to taste.

Never stuff poultry, or anything else, too tightly; the bread crumbs need room to swell in the cooking.

With ham. A variation on the stuffing above, with stronger flavours predominating.

4½ cups fresh white bread crumbs
milk
8 tablespoons [1 stick] butter
½ lb. onions, chopped [about 1 cup]
4 large cloves garlic, crushed
7 tablespoons chopped celery
½ lb. lean cooked ham or lean smoked bacon
    [see footnote, p. 33], uncooked
5 tablespoons chopped parsley
2 teaspoons dried thyme
rind & juice of 1 large lemon
2 medium eggs
salt, black pepper

Moisten the crumbs slightly with a little milk: they should be damp without surplus liquid. Melt butter and cook onion, garlic and celery in it for about 20 minutes. Don't let them brown. Meanwhile chop or mince the ham (or the bacon) finely. Mix all the ingredients together with salt and pepper to taste.

Purée of celeriac

This purée goes well with game, as I've mentioned, or with turkey or chicken. It's a recipe that can be adjusted to taste. but the result should never be watery.

> large celeriac
> ⅓ its weight in potatoes
> 8–12 tablespoons butter [1–1½ sticks]
> parsley, chervil, salt, pepper

Quarter, peel and cut the celeriac into 1-inch cubes. Cook in boiling salted water for 10 minutes. Drain well, then stew in 3 tablespoons butter (cover the pan) for 20 minutes, or until celeriac is cooked. Put through a strainer or food mill—don't put the celeriac in the blender or it will be too soft and smooth.

Meanwhile scrub, boil and peel the potatoes. Strain in the same way and add to the celeriac. Add chopped herbs, salt, pepper and plenty of butter to taste. Reheat and serve.

NOTE: If you have some thick béchamel or cream sauce, this may be substituted for the potatoes.

Peking celery

Celery as a hot vegetable is often a watery disaster, as anyone who eats in railway dining cars will know. The French way of avoiding this is to blanch the celery, cut in strips, in boiling water for 20 minutes, then to drain it well and stew slowly in butter until cooked but biteable. Lemon juice and chopped parsley are stirred in with the final seasoning of salt and pepper. The same method can be applied to celeriac (see preceding recipe).

But here is another method, more economical and quite as good. The celery retains its crispness, acquires an extra piquant flavour, and can be eaten hot, warm or cold. The recipe was given me by a Chinese friend, who serves it with poultry; it shows a method which can be adapted to many other vegetables such as Florentine fennel, or chicory, or savoy cabbage.

> head of celery
> corn or peanut oil
> soy sauce
> freshly ground black pepper

Trim the celery (keep the leaves for soup), and separate, wash and string the stalks. Cut them into ¼-inch strips on the bias, i.e., at an angle of 45° when the stalk is laid pointing towards you. Cover the bottom of a large heavy frying pan with a thin film of oil. When it begins to smoke, throw in the celery pieces and sizzle, stirring, for 4 minutes. Add a good dash of soy sauce, and plenty of black pepper. Stir the celery about (ideally with chopsticks) until the sauce is absorbed. This takes about 8 minutes. If you wish to serve the celery cold, keep it in a cool place but not the refrigerator.

Mixed celery salads

Celery and beetroot [beets]. A good layer of sliced, boiled or baked beets, with a roughly equal quantity of sliced celery laid on top. Good with turkey or chicken.

Dressing: 1¼ tablespoons wine vinegar, 5 tablespoons olive oil, salt, black pepper: i.e., vinaigrette.

Salad cauchoise, i.e., from the Pays de Caux, the chalk country in northern Normandy, not far from Rouen.

1 washed, sliced head of celery, mixed with ¾ lb. potatoes, scrubbed, boiled and peeled, then sliced.

Dressing: 6 tablespoons heavy cream lightly whipped, and seasoned with salt, pepper, wine vinegar and lemon juice.

Garnish: 1 truffle, chopped, and 1 half-inch slice of lean, raw smoked ham, chopped. Canned truffles and raw ham can be bought from delicatessen shops.

Celery and turkey. Equal quantities of diced, cold turkey (or chicken), diced crisp unpeeled eating apples, sliced celery, plus ¼ cup grated Gruyère cheese to each cup of poultry.

Dressing: vinaigrette or mayonnaise (see above).

Celeriac and apple. Another Normandy salad. Prepare celeriac as for *céleri-rémoulade*. Measure the blanched shreds, and add half as much in strips of unpeeled apples.

Dressing: vinaigrette.

Waldorf. This famous combination of diced, unpeeled eating apples and sliced celery, dressed with mayonnaise, was invented by the maître d'hôtel of the Waldorf-Astoria in New York. Walnuts were a later addition. Use equal quantities of celery and apple. Be sure to choose crisp eating apples; the woolly kind are disasterous in this kind of dish. Serve chilled.

Celery and walnut. 1 head of celery, trimmed, washed and sliced. Half its weight in shelled walnuts.

Dressing: 4 tablespoons mayonnaise mixed with 3 good tablespoons of heavy cream.

Garnish: a ring of watercress, picked into sprigs.

Serve chilled.

Cromwell salad. ¾ lb. prepared celery, mixed with ½ lb. shelled walnuts. Put into a lettuce-lined bowl.

Dressing: ½ cup mayonnaise mixed with ¼ cup well-mashed Roquefort cheese, and 3 tablespoons oil, 1 tablespoon wine vinegar, and up to 1 tablespoon Worcester sauce, depending on taste.

Why Cromwell? In this salad the only ingredients he would have been familiar with are the walnuts, oil and vinegar. Perhaps there is a reference to his victory at Worcester, on September 3rd, 1651, in the last ingredient.

Celery and Florentine fennel. 1 head of celery, prepared and sliced, mixed with 1 large head of fennel, sliced.

Dressing: vinaigrette (see salad 1).

Garnish: 2–3 oz. Gruyère cheese, in small dice.

Serve chilled.

Stuffed celery salad. Make a thick pommade of ¾ lb. Roquefort, Stilton or other blue or cream cheese with 8 tablespoons [1 stick] unsalted butter (or 4 tablespoons unsalted and 2 tablespoons cream). Season lightly with salt, pepper, and, in the case of cream cheese, with chives and parsley. Smooth this paste into the channels of celery sticks. Cut slantwise into short lengths, and put into a bowl without dressing.

ENDIVE

Some years ago we were visiting the painted caves of France, and came at last to La Mouthe with its image of a thatched shelter, an inverted **V**, painted and scraped on to the rock face. After the grandeur of Lascaux, and the squeeze-belly narrows of Font-de-Gaume, La Mouthe was domestic, tamed, providing useful storage space for a busy farm (which also had an identical shelter to the one drawn in the cave, a design with 20,000 years' success). A heavy wooden door barred the entrance. Inside were piles of potatoes and, further in, a long hummock of reddish earth. It glimmered in the thin light with many pale points. "Endive," said the farmer's wife, and raised her carbide lamp as she disappeared into the gallery opening off the cave.

It's strange to think that this endive, the endive or witloof chicory we buy at the greengrocers and more often call chicory in England (as well as the chicory sometimes added to coffee) is the same as the slender plant of European fields and gardens. The flat blue rosettes with their square-ended petals which cling tightly to the stem do not at all make one think of crisp winter salads.

Although the shoots of *Chicorium intybus* had long been eaten as a salad, it wasn't until about 1845 that market gardeners near Brussels began to blanch the shoots in banks of earth, like celery. This reduced the bitterness of the leaves. Belgium is still the largest producer in Europe, growing 90,000 tons a year on the rich light acres of Brabant (half is for export, mainly to France, but also to the U.S., where it is known as both French and Belgian endive, and is very expensive).

An interesting thing is that the producers evolved a system which includes the advantages of La Mouthe or any other cave—steady temperature of about 60 degrees, insulation from frost and absence of light. Seeds are sown in the ordinary way in the spring, and the roots are taken up and trimmed of their leaves in the autumn. They are then packed together on the ground in long rows. Specially prepared soil is mounded up over them. These oblong beds are warmed from below by hot water pipes or electrically heated metal lattices. The weather is kept out by corrugated iron sheets, bent over them like miniature hangars, and lagged with straw. Very quickly the shoots grow to an ideal 6 inches of compact white leaves, ready to be forked out. Women and old people—endive growing is a family business—trim and pack the heads for market. The strong cardboard boxes, often lined with waxy royal-blue paper, are not a luxury touch but a necessity: the blanched endive must be protected from too much light or it will turn green and bitter.

Basic preparation and cooking of endive

Allow a minimum of two heads per person when cooking endive (salads are a different matter—one each is enough). Store, wrapped up, in a cool place; best of all—seeing that the exclusion of light is important—is the crisper drawer of a refrigerator, where it will keep in good condition for ten days.

Prepare endive immediately before cooking it. Never leave it to soak in a bowl of cold water; just remove the brownish edges of the leaves, and a thin slice from the cut end, and rinse as briefly as possible under a cold tap. Pat dry with a clean tea towel. Take out the tiny, bitter core with a sharp pointed knife.

To cook endive, put it into a large saucepan in flat layers, with 2 teaspoons of sugar, the juice of a lemon and enough boiling water to cover. Simmer until the endive is almost cooked, about 20–30 minutes, testing it with a larding needle or sharp knife. Pour away the liquor. Add a good lump of butter, or the juices from roasting meat, and finish the cooking at a more vigorous temperature. Turn the heads over occasionally in the syrupy moisture so that they acquire a slight glaze. Sprinkle with parsley and serve as a hot vegetable, with meat.

Like many other vegetables, endive can provide a delicious course on its own, particularly when presented in more elaborate ways.

Endives with cream sauce (for 6)

A good but simple recipe. Try it on its own, or with chicken, boiled ham or salt pork.

>12 heads endive, prepared
>6 tablespoons butter
>1 teaspoon sugar
>juice of half a lemon
>¼ cup heavy cream
>6 lemon slices or quarters
>salt, pepper, chopped parsley

Melt the butter in a large heavy frying pan, and add the sugar, and endives, which should lie in a single layer. Turn the endives over so that the pieces are coated with butter. Pour in the lemon juice and cover the pan with a lid or foil. Simmer for about 40 minutes, by which time the endives should be cooked (small heads will take 20–30 minutes). Remove to a serving dish and keep warm. Bring the cream to the boil in a small pan, then tip it into the endive pan juices. After a few moments' hard boiling, the sauce should have reduced to a smooth thickness. Taste and correct the seasoning. Pour over the endives, sprinkle with parsley, garnish with lemon slices or quarters and serve immediately. Cream sauces should never be allowed to hang around and become tepid; make sure, too, that the plates are well heated.

Endives au gratin (for 4)

The French are clever at using piquant stuffings in unusual ways. No doubt this is the result of antique thrift—like the English country habit of serving suet pudding before the meat—but it often seems more like inspiration. Nicely seasoned with herbs, ham and spices, the bread crumbs don't just puff out the dish, they embellish it.

> 8 heads of endive, prepared
> 2 medium onions
> 1 large clove garlic
> 2 slices gammon [or Canadian bacon],
>   or 4 smoked back rashers of bacon [see footnote, p. 33]
> 2 cups bread crumbs
> milk
> 6 sprigs parsley, chopped
> ½ cup grated cheese, preferably Gruyère
> 6 tablespoons butter
> salt, pepper, nutmeg

Blanch the endives in boiling, salted water for 8 minutes. Remove and drain in a colander. Put onion, garlic, and gammon or bacon through the grinder. Soak the bread crumbs in a very little milk to moisten them; squeeze out any surplus moisture. Mix with the ground meat, etc., the parsley and three-fourths of the cheese. Season well with salt, pepper and nutmeg. Use 2 tablespoons of butter to grease an oval gratin dish, then put in half the stuffing. Lay the endives on top, head to tail, close together, and cover with the rest of the stuffing. Melt the remaining butter and pour it evenly over the top layer of stuffing. Bake in a moderately hot oven, 400°, for about half an hour. Sprinkle the remaining cheese on top, and return to the oven to brown (or place under the broiler).

NOTE: At Saint-Malo, large heads of endive are hollowed out, and filled with the stuffing, then wrapped in slices of local Brittany ham. A glass of Muscadet, plenty of butter and a good scatter of cheese, and the dish goes into the oven to bake at a slow temperature.

Baked endives   (for 4)

This attractive, easily made dish is a good way of introducing endive to people who've never eaten it before. Bring it bubbling and brown to the table, and provide good whole-wheat bread for everyone to mop up the delicious sauce.

> 8 heads of endive, prepared
> 8 long rashers of smoked bacon [see footnote, p. 33]
> 1 heaping tablespoon butter
> 1 heaping tablespoon flour
> 1½ cups hot milk
> ½ cup grated cheese (Parmesan & Gruyère or Cheddar)
> 1 generous teaspoon French mustard, or nutmeg
> salt, pepper

Wrap the bacon round the heads of endive, so that each one has a spiral jacket. Lay them in a lightly buttered baking dish; they should fit comfortably into it with a little room to spare. Make a sauce by melting the butter, stirring in the flour, and adding the milk, little by little, to avoid lumps. Add two-thirds of the cheese, salt and pepper to taste, and either the mustard or the nutmeg. Plenty of pepper is a good idea, but go carefully with the salt because bacon will add extra seasoning as the dish cooks. Put into a moderately hot oven, 400°, for about 40 minutes or until the endive is cooked. Sprinkle the top with the remaining cheese and brown under the broiler.

NOTE: Country ham may be substituted for the bacon. In this case, blanch the endives first for 10 minutes in boiling salted water. Drain, then wrap in the ham and continue with the recipe. Cooking time 15–20 minutes at 450°.

Curried endives   (for 6)

> 12 heads endive, prepared
> ¾-lb. piece bacon [see footnote, p. 33]
> 2½ tablespoons olive oil
> 2 tablespoons butter
> 1 medium onion, chopped
> 3 cloves garlic, crushed
> 1 generous tablespoon flour

1 heaping teaspoon curry powder
2½ tablespoons Calvados or brandy [or applejack]
½ cup red or white wine (or stock)
1 lb. tomatoes, skinned & quartered
salt, freshly ground pepper, sugar

for serving: boiled rice

Blanch the endive in boiling, salted water for 15 minutes, until it's nearly cooked. Leave to drain while the sauce is being made. Cut the bacon into strips about 1 inch long and ¼ inch wide and thick (remove rind).[1] Melt oil and butter in a heavy pan, and brown the bacon, onion and garlic lightly. Stir in the flour and curry powder to take up the fat. Add Calvados or brandy, wine or stock, and tomatoes. Season with salt, pepper, and a little sugar to bring out the flavour in the tomatoes. Simmer for half an hour with the lid off the pan. Correct the seasoning, add the endive to heat through and finish cooking, and serve, very hot, with boiled rice.

Endives in the Polish style   (for 4)

Most recipes for endive as a hot vegetable, certainly most of the ones in this chapter, use ham and bacon, or a sauce, to contrast with its watery but definite flavour. Here's something quite different. For its blend of crispness and smoothness, for its beautiful appearance, this is my starred dish. A good main course for supper, or first course to a grander meal.

8 fine large heads endive, prepared
2 teaspoons sugar
10 tablespoons [1¼ sticks] butter
juice of 1 lemon

---

[1] If you are using American-type bacon, which has much more fat, sauté bacon strips for 2–3 minutes first to draw off some of the fat, then pour it off before adding oil and butter.

4 *hard-boiled eggs*
¼ *cup of chopped parsley*
¼ *cup white bread crumbs*

Cook the endive in boiling water with the sugar, 2 tablespoons of butter and the lemon juice. Meanwhile shell the eggs. Fork them into crumbs (quicker than chopping them with a knife), then mix in the parsley. Fry the bread crumbs to golden brown in 3 tablespoons butter, and keep them warm. Drain the cooked endive, pressing it a little to get rid of as much moisture as possible, and fry in 2 tablespoons of butter to brown lightly. Arrange the heads on a large round serving dish, like the spokes of a wheel, leaving a hole in the middle for the egg and parsley mixture. Scatter the browned crumbs over the dish. Melt the last of the butter and, when it bubbles up, pour over the whole thing and serve immediately.

Two endive salads   (for 4–6)

Endive makes a much better winter salad than floppy lettuce from a plastic bag. It's crisp and juicy, and can quite well be served on its own with just a French dressing and plenty of freshly ground black pepper. Of all salad vegetables, it combines best with other ingredients; in this respect it even tops celery.

6 *heads endive, prepared*
2 *large eating apples*
¼ *cup raisins, soaked in hot water 1 hour*
3 *oz. shelled walnuts*
½ *cup diced mild cheese*
French dressing, mayonnaise, or cream seasoned with French
    mustard & lemon juice

Slice the endives into half-inch pieces, and push out the half rings of leaves. Core and dice the apples, but don't peel them. Drain the raisins. Mix these ingredients with walnuts, cheese, and the salad dressing. Chill and serve.

> 4 large heads endive, prepared
> 5 hard-boiled eggs
> 2½ tablespoons heavy cream
> 2½ tablespoons melted butter
> 1 tablespoon chopped parsley
> salt, black pepper
> 12 black olives, sliced

Carefully separate and remove the leaves from the endive heads, stopping when you come to a core of about 2 inches. Shell the eggs and mash with a fork, then mix them with cream and melted butter. This mass should be only lightly coherent, not smooth or pastelike. Season it well. Fill the endive leaves with the mixture, arranging them on a serving dish. Sprinkle with parsley, put a few slices of olive on each one, and the tiny cones of endive in the centre.

NOTE: ½ lb. cottage cheese may be substituted for the eggs.

HARICOT OR DRIED WHITE BEANS

Every civilization has its special beans. The Old World's classical bean, back to the Greeks, was the broad bean. The bean of the Incas and the Mexicans was the kidney bean, which Peruvian Indians were eating several thousand years ago.

When Europe obtained these new kidney beans quite early in the sixteenth century, they were soon everybody's eating—especially dried, for winter food. It was the French, I think, and the Italians (so we say French bean, and used to say Roman bean) who devised most of the special bean dishes. Variously called haricot beans, butter beans, navy beans, Boston beans, the dried beans were "haricots" first of all because the French added them, with small turnips, to the *haricot* or ragoût of mutton. They were called haricots in England (or French in their green undried state), because gardeners came to prefer varieties raised in France, for instance, to Dutch-raised varieties. The name persists, though our haricots are now imported from far beyond Europe: the climate here is too uncertain for their successful production on a commercial scale.

Don't despise them. Beans may not be the pinnacle of Wine and Food Society living, but there is something wonderful in what can be made out of a package of pallid, dull-looking butter beans (from a variety similar to lima beans with pods that are yellow or butter coloured) or the smaller haricot beans. It is wonderful how they combine without ceasing to be beans—particularly with olive oil. There is a basic marriage for you—if you like to mix history with your meals—of two civilizations, Andean and Mediterranean.

My starred dishes are the last two in this section. One is really a version of an ancient *haricot*; the other, from North Carolina and made of the lima-like butter beans, is an improvement of Boston baked beans, which, of course, is another *haricot* with a New World seasoning of molasses.

You can keep haricots and butter beans indefinitely, like other dried vegetables, but it's better not to. With time they become drier, harder, increasingly tasteless. To enjoy them at their best, see if you can find new-season Soissons beans[1] in the autumn (so called in Europe after the main town of a famous bean-growing district of France); if you are in London and can visit Soho, this should not be too difficult. For baked bean dishes, from cassoulet to the baked beans Southern style on page 182, these whitish beans, as they are raised in France, are especially good. This is aiming at perfection, though, because the quality of dry beans on every supermarket shelf can be relied upon.

I find small beans—haricot, navy, Boston beans—more useful than the larger butter beans, whose coarse skins can be obtrusive. Whichever you are using, disregard instructions to soak overnight. Unless they've been in the storecupboard for months, this is far too long. Two, three hours is often enough. Be guided by the fact that dried beans will absorb enough water to double their weight, more or less. If you are short of time, cover the beans with cold water in the proportion of 1 pound beans to 7½ cups water, bring them to the boil, then leave them to cool for 40 minutes; drain them well, before continuing with the recipe.

An important point. When cooking beans, add salt at the end of the cooking time, never at the beginning, or they will harden.

Bean soup   (for 6)

The people of Tuscany are the great bean eaters, the *mangia-fagioli*, of Europe. They have so many bean dishes that I'm surprised

---

[1] Navy, pea, or Great Northern beans are the best U.S. equivalents.

they've never invented any bean cakes, or buns, in the Japanese style. But they have invented a special pot for cooking beans in, a *fagiolara*. Apart from being a beautiful object, the *fagiolara* is practical: it can be used over low, direct heat or in the oven, and, on account of its chianti-flask shape, the top is easily sealed against loss of heat and flavour. In these pots, beans simmer in water seasoned with olive oil, garlic, sage, tomato, and perhaps some pickled pork, to make Tuscan—not Boston—baked beans. But for a small party of tired urban stomachs here is the Tuscan recipe I would choose:

> ½ lb. dried haricot or butter beans [navy, pea, or
>   Great Northern]
> 5 cups water
> 2 large cloves garlic, chopped not crushed
> ¼ cup olive oil
> ½ cup chopped parsley
> salt, black pepper

Soak, then simmer the beans in the water *without salt* until cooked. When they are soft, set aside one-fourth to half of the beans, and put the rest through blender or food mill. Season well, diluting the soup with more water if necessary. Reheat, with the whole beans. In a separate pan cook the garlic slowly in 2 tablespoons of the olive oil, until it turns golden. Add to the soup, with the parsley and the rest of the oil. Serve immediately.

NOTE: If you can't buy good olive oil, don't make do with vegetable oil, which is tasteless. Use butter instead. The result will be quite different, more like a French soup, but still very good.

Soissons soup

Because Soissons, a cathedral town about 65 miles northeast of Paris, remains the most renowned bean-growing capital, the French have a tendency to name bean soups after it, just as carrot soups are inevitably Crécy, and pea soups are likely to be Saint-Germain.

½ lb. dried haricot beans [navy, pea,
   or Great Northern]
1 medium carrot
1 medium onion, stuck with 3 cloves
bouquet garni
salt, pepper
⅓–½ cup cream
2 tablespoons butter
croutons of bread fried in butter

Soak the beans. Drain and put them into a large pan with the carrot, onion and bouquet garni, and cover them with water. Simmer, without salting the beans, until they are cooked. Remove carrot, onion and herbs. Strain the beans or purée in the blender and return to the pan. Season and add more water if the soup is too thick for your liking. Reheat, adding the cream at the end. Pour into the soup tureen, stir in the butter. Serve with croutons.

Cream of haricot beans in the Berry style

(for 4)

¼ lb. dried haricot beans [navy, pea, or
   Great Northern, soaked
1 large onion
¼ lb. potatoes, peeled
salt, pepper
6 tablespoons cream
2 tablespoons butter
parsley or croutons to garnish

Cover beans, onion and potatoes with water. Simmer until cooked. Put in the blender or through the food mill, then season and reheat, adding cream at the end. Pour into the soup tureen, stir in the butter, and sprinkle with chopped parsley or croutons.

Napoleon's bean salad (*for 4*)

Napoleon, when he was on Saint Helena, used to eat this bean salad at lunchtime every other day. As with Tuscan bean soup, the important ingredient, after the beans, is olive oil.

½ lb. dried haricot beans [navy, pea, or Great Northern]
good handful of green herbs: chervil, tarragon,
    chives, parsley, etc.
6 tablespoons good olive oil
1¼ tablespoons tarragon vinegar
1 teaspoon French mustard (*moutarde de Maille*
    or strong Dijon)
salt, freshly ground black pepper

optional: 1 tablespoon chopped onion or shallots

Soak the beans, and simmer in water until they are soft but not disintegrating. Add salt when the beans are nearly ready. Drain and cool. Chop the herbs (cooks of Napoleon's time included the astringent salad burnet) into a salad bowl, and mix in the beans. Leave for an hour or two, for the beans to absorb the flavour of the herbs. Add the rest of the ingredients (which can be adjusted to taste) just before serving. A tablespoon of chopped mild onion or shallots makes a good addition to the green herbs.

Beans with cream & celery (*for 4*)

A delicious example of the elegance of French vegetable cookery. Here's something quite ordinary, not rare or luxurious, a subsistence food if you like, treated with love and intelligence. Serve these beans on their own, or as an accompaniment to chicken and turkey: the trick is to cook the celery at the very last moment. Beans and cream can be kept warm for a while, but not the celery.

½ lb. haricot or butter beans [navy, pea,
    or Great Northern]
8 tablespoons [1 stick] butter
nutmeg
⅓–½ cup heavy cream
lemon juice
2 stalks celery
salt, black pepper

Soak the beans in the usual way. Drain them, and put into a pan with just enough water to cover them. Add 4 tablespoons of the butter, pepper and a good grating of nutmeg, but no salt. Simmer with the lid off the pan until the beans are nearly cooked. Put in ¼ teaspoon salt, and finish the cooking. The liquid should almost have disappeared. Stir in the cream, bring back to the boil and cook until the beans are bathed in a thick sauce (it's important not to overcook the beans in the first place). Correct the seasoning with a little lemon juice, salt and pepper.

String the celery well. Slice it across, at an angle, into thin strips. Just before serving the beans, fry the celery in the remaining 4 tablespoons of butter until it's lightly browned but still crisp. Keep stirring it about, and don't let the butter burn. Scatter on top of the beans as a garnish.

Chirashi-zushi with sweet beans

(for 4 to 6)

The Japanese are famous for their bean cakes and buns, which are often sold in the most exquisite wrappings and boxes. They also cook beans in syrup and serve them with savoury rice dishes. Beans prepared this way are so good that I sometimes serve an Anglicized version of *chirashi-zushi* as an hors d'oeuvre to give us an excuse for eating them. People who are fortunate enough to live near an Oriental foodstore might like to substitute the Japanese ingredients (in parentheses) for capers, etc.

Choose a plain beautiful serving dish for *chirashi-zushi*, and take extra time to arrange the items elegantly. There are six of them to prepare:

1.

½ cup haricot or butter beans [navy, pea, or Great Northern]
⅓ cup sugar
5 tablespoons water
½ teaspoon soy sauce (preferably Japanese)
salt

Soak and simmer the beans in the usual way, adding a little salt at the end. Drain well. Make a syrup of the sugar and water by bringing to the boil and stirring until the sugar has dissolved. Add the beans and keep them below boiling point for 10 minutes. Stir in the soy sauce and leave to cool.

2.

1 cup rice
2½ tablespoons wine vinegar
teaspoon sugar
soy sauce to taste (or 2–3 tablespoons *dashi*)
¼ cup cooked carrots, chopped small
1–2 tablespoons capers (or 2 tablespoons *chirasu-boshi*)

Boil the rice in the usual way. Rinse well under the hot tap, then mix in the other ingredients. More sugar or vinegar or soy sauce—or less—may be added to taste.

3.

¼ lb. mushrooms (or 1½ oz. dried Japanese mushrooms)
1 tablespoon soy sauce (preferably Japanese)
1 tablespoon sugar

Remove the stems of the mushrooms, and cut them in strips (dried mushrooms must be soaked in tepid water for about 20 minutes, before slicing). Simmer until cooked in soy sauce and sugar. Cool. Mix in with the rice in recipe 2.

4.

¼ lb. green string beans, cooked, preferably *haricots verts*
teaspoon each soy sauce & wine vinegar (or 2 tablespoons
      dashi, ⅛ teaspoon salt)

Mix the ingredients together and leave to soak for an hour.

5.

¼ lb. shrimps, cooked & peeled
2 tablespoons wine vinegar
1½ tablespoons sugar

Mix together, leave for half an hour, then drain.

6.

2 eggs, beaten
pinch salt
1 teaspoon sugar
1 teaspoon soy sauce (or 2 teaspoons *dashi*)
corn oil

Beat the eggs well, add sugar and soy sauce or *dashi*. Brush a heavy frying
pan with a thin coating of oil, place over a moderate heat for a few
moments, then pour in a thin layer of beaten egg. It will cook quickly, and
should not be moved about but left in an even layer. Remove with a
palette knife or fish slicer. Repeat until the egg is finished and you have
3 or 4 pancakes. Roll them up, then slice them downwards into thin shreds:
they will look like tiny slices of jam roll.

Serve with warm sake. Bowls of clear Japanese soup (with bean curd
and mushrooms) can accompany the dish—the soup is easily prepared
from dehydrated packages sold in Oriental food shops.

Leg of lamb in peasant style   (for 8)

Beans of all kinds are a favourite accompaniment to lamb in
France. In early summer, there will be a dish of the beautiful stringless

haricots verts. They will be followed by shelled green flageolet beans, first fresh, then half-dried as summer passes. In winter the lamb will be served on a bed of white haricot beans. Sometimes they will be cooked together.

3–4 lb. leg of lamb, boned
2 cloves garlic
1 lb. haricot beans, soaked [navy, pea, or Great Northern]
onion stuck with 3 cloves
large carrot, sliced
bouquet garni
4 tablespoons butter
½ lb. piece smoked streaky bacon [see footnote, p.33]
2 large onions, sliced
1 lb. potatoes, peeled & cubed
3 cups light stock, preferably prepared from lamb bones
salt, pepper

Cut the garlic into slivers, and insert them into the lamb (make little cuts with a sharp pointed knife first). Season well and tie firmly into a roll. Put beans, onion stuck with cloves, carrot and bouquet garni into a saucepan; cover with water and simmer for an hour. Meanwhile brown the lamb in butter, in a large oval, enamelled iron pot. Cut the rind from the bacon and discard, then cut the bacon downwards into strips about 1 inch long by ¼ inch wide and thick. Add bacon to the lamb when it's browned, and transfer the pot to a moderate oven to roast (calculate cooking time according to whether you like lamb well done or slightly underdone). Half an hour before the lamb is cooked, remove the pot from the oven. Put in the sliced onions first, slipping them underneath the meat, then the beans—drain them well—the potatoes and the stock, which should be at boiling point. Cover the pot and return to the oven for about half an hour, or until beans and potatoes are done. Serve in the cooking pot.

NOTE: In Brittany, salt-marsh lamb is often served with haricot beans, but the two are cooked separately. No potatoes or bacon are included. I think the peasant style is more succulent, particularly for our often inferior lamb.

Beans village style   (for 6)

This is the easiest recipe for beans I know. It's a good one, and cheap. All you need are two or three homely ingredients, an ovenproof pot (the Italian *fagiolara* does well, or a French storage jar, stoneware jug [or any U.S. casserole ware]), and a collection of open-air appetites.

Beans village style are the antique basis from which cooks evolved cassoulet in the Languedoc and Boston baked beans in North America. Locally produced French additions were tomatoes, onions, garlic sausage, preserved goose and occasionally a ragout of mutton. American additions reflected the early New England trade—molasses, soft brown sugar and rum from the West Indies. People in the circumstances of those days, a century or two or three ago, could not consult books of international cookery for inspiration: they consulted their storecupboards and kitchen gardens and cellars instead.

> 1 *lb. haricot beans* [navy, pea, or Great Northern]
> bay leaf, sprig thyme, sprig parsley
> 6–8 oz. streaky bacon in a piece [see footnote, p. 33]
> salt, pepper

Soak the beans in the usual way. Tie the herbs together. Put all ingredients, except salt, into the cooking pot and add just enough cold water to cover. Add a lid of double foil, firmly secured to prevent steam from escaping. Simmer in a slow oven, 300°, until the beans are cooked (1½–2 hours). Season with salt at the end, as required.

Baked beans Southern style   (for 6)

Nearer the home of the kidney bean, cooks make use of other American ingredients—peppers, molasses and tomatoes. Being a hot substantial dish, these baked beans are best followed by fruit, say a chilled pear, or chilled melon.

Follow the ingredients and method for beans village style, but remove beans from the oven when they are half-cooked. Take out the herbs, and mix in:

> 1 green pepper, deseeded & chopped
> 1 large onion, chopped
> 2 large tomatoes, peeled & chopped
> ¼ cup molasses, more or less to taste
> salt & pepper to taste

Remove the bacon and slice it. Turn the beans, etc., into a large wide dish, put the slices of bacon on top and finish cooking in the oven without a lid. Beans and bacon will develop a rich brown glaze, almost a crust.

Meat stew with beans *(for 6)*

This recipe, I know, reads unpromisingly. The main ingredients sound like a school dining room stew. But please try it—both flavour and texture are unexpectedly delicious. The interesting thing is the way the beans come almost to dominate the meat. They also thicken the sauce so that the dish coheres agreeably, without stodginess. Don't leave out the garlic and allspice.

> 6 oz. haricot or butter beans [navy, pea, or Great Northern]
> 1 lb. chuck steak or stewing lamb
> 1 medium onion, chopped
> 1 large clove garlic, chopped
> 4 tablespoons butter
> 1 large tomato, skinned & chopped
> 2½ tablespoons tomato paste
> allspice
> salt & pepper

Soak the beans for as short a time as possible (see p. 174). Simmer in unsalted water for 20 minutes and drain. Meanwhile cut the meat into cubes (when buying lamb, allow extra for the weight of the bones), including the fat. Fry onion and garlic in butter gently for about 15 minutes, turn up the heat and brown beef or lamb. Add tomato, tomato paste, beans and enough water to cover. When bubbling nicely, season with plenty of ground allspice and black pepper. Transfer to a casserole and cook, covered, in the oven at 350°, until meat and beans are cooked. This takes about 1½ hours. Fifteen minutes before the end of cooking time, season with salt and more pepper and allspice if necessary.

As with baked beans Southern style, it's prudent to follow this dish with fruit on its own.

LEEKS

Leeks must be one of the oldest vegetables. They grew leeks (and still do) in Egypt. Leeks spread north, green and fresh in beastly winters. They fed the English, the Welsh, the Irish, the Danes. Simple food. When an Irish hermit 900 years ago wrote a poem to boast of how simple and good it was to be a hermit, he talked of having "fresh leeks, green purity" outside his hut in the woods. When Englishmen 1,400 years ago spoke of a vegetable patch, they called it a *leac-tun*, leek enclosure, as we might speak of a cabbage patch or potato patch or, in Scotland, a kail-yard. They scattered England with leek-patch names—Leckhampstead, Latton, Leighton Buzzard. Up north, Loughrigg was a Norseman's *laukr* or leek ridge, Lawkland his leek land. "Green as a leek" was a standard phrase in England's Middle Ages—a green leek even in frozen winter.

Why are leeks associated with Welshmen, St. David and St. David's Day? Books give legends, but none of them sounds reasonable. I suspect it was only because a primitive dependence on leeks, so hardy and so easily grown, lasted in poor, wet Wales when it was on the way out in England. Anyhow John Parkinson, our great gardener of the time of James

I and Charles I, records that leeks had become a poor man's food in England, though leek pottage was still "a great and generall feeding in Wales with the vulgar gentlemen" (before a bunch of Welsh *cennin* hits me in the eye, mud, leaves and all, I hurry to say that "vulgar gentlemen" means no more than the run of gentlemen).

I think leeks remained a poor man's food[1] till recently—or just a taken-for-granted everyday veg, or an ingredient only. You won't find much about them, say, in Mrs. Beeton or Eliza Acton (or even in such a recipe book as the very British *Farmhouse Fare*). For every mention of leek there is a dozen of cabbage. But then social attitudes often make fools of us in matters of food—and I shall swear that some of the leek soups are not easily surpassed, the French *bonne femme*, the French-American vichyssoise, and soup above soups, Scotland's cockie leekie. Talleyrand, who knew more about good food than most politicians—or most cooks—gave a high mark to cockie leekie, or cock-a-leekie.

To prepare leeks:

Cut off the roots, the coarse green leaves (can be used up in stock making) and the damaged outer layer. Run under the tap to remove the earth and grit.

They can then be sliced into a colander, and rinsed again.

Or, if they are to be cooked whole, they can be placed, root end up, in a bowl of water for half an hour. Any obstinate pockets of earth can be removed through tiny cuts in the stem.

Potage à la bonne femme and crème vichyssoise glacée (for 4-6)

These two soups are now linked with the name of Louis Diat, the French chef who over 50 years ago invented the most delicious

---

[1] Not so in America. Here leeks are rare (some Americans would not even recognize a leek if they saw one) and so expensive that they are ironically called "rich man's asparagus," best known for their importance as the vital ingredient in Louis Diat's vichyssoise, the iced cream soup he introduced in New York. The solution for gastronomes who have garden space is to raise their own. Leeks are easy to grow, but they take a long time—130–150 days. Started about the last week in May, they reach full size just before cold weather, but they keep their quality when left in the ground through winter.

chilled soup from a commonplace of French peasant cookery. "Of the many specialities I created for the old Ritz-Carlton," he wrote of the hotel in New York, "none has gained the wide and lasting acclaim of *crème vichyssoise glacée*, the chilled cream of leek and potato soup now served in restaurants everywhere. I suspect that some of the *fins becs* who order it would be much surprised to learn of its humble origins as my mother's simple leek and potato soup. Casting about one day for a new cold soup, I remembered how *maman* used to cool our breakfast soup, on a warm morning, by adding cold milk to it. A cup of cream, an extra straining, and a sprinkle of chives, *et voilà*, I had my new soup. I named my version of *maman*'s soup after Vichy, the famous spa located not twenty miles from our Bourbonnais home, as a tribute to the fine cooking of the region."

> 2 fat leeks
> 1 small onion, chopped
> 4 tablespoons butter
> 2½ cups water
> 2 potatoes (about ½–¾ lb.)
> 1 teaspoon salt
> 1¼ cups milk

plus:

for bonne femme: extra butter or cream, & croutons

for vichyssoise: 1 cup light cream
> 1 cup heavy cream
> chives, chopped

Use the white part of the leeks only—there should be between ½ and ¾ lbs. Chop and put with the onion and butter into a heavy pan. Cover, then stew very gently for about 5 minutes, but do not let the vegetables brown. Add water and cleaned, peeled and diced potatoes, and salt. Simmer until the potatoes are well cooked. Put through the food mill or blender.

To finish bonne femme soup: Add the milk, heated, and reheat the soup to just under the boil. Correct the seasoning. Stir in a little cream or a good knob of butter to finish, and serve with croutons of bread fried in butter.

To finish crème vichyssoise: Add the milk, heated, and the light cream, also heated. Bring the soup back to the boil, stirring to prevent it sticking. Strain the soup again, or quickly purée in the blender again. Stir in the heavy cream, correct the seasoning, and chill thoroughly. To serve, sprinkle each bowl of soup with finely chopped chives.

The amount of cream may be reduced, and replaced by milk. Alternatively water can be replaced by chicken stock.

Leeks à la grecque   (for 4)

3 or 4 medium leeks
1¼ cups water
½ cup olive oil
1½ tablespoons tomato paste
1 heaping teaspoon sugar
¼ cup rice
12 small black olives
chopped parsley
lemon juice & 3 or 4 slices of lemon

Prepare the leeks in the usual way, cutting them into 1½-inch slices. Bring to the boil in a heavy pan with the water, oil, tomato paste and sugar. Season with salt and pepper, then cook, covered, for 5 minutes. Add the rice. Boil, covered, for another 8 minutes—the liquid should be almost entirely absorbed by the rice. Turn off the heat, but leave the pan covered for another 10 or 15 minutes. The rice should be cooked but firm, in agreeable contrast to the moist leeks. Add lemon juice to taste. Serve chilled, with olives, parsley and lemon slices arranged on top.

Poor man's asparagus   (for 4)

8 thin leeks
2 hard-boiled eggs
1 tablespoon chopped parsley

vinaigrette: 1 tablespoon lemon juice
4 tablespoons olive oil
salt, pepper, sugar to taste

Clean the leeks as above, leaving them whole. Cook in just enough salted water to cover, until tender but firm—about 8–10 minutes. Leave to drain and cool. Mix the vinaigrette ingredients, seasoning well.

Arrange leeks on a serving dish, pour the vinaigrette over them and chill. Just before serving, mash the eggs to crumbs with a fork, and arrange with the parsley on top of the leeks.

Cornish leek pie   *(for 4)*

Very similar leek pies and flans have been made for a long time in northern and central France, in Flanders, in Wales and in Cornwall. Basic ingredients are the same—leeks, cream, eggs and short pastry —but in Cornwall and Wales, and in French Berry, bacon is added as well. This improves the flavour.

Pastry goes either below the filling, as in the leek *flammiche* (flan) that Francatelli shaped like a soft leather moneybag purse, or above it, as in this Cornish recipe:

½–¾ lbs. leeks, cleaned & sliced
4 tablespoons butter
¼ lb. bacon rashers [see footnote, p. 33]
1 cup Cornish or heavy cream
1 egg and 1 egg yolk
salt, pepper
short pastry made with ½ cup flour

for glazing: 1 egg yolk or cream

Cook leeks gently in the butter for 10 minutes, in a covered pan, without browning them. Remove from the heat. Add bacon cut into ¼-inch-wide strips, and turn into a pie dish or plate. A good size is 8–9 inches in diameter, and 1½ inches deep. Mix cream and eggs well together, season

—allowing for the bacon's saltiness—and pour over the leek mixture. Cover with a pastry lid. Brush with beaten egg or cream and bake for 20–30 minutes in a moderate oven (375°). Like all custard mixtures, this pie tastes best warm, rather than hot.

NOTE: For a Welsh leek pie, put a layer of pastry below as well as above the filling.

Welsh mutton broth   (for 4)
(cawl mamgu—Granny's broth)

This is a dish for those who live in good mutton areas—in Wales, obviously, but also in parts of Scotland and England, where lean, fine-flavoured lamb can be bought, even if true mutton cannot.

"Cawl" is Welsh for soup. It comes from *caulis* or *colis*, Latin for a plant stem or stalk—usually of the hollow, cabbage type. (Cabbage names such as kale, cole, cauliflower, broccoli, and the Scottish kail have the same origin.) Although the recipe for Welsh mutton cawl was first published in 1867 in Lady Llanover's *Good Cookery*, the dish has a long history like other peasant soups of Europe, French *potée* and *garbure,* for instance, or Scottish cock-a-leekie which follows.

> 2 lbs. best end of mutton neck [mutton rib or lamb rack]
> salt & pepper
> ¼ cup pearl barley
> 1 large carrot, sliced (6–8 oz.)
> ¼ cup turnips [or rutabaga], diced
> 4 medium potatoes, scrubbed
> 2 lbs. leeks
> 1–2 tablespoons chopped parsley

Put the meat (don't cut it into chops, but have the backbone cracked) into a deep pot. Cover with water, add salt and pepper and bring to the boil. Skim off the greyish-brown foam. Put in the pearl barley, carrot, turnip, potatoes and 1 large leek, whole, from the 2 lbs. Simmer for 1½–2 hours, until the meat is cooked. Meanwhile clean and slice the rest of the leeks, discarding the coarse green part. When the meat is done, divide it into chops; remove and peel the potatoes, then return them with the meat to the pot. Take out the large leek and discard. Put in the sliced leeks and parsley, cook for 5 minutes only—the leeks should still be crisp. Serve in soup plates, with a marigold flower or two on top if it's the season. Fingers of bread should also be provided.

Cock-a-leekie (for 6 to 8)

For centuries, souplike stews kept most of Europe alive—just. Within present memory "stew" has still meant a great deal of water, barely flavoured with vegetables, and a scrap of meat on Sundays. Potatoes, pearl barley or bread, sometimes oatmeal, were added to deceive the belly into temporary quiescence. No wonder that stews have a poor reputation with many people today.

This is a pity. When these old survival recipes are well made, with enough meat, they can be delicious. Welsh mutton cawl (above) is one example, cock-a-leekie from Scotland an even better one. No doubt it often provided a last home for the aging rooster, but made with a younger bird of flavour it has earned smart gourmet approval, outside its country of origin, for over a century and a half. (Anyone who's only tried cock-a-leekie from a can may find this difficult to believe.)

A capon produces the finest flavoured cock-a-leekie. Next, in order of merit, come a roasting bird, a really good boiling fowl (cooking time will need to be increased), a deep-frozen chicken, and lastly those egg-tired birds euphemistically known here as "steamers."

> 1 lb. giant prunes
> 1 capon or chicken
> 2–3 lbs. leeks
> Beef stock,
>   or 2-lb. piece shin of beef & water

Soak the prunes overnight. Next day fit the bird, breast down, into a pot, with the piece of beef if used. Cover with water, or beef stock, and bring slowly to the boil. Skim off any brownish-grey scum. Meanwhile prepare and slice half the leeks; wash the rest, leaving them whole, and tie into a bundle—add these to the chicken pot after skimming. Simmer until the meat is almost cooked (if a very young bird has been used, it's best to cook the beef for 1½–2 hours first before adding the chicken, the point being to have them ready together). Correct the seasoning, and add the prunes, stoned [pitted]. Simmer for 20 minutes. Add the sliced leeks, and simmer for 5–10 minutes. Remove and discard the bunch of leeks before serving.

By tradition cock-a-leekie is served in bowls—a slice or two of chicken and beef, a few prunes and some leeks, plus the delicious broth, everything all together. However the broth is so excellent that it can make a first course on its own (with an extra flavouring of freshly ground black pepper), followed by chicken, prunes and leeks as the main course. The beef can be left to cool in the remaining broth and provide a meal next day. Talleyrand, the French foreign minister, considered that the prunes should be removed before serving. While from the gourmet point of view this may be a good idea (the prunes having given up their flavour to the broth), I think it is a shame. Because the prunes look so beautiful against the green of the leeks and the pale chicken.

Some modern recipes omit the prunes altogether. Was this considered a refinement, I wonder? To do so is a pity because they add a wonderful richness. A description of a knight's table in country Scotland in 1598, by Fynes Moryson, mentions that while the servants and lower tables had broth with a little bit of stewed meat, the "upper messe, insteede . . . had a Pullet with some prunes in the broth." He did not consider, as Talleyrand did, that this dish came within the "Art of Cookery," any more than the oatcakes baked on the hearth, which everyone below the "best sort of citizens" ate.

SOME WOODLAND MUSHROOMS

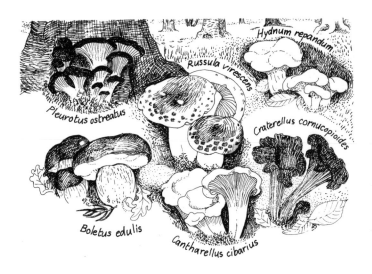

The pleasure of commune woods is well understood in the Bas-Vendômois, as in many other parts of France. They are well kept up and well used. People shoot there on Sundays in the season—shooting is not a snob occupation for the rich alone. They cut down the trees for firewood. And they walk in the woods to find chestnuts—or mushrooms.

We haven't in England, I think, quite the same feeling of enjoying our patrimony, the same strong local pleasure in the seasonal opportunities of the woods. Rarely does one see in this country family parties out on Sunday with baskets and sacks, after a copious meal, as one does in the autumn in France. Heads down, they fan out methodically through the quiet brown woods, calling to each other to keep their area under surveillance. There are shouts from the children as they find a colony of girolles or *trompettes de la mort*, then total meaningful silence as they bend to their treasure. One may recognize families one cannot see. Our family is of course more recognized than recognizing; the alien voices of Grigson *père et mère*, replying to the happily more authentic noises of their daughter, stick out like parrot squawks in a rookery. When we go shopping through the week, people say to us, "I think you were lucky on Sunday? We heard you . . . in the Lorette woods . . . out on the Célé road . . . at the back of Cornille." Then follows a lecture on cooking mushrooms: everyone knows that the English can do little more than fry chips. And to be honest the recipes which follow, with two Italian exceptions, have all been given me by those kindly voices which I cannot recognize without a bodily envelope, as they can recognize mine.

Whether you're in France, Britain, or the United States, all woods are worth exploring. But the best are old forests. Mushrooms don't grow much in the centre of woods, as Varenka remarked to Levin's half-brother in *Anna Karenina*. He agreed that cepes preferred the outskirts—and decided to discuss mushrooms rather than propose. "The stem of a boletus," he remarked calmly as they walked through the trees, "looks rather like the growth on a dark man's face who's not shaved for a couple of days." Which is true, of some boletuses at any rate.

If Varenka hadn't been so abashed at the lost moment, she might have added that mushrooms also grow on or near the riding trails through a forest. A certain amount of light slipping through the trees helps to create the right conditions. Should you find too many for present use, allowing for the fact that they shrink in the pan more than commercial mushrooms, you can dry the most perfect ones for winter soups and stews and omelettes. Slightly blemished ones must be used straightaway.

In late summer and autumn far and away the two best woodland kinds are, to my taste, the two which are most famous in cooking: the girolle or chanterelle (*Cantharellus cibarius*), bright apricot yellow, which looks very clean and appetising growing in colonies often out of green moss under tawny leaves, and the cepe, *Boletus edulis*—edible boletus (though other kinds of boletus are nearly as good). Both are easily recognized (remember that boletus mushrooms don't have gills below the cap, but closely packed, spongy tubes). Both are common in leafy woods, especially beech woods.

I like to eat four other kinds of woodland mushrooms. First, the one the French call *pied de mouton* (*Hydnum repandum*), another clean and sweet-looking mushroom of leafy woods, easy to identify by its hanging spines, in place of gills or tubes (sometimes this is called the rubber brush mushroom, on account of the appearance of these spines). Then the oyster mushroom (*Pleurotus ostreatus*), which grows out of trees such as ash and beech in a cluster of soft shelves. Then two of that large, gay-coloured, mostly white-gilled family, which go under the name of

Russula. These two, well worth a trial, are the verdigris russula (*Russula virescens*) with a blue-green cap (the French call it the *bise verte*, or the *palomet*) and the *Russula cyanoxantha*, with a cap of darkish green blue to violet. These two russulas are often abundant in beech woods; and when cooked you will find their flesh firm, more bity than the run of fungi, and tasting of new potatoes.

All the kinds I've mentioned are illustrated in colour in *Collins Guide to Mushrooms and Toadstools.* If the colours and the drawing aren't always exact, illustration and text together should be quite enough to clinch identities. The thing to remember is that there's no substitute for accurate knowledge. Any bits of country lore, any generalizations, should be ignored: while there are very few fatal mushrooms, there are a number which taste bitter or can cause indigestion.[1]

Incidentally, if you go on holiday to France or Germany, look out for the excellent mushroom charts on sale in most places: they can be kept in the car as a preliminary aid to identification. (Papers in France in the autumn are continually exhorting people to take the mushrooms they've picked to the pharmacist for inspection before eating them; an English chemist would be startled indeed at such a request; you would have more chance of success at the local natural history museum.)

Preparation

Remove the earthy base of the stem, and cut out any damaged parts of the cap. No need, with cepes, to remove the spongy underlayer of tubes, so long as they're firm and fresh-looking.

Never soak any mushrooms in water—it spoils the flavour. Large ones can be wiped over with a damp cloth; small—or messy—ones should be put into a colander and rinsed as briefly as possible under a cold tap.

Many recipes for woodland (and field) mushrooms start with a preliminary cooking, to draw the juice. A thin layer of corn oil is put into a frying pan, and the mushrooms are cooked over a medium to high heat

[1] *In addition to the government pamphlet identified on page 97, very sensible guidance is given by Euell Gibbons in* Stalking the Wild Asparagus *(N.Y., 1962), and he stresses the need for expert guidance. Other authorities like composer John Cage and Guy Nearing of the New York Mycological Society guide mushroom hunts occasionally; still others, like a zealous friend on the West Coast, find reason to be circumspect about their knowledge. "To ask a mushroom hunter," he said, "to take you to the patch, or tell you exactly where it is, is to ask that which is not in his nature to give. He may be generous and honest to the core in all else; but where mushrooms are in question, he is the embodiment of greed and conceit."* The Field Book of Common Mushrooms *by William Sturgis Thomas is also highly recommended.*

for about five minutes. When they're swimming in liquid, they're transferred to a sieve to drain (use up the juice in sauces and soups). Then the cooking is completed in a clean pan with butter or *olive* oil.

This is a good method for girolles,[2] which have plenty of moisture to lose (with, alas, a considerable diminution in size). With other mushrooms, particularly in a dryish season, it's usually enough to cook them quickly to evaporate the juice. The risk of this method is overcooking. Sometimes one has to switch rapidly to the first method, if the mushrooms produce more liquid than expected (this can depend on the weather, as well as on the type of mushroom). But with very little experience, one learns to judge the best method for any particular batch of mushrooms.

Girolles on buttered toast   (for 4 to 6)

The most treasured finds are the egg-yolk-coloured girolles or chanterelles. Their trumpet heads are easy to see against green moss, less easy when partly concealed by a scatter of autumn leaves. They're quickly identified by their gills, a miniature of fan-vaulting. For beauty, their only rival is the black flaring horn of plenty (*Craterellus cornucopioides*); for flavour, for their slightly earthy yet perfumed flavour, they have no rival.

> 2–3 *lbs. girolles*
> 6 *tablespoons butter*
> 1 *clove garlic, crushed*
> *salt, black pepper, chopped parsley*
> *buttered toast, or biscottes, or rusks*

Prepare and drain the girolles as above. Melt the butter in a clean pan, add garlic and mushrooms and stew until cooked—about 5 minutes. They

---

[2] Girolles, or chanterelles, are funnel-shaped mushrooms of various species, found in dry coniferous forests. If necessary, they may be replaced by dried mushrooms from Italy or Japan which are packaged and sold in many markets; but it's a good idea to avoid canned varieties because they are apt to be waterlogged and to have lost most of their flavor.

will be slightly chewy but not tough. Season with salt, plenty of freshly ground black pepper, and parsley.

Serve on generously buttered toast—better still on buttered *biscottes*, Melba toast or Dutch rusks, whose crispness and flavour set the girolles off perfectly.

This simple recipe can be used for all edible mushrooms, as well as for russulas, oyster mushrooms, *pieds de mouton* and cepes mentioned in this chapter.[3] Rice may be substituted for buttered toast, or a puff pastry vol-au-vent case (warm it in the oven); or the mushrooms can be used to stuff an omelette.

CEPES, OR BOLETUS

Many boletus mushrooms are deliciously edible, including one specimen which cuts to a sinister deep blue colour, but the favoured kind is *Boletus edulis*, to be found usually in beech woods. Whatever colour the cap of a boletus may be, its distinguishing characteristic is the spongy mass of tiny tubes underneath, where one expects to find gills. This part peels easily from the upper part of the cap, though it's not necessary to remove it any more than it is to peel mushrooms. Cepes don't shrink much in cooking. Indeed they retain an unctuous, yielding firmness, which sets them apart from all other mushrooms, particularly girolles and horns of plenty. For this reason they are admirable when used in stews, as they don't dissolve into the general mass; and when grilled or baked in the oven.

Although I must allow *Boletus edulis* its superior flavour, the cepes I most like to remember came from the springy turf under a group of pine trees. We'd passed Falaise in Normandy, on our way home, and had turned off the main road to picnic on the edge of a ravine near a small village. This romantic place had been embellished at the beginning of the nineteenth century by a widowed husband. He buried his wife, an actress known as Marie Joly, at her favourite viewpoint and had put up an elegant sarcophagus to her memory. Full of tender thoughts, we drove

[3] The fresh mushrooms available commercially in the U.S., which are whiter than most wild fungi, are a variety of the *agaricus* type commonly called field mushrooms; they are grown under government regulations and are tasty enough, but they cannot vie with mushrooms from the woods.

across the field towards the ravine and its heart-shaped garden, when suddenly we saw these cepes, cepes by the hundred. Conjugal affection and lunch forgotten, we jumped out of the car and filled every bag I could find. They were so dry and perfect that we ate them two days later in England, enjoying their flavour and the reflective nostalgia that distinguishes the end of a good holiday.

Potatoes with cepes

Only a few cepes? This is what you do. Prepare enough potatoes to fill a heavy frying pan. Cook them in 2 or 3 tablespoons of olive oil, with the sliced cepe caps. Stir them about until they're lightly browned, cover and lower the heat. Chop the cepe stalks with a clove of garlic and some parsley, add them to the pan with some salt and pepper, and leave to continue cooking. You'll find that the potatoes have absorbed flavour from the cepes in a most agreeable way.

This recipe can also be used with russulas, and with any other mushroom that doesn't toughen with prolonged cooking. Girolles are best cooked very quickly with a few peeled and sliced tomatoes, if you want to stretch them.

Champignons à la persillade

An excellent recipe from the Dordogne. Serve it with boiled potatoes, finished in butter and chopped parsley.

2–3 lbs. mushrooms, preferably cepes
4 oz. lean smoked bacon [see footnote, p. 33]
1 cup bread crumbs
1 large clove garlic, crushed
1 large bunch parsley, chopped
6 tablespoons butter
salt, black pepper, wine vinegar

Prepare the mushrooms as on page 195. Chop the bacon, and mix it with the bread crumbs, garlic and parsley. Cook the mushrooms for 2 minutes in the butter, season with salt and freshly ground black pepper, and sprinkle on the bread crumbs mixture. Cook uncovered for a further 15 minutes. Correct the seasoning, add a dash of wine vinegar to sharpen, and serve very hot.

Champignons à la crème

The classic recipe for mushrooms—any mushrooms—in cream. I think, though, that it's not the best way to cook cepes: their rich texture demands olive oil, garlic, parsley, not butter and cream. Cooked in this way, mushrooms can be eaten as a course on their own with triangles of bread fried in butter, or as the filling for pastry cases. As vegetable-cum-sauce, they make a good partner for veal, chicken, turkey and grilled meat.

> *3 lbs. mushrooms*
> *6 tablespoons butter*
> *½ cup heavy cream*
> *salt, pepper*
> *chopped parsley*
> *chopped chervil or chives*

Prepare mushrooms as on p. 195. Stew them in butter for 10–20 minutes uncovered, allowing them to produce a small amount of concentrated liquid. When they're cooked, stir the cream into the pan juices, and simmer for a couple of minutes to form a sauce. Season with salt, pepper and the herbs.

Mushroom stuffing from Berry

Although this stuffing is usually made with the fine fat stalks left over from grilling cepe caps, any other edible mushroom may be substituted. It's a good way of using up small quantities of girolles or *pieds de mouton* or oyster mushrooms, after a lean expedition.

> 1 large onion, chopped
> 1 large clove garlic, crushed
> lard or olive oil or butter
> 1 cup bread crumbs
> 2 tablespoons milk
> ½ lb. good sausage meat
> 1 cup cepe stalks, chopped
> parsley, salt, pepper
> 1 egg

Melt onion and garlic over a low heat in 2–3 tablespoons of fat, which should be chosen to suit the meat being stuffed—for instance, butter or olive oil for chicken, olive oil for lamb, lard for pork, and so on. Moisten the bread crumbs with the milk. Mix all ingredients together.

Use with poultry, boned roasts of all kinds, paupiettes of veal or beef (adding olives to the latter). For Christmas turkey, double the quantities and use 2–3 ounces of dried cepes (see p. 206), soaked and drained.

The mixture can also be used to stuff large cepe caps—bake at 425°, for 15–20 minutes, in a well-greased dish. Or to make *crépinettes*: divide into 2-ounce knobs, and wrap each one up in a 5–6-inch square of caul fat (soften it first in tepid water), then grill or fry, and serve with mashed potatoes.

Porcini alla casalinga

The Italians are as keen on woodland mushrooms as the French. In one village north of Carrara, the marble town, they hold a mushroom feast in the autumn. Wagonloads of various kinds are brought in from the countryside in a good year, and fried up in huge iron pans. As with the French, *porcini* or cepes are the prime favourites; this recipe is for cepes *alla casalinga,* in the homely style:

2 *lbs. cepes*
8 *tablespoons butter*
3 *tablespoons olive oil*
2 *large mint leaves*
4 *anchovy fillets*
some pounded parsley
salt
juice of half a lemon

Clean and slice the cepes, stalks and all. Melt butter and oil together in a large pan; add mint, anchovy and parsley, stirring them about well. Put in the cepes, sprinkle with some salt and cook slowly.

Serve on croutons of bread fried in butter, squeeze the juice of half a lemon over them, and serve very hot.

Sometimes the Italians use tomatoes with cepes, as the French do. They cut up some ripe sweet tomatoes, having removed the skin, and add them to the pan with garlic and some parsley so that everything cooks together. This can be used as the basic sauce for stewing lamb or veal or chicken: turn the meat in seasoned flour, then brown it nicely in olive oil, before adding it to the pot of cepes and tomatoes. Remember to add a little sugar and plenty of black pepper if your tomatoes are watery.

Grilled cepes

Cepes are unlike any other woodland mushrooms in their thick fleshiness, which does not collapse entirely in cooking. This means they can be grilled or baked, or turned into a cold hors d'oeuvre.

For grilling, choose large, evenly sized cepes. Put the stalks aside for a stuffing (see p. 199), and remove the underlayer of tubes unless the cepes are in exceptionally good condition. Place the caps, peel side up, on the broiler rack. Brush generously with olive oil, and broil at a medium temperature for about 10 minutes. Turn them over, put some more olive oil into the centre cavities, and grill at a higher temperature for about 5 minutes. Sprinkle with pepper, salt, and chopped parsley. Serve on toast or *biscottes*, with any juice from the pan, or as a vegetable with grilled meat.

Cepes as
hors d'oeuvre

1 lb. small, firm cepes
1 qt. water
1 tablespoon vinegar, wine or malt
1 heaping teaspoon salt

marinade ingredients: 5 tablespoons olive oil
2 tablespoons wine vinegar
8 whole peppercorns
bouquet garni
thinly cut peel of a lemon

garnish: 3 large cloves garlic, chopped
2 tablespoons chopped parsley

After cleaning the cepes, cut the caps into quarters, and the stalks across into sizable slices. Blanch in 1 quart boiling water, seasoned with vinegar and salt, for 2 minutes. Drain the cepes well in a strainer. Put into a serving dish and keep warm. Simmer marinade ingredients in a small pan for 5 minutes, then strain it, boiling, over the mushrooms. Sprinkle with the finely chopped garlic and parsley. Cover and leave for at least 24 hours. Serve well chilled.

Fricassee of chicken
with cepes   *(for 4 to 6)*

Cepes are the ideal mushroom for cooking with meat. From Brittany down to Italy and across to Yugoslavia, one comes across recipes for chicken or lamb or beef stewed with cepes, and with cepes and tomatoes (1 lb. of each to 2–3 lbs. of meat).

> 1 chicken, jointed & turned in seasoned flour
>   [cut in pieces & dredged in flour]
> 1 lb. cepes, cleaned
> about ½ cup chicken stock
> 2 large cloves garlic
> parsley, salt, pepper
> olive oil
>
> for serving: triangles of bread
>   or boiled potatoes

Cover the base of a heavy frying pan with a thin layer of olive oil, and put it over the heat. When it begins to smoke, add the chicken pieces and brown them to a nice gold colour. Add the cepe caps, sliced or quartered, and cover the pan. Simmer for 20–30 minutes, until the chicken is cooked, adding stock from time to time if necessary, so that there is always about half an inch depth of liquid in the pan. Meanwhile chop the cepe stalks and the garlic, and mix them together with a spoonful or two of chopped parsley.

Transfer the chicken to a serving dish with the pieces of cepes. Put the stalk and garlic mixture into the pan juices and boil hard for 5 minutes to reduce the sauce. Correct the seasoning and pour over the chicken. Serve with triangles of bread fried in olive oil, or with plain boiled potatoes which have been sliced thickly and reheated in the sauce at the last minute: either of these garnishes should be added to the dish of chicken, and not served separately.

Trout with cepes   (for 6)

Cepes go well with fish. Surprisingly well. And though this recipe was invented for the fine fresh trout of Pyrenean streams, I can recommend it for fillets of salt water fish such as cod, plaice, brill, turbot, etc.

6 trout
¼ lb. [1 stick] butter
seasoned flour
16 cepe caps (use stalks for stuffing, p. 199)
1 clove garlic, crushed
1 tablespoon aniseed apéritif (e.g., Pastis, Ricard)
4 tablespoons heavy cream

First clarify the butter by bringing it to the boil in a small pan, and then pouring it gently into a bowl through a cloth-lined strainer. This removes a white sediment, and prevents the butter from burning when you fry fish (or anything else).[4]

Put just about half this clarified butter into the frying pan. Turn the trout in seasoned flour while the butter heats up, and then add them to the pan—3 minutes on each side should give them a crisp brown coating. Transfer them to a serving dish, and keep them warm.

Add the rest of the butter to the pan, and stew the sliced cepe caps with the garlic for about five minutes, until they're cooked, keeping the heat fairly high. Arrange them round the trout, and put the dish back in the oven to keep warm. Pour the aniseed apéritif into the pan, and bring it to the boil, scraping in the appetising brown bits and the juices. Then stir in the cream and boil for a couple of minutes until the sauce is thick and smooth. Season, pour over the trout, and serve at once.

TROMPETTES DE LA MORT, OR HORNS
OF PLENTY (CRATERELLUS CORNUCOPIOIDES

The trumpet of death (or horn of plenty, according to temperament and nationality) carpets the autumn woods of the château country near Trôo with its black flowers. I suppose the French name derives not only from its colour, but also because it flourishes around All Saints' Day, with its lugubrious libations in honour of death and ancestors. To me it belongs to the happier celebrations of the wine harvest, or to the white wine harvests of the Coteaux du Loire at least. During the last days of preparation, at the lunch hour, people dive into the woods bordering the vineyards and emerge with baskets of these dry-fleshed, exquisitely

---

[4] See footnote, p. 11, for alternate method.

furling mushrooms. The wives put them into pork or pork and rabbit pâtés, to be served at the harvest picnic. Their appearance is truffle-like enough to give one great confidence in what one is eating. The *trompettes* left over will be either bottled or dried for winter use. Preserved in this way they are useful, but cannot be compared with dried cepes, which keep a remarkable amount of their fine flavour and texture.

Crépinettes

1 lb. lean & fat pork from throat or belly
¼ lb. green back rashers [see footnote, p. 33]
6 oz. trompettes de la mort (about 3 oz. dried)
1 clove garlic, crushed
2 tablespoons parsley
piece of caul fat[5]
salt, pepper, butter

for serving: mashed potatoes or buttered noodles

Remove skin and bone from pork. Mince it or put it through a meat grinder, with the bacon. Cut the *trompettes* into small but identifiable pieces; mix with the meat, garlic and parsley. Season with salt and pepper. Soften the caul fat in tepid water, cut it into pieces roughly 6 inches square and wrap up 2½-inch patties of the meat mixture in them to make flat oval packages. Fry in butter for about 6 to 8 minutes a side, until they are golden brown and cooked through. Serve with mashed potatoes, or buttered noodles.

How to dry mushrooms

After a successful mushroom expedition, it's a good idea to set aside the best ones for drying. Then in January and February, soups, stews and omelettes can be flavoured with the unexpected delight of cepes or russulas. Even when dried, they have more to offer than fresh commercial mushrooms.

---

[5] Caul fat is not so easy to obtain in the U.S. If your butcher cannot get it for you, try wrapping the patties in cheesecloth, which will of course have to be peeled off before serving.

Speed of drying is the thing to aim for—although temperatures needn't be constant—so that the mushrooms don't have a chance to go mouldy. It follows that they should not be washed: just cut off the earthy parts of the stems. In less humid climates, mushrooms will dry perfectly in an airy room or veranda, but in Great Britain it's prudent to make use of artificial warmth. Remember that the enemies are steam and smoke. Avoid these two, and you can use either of the following methods, or a mixture of them according to convenience:

1. Thread the mushrooms on to string, with knots in between or pieces of card, and hang them over a radiator, or in a warm, dry kitchen.

2. Dry them in the oven, on trays made with four flat bits of wood and a sheet of wire gauze. Line the tray with newspaper before putting the mushrooms on it. Keep the oven door ajar (for evaporating moisture to escape) and the temperature below 140°, or they will cook rather than dry. The most economical way of doing this is to put the trays into the switched-off oven every day, after cooking lunch or the evening meal.

The mushrooms are ready for packing away when they're leathery and dry (and much reduced in size). Store them in paper bags in a dry place or, if you're confident that all moisture has gone, in plastic bags. Two to three ounces per bag is a sensible amount.

When the mushrooms are required, put them into a bowl of tepid water to soak. Allow an hour at least, although you may find that some mushrooms take far less time to plump up to a semblance of their original size. Drain and rinse them quickly, and use as if they were fresh.

NOTE: One can buy packages of dried mushrooms in delicatessen shops. They are reconstituted and used in the same way as home-dried mushrooms.

PARSLEY

Has parsley really crossed from Europe to Britain? Or stopped short at Boulogne? Of course we have used it for centuries in medicine and in cooking. The Greeks and Romans taught us that it was a great plant for bladders and kidneys and driving out wykked wyndys—a great body opener (Shakespeare was sure of a laugh when he wrote in *The Taming of the Shrew* of a wench getting married on the way to the garden for parsley to stuff a rabbit).

But for the Greeks and the Romans, parsley was part of life. You were crowned with parsley if you won a race. It was an herb of life at funerals. (By country superstition, parsley is never transplanted or there will be a death in the family.) It was given as a strengthening feed to Homeric chariot horses. It reminded Pliny of holidays away from Rome— "You see sprigs of parsley swimming on milk everywhere in the country."

And in England it reminds us—of what? Boiled cod, on Good Friday, the relationship of centuries and civilizations reduced to green flecks in a white sauce. Sometimes I eat the parsley from the cold buffet dish in restaurants. Waiters look surprised. It isn't there for eating. Butchers decorate windows with plastic parsley (try stuffing some of that in a rabbit).

Parsley can be grown anywhere—window box, backyard tub or kitchen garden border—provided the soil is rich and moist. Sow in April and September for an almost year-round supply.[1] French cooks care for its taste, not for its looks alone, or for its richness in iron or richness in vitamin C. They know that curly-leafed parsley is the kind for strong taste and smooth-leafed parsley the kind for delicate taste; that there is as much flavour in the stalks as the leaves. And they know that, in cooking, parsley is a flavouring ingredient as basic as wine or brandy or cream or butter.

All the recipes in this chapter, with one important and one less important exception, are French. All require parsley by the handful.

Green salad

It's difficult to think of a simpler dish than this one, yet it's invariably badly made—at least in public eating places. The first important ingredient is the lettuce. It should be crisp (avoid winter lettuces, flopping heartlessly in plastic bags, and use chicory [or endive] instead), a lettuce of substance, of character, such as Webb's Wonder or long-headed cos.[2] Wash, shake dry and pull apart.

For the dressing:
> 1 heaping teaspoon sugar
> sea salt [kosher] & black pepper to taste
> 1 large clove garlic, crushed
> 1¼ tablespoons wine vinegar

---

[1] In the U.S. it will survive until the temperature drops to 18°F.

[2] Webb's Wonder is much like a garden-grown head lettuce and cos lettuce is sometimes known in the U.S. as romaine; also good and common in markets are Boston or butterhead, leaf lettuce, escarole, endive, chicory, and Chinese cabbage.

Blend these together in the salad bowl. Add to them:

>   *5–6 tablespoons olive oil*
>   *1 heaping tablespoon chopped shallots*
>   *(or mild onion, or onion sprouts)*

Just before the meal (no sooner), stir in 4 tablespoons of chopped parsley. Lay the salad servers in the bowl across each other to form a base for the lettuce leaves, keeping them separate from the dressing.

After the meat course, serve the salad, turning it over carefully at table until the leaves are shiny and coated with dressing. Many French families like eating a bland cheese with their salad. (Camembert is the obvious choice, but some of the soft Scottish cheeses now on sale do very well instead),[3] finishing the meal with fruit, or, on Sundays, a delicious cake or pudding.

Fines herbes

Ideally a mixture of parsley, chives, tarragon, chervil and watercress, fines herbes is often reduced to parsley and chives alone. Or, at the family table, to a bowl piled high with chopped parsley to be sprinkled individually over cold dishes—chicken and mayonnaise, herrings and potato salad, tomatoes layered with slices of egg. Here is a basic mixture, which may be varied according to taste and supply, and used in the recipes which follow:

>   *3–4 tablespoons chopped parsley*
>   *1 tablespoon chopped chives (or scallions, spring onion stems,*
>   *onion sprouts or Welsh onions)*
>   *1 tablespoon chopped tarragon*
>   *1 tablespoon chopped watercress*
>   *1 large clove garlic, crushed (optional)*
>   *grated rind of half a large lemon (optional)*

---

[3] *Not to mention dozens of cheeses from New England, New York, Wisconsin, and the West Coast, many of which go well with salad, or with a final glass of dinner wine.*

Beurre aux fines herbes

Fork the mixture given above into about 12 tablespoons unsalted butter, until it's well distributed. Flavour with lemon juice to taste, form into a long roll and keep wrapped up in the refrigerator. Cut slices off as required, to serve with steak or lamb chops, or grilled fish. Toss summer vegetables in it—new potatoes, carrots, real French beans, young broad beans, spinach, asparagus. Or use it in sandwiches instead of plain butter.

Cream cheese aux fines herbes et l'ail

We're familiar now with those delicious cream cheeses from France which are blended with herbs and garlic. It's easy to make them at home, as many Frenchwomen do—and rather cheaper:

8 oz. cream or milk cheese (cottage, Gervais)
1–3 tablespoons heavy cream
salt & pepper
about half the fines herbes quantities above

If cottage cheese is used, it must be sieved, or blended with cream, to get rid of the granular texture. With other soft cheeses, mash them with a fork and add cream gradually. Nonfat and low-fat cheeses will require 3 tablespoons—or more if you can manage it—of cream; cheeses with a medium fat content, such as Chambourcy, Gervais and Petit Suisse, will require less. This is entirely a matter of taste and texture and your own judgement.

Mix in the rest of the ingredients, seasoning with salt and pepper as required.

Pack into small pots or plastic cartons and leave in a cool place overnight. If you're lucky enough to be able to make your own cream cheese from unpasteurized milk, pierce a few holes in the cartons so that the whey continues to drain from the cheese. This is not necessary with commercially produced cream cheeses, as a rule.

Sauce à la crème

A marvellous sauce, simple to make, expensive, and quite delicious. Happily one encounters it frequently in Normandy and northwestern France, served with boiled chicken or fish (try it with poached salmon, bass or John Dory).[4]

> 8 tablespoons [1 stick] unsalted butter
> 1 cup heavy cream
> about half the quantity of fines herbes above
> lemon juice, salt, pepper to taste

A warning: this sauce takes a few minutes to make and must be served immediately, so have everything else dished up and ready.

Melt the butter in an enamelled or nonstick frying pan. When it bubbles, pour in the heavy cream. Stir over a gentle heat until they are well amalgamated and thick. Add the herb mixture, season to taste with lemon juice, salt and pepper.

Omelette aux fines herbes

Add the fines herbes above to 6 or 8 beaten eggs, according to taste. Season and cook in the usual way.

---

[4] John Dory is a fish never seen in American waters; porgy, though sometimes smaller, is an acceptable substitute.

Crempog Las

The Welsh, living in a less prosperous land, make pancakes rather than omelettes with herbs. I increase the quantities of herbs:

1½ cups all-purpose flour
fines herbes mixture above, without garlic & lemon peel
2 eggs, beaten
Milk, salt and pepper

Mix to a pancake consistency. Cook in the usual way. Eat buttered and hot. They are sometimes served with sausages and bacon, very good.

Quiche au persil

shortcrust pastry: ¾ cup flour
4 tablespoons butter
1 teaspoon confectioners' sugar
1 beaten egg to mix

filling: 6 tablespoons butter
1 cup chopped onion
1¼ cups cream
2 eggs, beaten
fines herbes mixture above
salt & pepper

Prepare the shortcrust pastry and roll out.

Line a fluted flan ring, about 9½ inches in diameter and with a removable base, with the dough. Melt the butter in a heavy pan, and sauté the onions in it until they're golden and transparent. Put into the pastry shell. Beat cream, eggs and herb mixture together, season well and pour over the onions. Bake about 40 minutes in a moderate oven, about 375–400°. Like all other quiches, this one may be eaten hot, warm or cold, but best of all warm, I think.

Jambon persillé de Bourgogne

A famous Easter dish from Burgundy, which makes a splendid centerpiece for a cold table at any time of the year. It is often left to set in thick white china bowls or terrines, and served in slices from them. It can, alternatively, be turned out on to a large dish like any other jellied food. Whichever you decide to do, remember that a simple white background will show off the magnificent pink and green of parsley and ham much better than the ancestral Worcester or Sèvres.

> 3–4-lb. piece of gammon [ham or Canadian bacon]
> 1 calf's foot, or 3 pig's trotters [feet]
> veal knuckle
> 8 peppercorns
> bouquet garni
> 1 bottle dry white wine, or half water and half wine
> 1 tablespoon white wine vinegar
> plenty of chopped parsley, at least 8 heaping tablespoons
> salt, pepper

Cover the gammon [ham] generously with water, bring to the boil and simmer for 45 minutes. Cut the meat into chunks, put into a large pan with the calf's foot or pig's feet, the veal knuckle, peppercorns and herbs. Pour in the white wine until it covers the contents of the pan. Simmer gently until the gammon is well cooked.

Drain off the liquid through layers of cheesecloth or a muslin-lined strainer. Taste and adjust seasoning. Add the vinegar and leave to set slightly in a cool place.

Crush the ham into a roomy bowl. Keep the rest of the meat to make a separate dish of brawn [headcheese].

Add the parsley to the setting liquor, pour it over the ham in the bowl and mix well. If you are intending to turn out the *jambon persillé* later on, keep back some of the parsley jelly to melt slightly and brush over it in a green layer.

When the *jambon* is cut, it has a beautifully marbled appearance. Very fresh and appetising. Serve with good bread and unsalted or lightly salted butter.

Charter pie   (for 8–10)

Parson Woodforde, the Norfolk clerical glutton, enjoyed a sociable day on July 13th, 1785. "We had for Dinner some Pyke and fryed Soals, a nice Piece of boiled Beef, Ham and a Couple of Fowls, Peas and Beans, a green Goose rosted, Gooseberry Pies, Currant Tarts, the Charter, hung Beef scraped &c. . . ." All straightforward English food (he despised French cookery), things we might eat today if not all together at one meal, except for "the Charter." Was it sweet or savoury? Was it in fact food at all? It bothered me for a couple of years, until the other day I acquired a copy of a small Victorian cookery book, compiled by Lady Sarah Lindsay, and suddenly turned the page to find this "Charter Pie (Cornish Recipe)," which I've adapted slightly. It's a winner of a dish, well worth the expensive ingredients, and quite up to Parson Woodforde's exacting standards:

shortcrust pastry: 1½ cups flour
        4 tablespoons butter
        4 tablespoons lard
        2 teaspoons confectioners' sugar
        1 egg
        pinch salt
        light cream or beaten egg to glaze

filling: 2 chickens, cut in pieces, about 3 lbs. dressed weight
        1 large onion, chopped
        6 tablespoons butter
        seasoned flour
        2 bunches parsley

½ cup milk
2 cups heavy cream
salt, pepper

Make the pastry and leave it to rest. Gently cook the onion in 3 tablespoons of butter until transparent, and put into the pie dish (a large
shallow one is best). Roll chicken in seasoned flour. Add the rest of
the butter to the pan and fry the chicken in it; when the pieces are
lightly browned, lay them on top of the onion in the dish. Chop the
parsley (excluding the tougher stalks) and simmer for 3 minutes in the
milk. Pour over the chicken, with half the cream. Season well.

Put a pastry rim round the pie dish, moisten it and lay on the lid (see
the chicken bones don't pierce it). Decorate and make a central hole, which
should be kept open with a small funnel, a pastry nozzle or a roll of white
cardboard. Brush over with light cream or beaten egg, and put into a hot
oven for 15 minutes at 450°. Protect the top with paper and lower the
heat to about 375°. Leave for an hour. Just before serving heat the rest
of the cream and pour it into the pie by way of the central hole—remove
the funnel first.

Charter pie is very good cold—the sauce sets to an excellent jelly.

NOTE: Mary Norwak of the *Farmer's Weekly*, published in London, says
that she makes a similar chicken pie, from a recipe given her by an
American. Instead of onion, she includes peeled, diced potatoes, which
do not need to be fried in butter like the onions above.

PARSNIPS

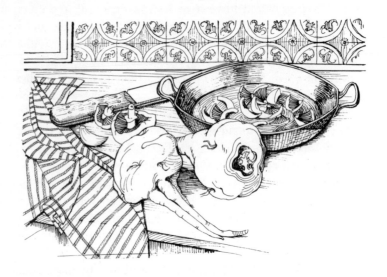

Parsnips should not at all be dismissed because only the Americans and the British seem to eat them in any quantity. They're an ingredient in French pot-au-feu, but otherwise few inventive cooks in Europe have troubled to make use of the parsnip's individual flavouring and sweetness.

I suspect that, like sea kale, it was one of the few vegetables of British origin (it's the cultivated form of the wild parsnip of chalk and limestone country), so it's been rejected in fine cooking with a degree of quite unjustified snobbery. Or perhaps the reputation of the parsnip was due to its once common and unholy alliance with salt cod in Lent. Certainly the English have been eating parsnips from the Middle Ages or earlier. A raw parsnip round your neck kept off adders or reduced swelling in the testicles. Cooked parsnip gave men an "appetyt for wymen."

Old, rather humble and homely recipes for parsnips survive in American cookery,[1] such as farmer's pie and parsnip chowder or stew. Not, I think,

---

[1] But few contemporary cookbooks give them much space. In Cross Creek Cookery Marjorie Kinnan Rawlings wrote: "Folk who would rather starve than eat parsnips would

the best of parsnip dishes, which are perhaps parsnip and walnut fritters (but they are American, too) and curried parsnip soup. Cubes of parsnip, blanched in boiling salted water for ten minutes, are good when dipped in batter and deep-fried.

The most striking use of parsnips I can recall was a resourceful wartime recipe. Boiled parsnip was sieved and flavoured with banana essence. The vegetable provided enough sweetness and the right texture to make quite a convincing substitute, say, in banana sandwiches. Or at least it seemed convincing at the time—I would not vouch for it now with real bananas around to set the standard.

The thing to remember with parsnips is that both by themselves and in combination they require plenty of butter or some form of richness, such as oil or cream—and plenty of seasoning. They have a wonderful affinity with beef, and, more surprisingly, with white fish. The cubes of parsnip in batter, for instance, are an excellent accompaniment to baked plaice or sole.

Parsnip salad

I've heard this salad called "poor man's lobster," which is stretching things a bit. The texture of cold parsnips may be a little like lobster—a very little—but the flavour is not. Anyway parsnips are perfectly good as parsnips: they don't need apologetic (or pretentious) names.

2–3 *nice parsnips*

mayonnaise: 1 egg yolk
1 teaspoon mustard
½ cup olive oil
lemon juice, salt, pepper

plus: some lettuce leaves

Trim and scrub the parsnips and boil in salted water until tender. Remove the skin and slice them. Leave to cool. Make the mayonnaise with the

---

make a sizeable army. . . . *There is little excuse for eating plain boiled parsnips, and fried parsnips are none too tempting, but parsnip croquettes are the ugly duckling become a swan."*

ingredients above: beat the egg yolk in a mortar or basin with a wooden spoon. Add the mustard, and continue beating. Pour in the oil drop by drop until the mixture thickens, then pour the oil a little more quickly until it's used up. Season with salt, pepper and lemon juice. Mayonnaise will not curdle so long as egg yolk and oil are at warm-room temperature, and so long as you do not hurry in the early stages.

Arrange the parsnip slices on the lettuce leaves, on a serving plate. Put some of the mayonnaise over them and serve the rest separately.

Roast parsnips with beef

Parsnips, as I've said, make a delicious accompaniment to beef when treated with respect. One good way is to boil, then slice them, and finish in butter, lemon juice and parsley. Another favourite way is to roast them. Allow one medium-sized parsnip per person. Trim, peel and cut into slices about half an inch thick. Blanch in salted boiling water for ten minutes, then drain in a colander.

Now there are two choices. You can either arrange the slices in the meat roasting tin, under the rack on which the beef sits, or cook them in a separate pan of fat at the top of the oven, just as if you were roasting potatoes (the two can of course be cooked together). The latter method will give you crisply coated parsnips, but the slices set under the beef will catch all its wonderful flavour.

The best solution is to cook half one way, and half the other.

Parsnip & walnut fritters   (for 6)

One would not think that parsnips and walnuts would go well together. But they do. So do parsnips and almonds, or parsnips and hazelnuts. My preference, though, is for walnuts. Try these fritters, and see if you agree that they make a very special dish.

2 lbs. parsnips
2 large eggs
6 tablespoons melted butter
1 tablespoon flour
up to ¾ cup milk
salt, black pepper
½ cup shelled walnuts, halved or quartered

Trim, clean and boil parsnips in the usual way. When they are tender, mash them well or put through a food mill, discarding tough bits of core. Mix to a smooth paste with the eggs, butter, flour, and milk. Season with salt and pepper and stir in the walnuts.

Bring a deep pan of oil to between 350° and 375° (I use a food thermometer to make sure the temperature is right, and is not too reduced by the fritter mixture). Slip in spoonfuls of the mixture, including a piece of walnut with each spoonful. Remove with a draining spoon when they are deep golden brown. Serve as a course on their own, or with white fish baked with butter and a little white wine.

Pot-au-feu, or boiled beef

Many Frenchmen, it seems, have a button labelled *pot-au-feu*. Press it, and you'll be swamped with nostalgia—cosy kitchen, fire on the hearth, pot bubbling as it hangs from the pot crane, mother flinging in vegetables, the pervading smell, the wonderful beef, wonderful mother, those were the days. I suppose in fact that pot-au-feu is the Gallic equivalent, emotionally, of our mother's apple pie; it can certainly be just as boring and resistible. Properly made, though, it's an excellently convenient dish. You will end up with beef for hot and cold meals, possibly a boiling fowl as well. And with several pints of beautiful broth for sauces and soups, its rich sweetness depending on the combination of onions, carrots and parsnips, particularly parsnips. (I read in a French flora of 1883 the rather tart remark that parsnips are cultivated in Brittany and Belgium to feed horses—it might have been added that the pigs at Parma are fed on parsnips to give the hams a specially good flavour—but at any rate the pot-au-feu, the classic of French bourgeois cooking, cannot be imagined without them.)

> 3–4 lbs. boiling beef (top or bottom round, neck, chuck)
> veal knucklebone
> 5 qts. water
> 3 medium onions
> 4 medium carrots
> 2 medium parsnips
> 6 leeks
> 2 stalks celery
> 1 small bay leaf
> several parsley stalks
> 2 sprigs thyme
> 3 cloves
> 1 large clove garlic
> 12 peppercorns
> 1 tablespoon salt
>
> optional: 1 boiling fowl

Put beef and veal knuckle into a huge pot, and cover with the water. Bring slowly to the boil (this takes about an hour), and skim off the rising clouds of scummy bubbles. Pour in a large cupful of cold water, and skim again. This is important, if you want to end up with a good clear stock. Meanwhile prepare the vegetables. Top and tail the onions, wash them, but leave the skins, which will add a golden colour to the stock. In the past pea pods, dried out in the baker's oven after the bread was finished, used also to be added to improve the colour and add a little sweetness: if you have a solid fuel stove with a plate-warming oven, you could dry your own pea pods, and store them when dry in an airtight tin.

Clean and slice carrots and parsnips. Wash and tie leeks and celery into a bundle.

When the water is scum free, and simmering, add vegetables, herbs, cloves, garlic and seasonings, and the boiling fowl if used. The combination of fowl and beef may sound odd, but it works well—think of cock-a-leekie (p. 191), the famous Scottish soup, which at its best combines beef or beef stock with chicken.

The bundle of leeks and celery may be removed after simmering about 20 minutes, to be eaten when cold with vinaigrette, as an hors d'oeuvre sometimes known as "poor man's asparagus" (p. 188).

Watch the boiling fowl: it may be as done as it should be in 2 hours, depending on its antiquity. And after 3 hours the beef will be done, after 3 hours of simmering, that is. As each becomes completely cooked, remove chicken and beef from the pot, and strain the broth into a large bowl through a cloth-lined colander.

Now the beef can be eaten hot with a little of the stock as sauce, plenty of French mustard, and freshly cooked glazed vegetables (the pot vegetables have given up their goodness to the broth and meat, and should be thrown away). Or it can be left to cool in the stock; serve, carved in thin slices, with potato or parsnip salad, lettuce and gherkins.

The boiling fowl is best eaten hot, accompanied by well-buttered rice, and a cream sauce made with some of the stock, light cream and a flour and butter roux.

NOTE: If you normally rely on bouillon cubes for soups and sauces, you will be surprised at the difference this broth makes to your usual recipes.

Curried parsnip soup *(for 6 to 8)*

This is a wonderful soup, delicately flavoured yet satisfying. One doesn't immediately recognise the parsnip taste, and no other root vegetable can produce such an excellent result.

1 large parsnip
½ cup chopped onion
1 clove garlic, crushed
6 tablespoons butter
1 tablespoon flour
1 rounded teaspoon curry powder
4 cups hot beef stock
½ cup cream
chives

for serving: croutons

Peel and dice the parsnip. Put the onion, parsnip and garlic into a heavy pan with the butter and cook for 10 minutes slowly with the lid on the pan. The vegetables must not brown, but gently absorb the butter. Add flour and curry powder to take up the fat, and gradually incorporate the hot beef stock (from the pot-au-feu, p. 219, for preference). Simmer until the parsnip is cooked. Whirl in blender or push through the food mill. Return to the pan, correct seasoning with salt, pepper and a little more curry powder if liked (but be cautious: keep the flavour mild). Add the cream and a sprinkling of chopped chives. Serve with croutons of bread fried in butter and oil.

NOTE: Soup puréed in the blender may need the further dilution of some extra stock, or some creamy milk.

Glazed parsnips   (for 6 to 8)

If you like the occasional dish of sweet potatoes with pork, veal or poultry, you will find this American recipe for glazed parsnips a much cheaper (and less fattening) substitute. It emphasizes the sweetness of parsnips—in fact, I've often thought it would make an excellent pudding, if served with cream.

> *3 lbs. parsnips*
> *4 tablespoons melted butter, plus extra butter*
> *1 teaspoon salt*
> *½ cup brown sugar*
> *juice of half a lemon*
> *½ cup orange juice or good cider*

Wash, boil and peel parsnips in the usual way. Slice them and leave to drain well. Choose a shallow baking dish, butter it and arrange half the parsnip slices in a single layer. Mix the salt, sugar, melted butter, lemon juice and orange juice or cider together. Pour half of it over the parsnips. Arrange the rest of the slices on top and pour the rest of the sugar mixture over them. Dot with small knobs of extra butter and bake at 400°, for about 20 minutes, or until the top is nicely glazed.

Parsnip & mushroom soufflé   (for 6)

1½ lbs. parsnips
¼ lb. mushrooms, sliced
1 clove garlic, crushed
8 tablespoons [1 stick] butter
3 tablespoons heavy cream
4 egg yolks
4 egg whites

Wash and boil the parsnips in the usual way. Meanwhile cook the mushrooms and garlic together gently in 2 tablespoons of the butter. Peel the parsnips when cooked, and put through food mill. Add the mushroom mixture, the remaining butter, the cream and egg yolks. Beat the whites until stiff. Season the parsnip purée well, and fold into the whites gently with a metal spoon.

Pour into a 1-quart soufflé dish, collared[2] and buttered in the usual way, and bake at 450°, until risen and golden brown on top (about 20 minutes). Serve immediately.

[2] In other words, to give added height make a collar by tying a strip of buttered foil or brown paper around the outside of the soufflé dish. The dish itself should, of course, always be well buttered inside.

PEAS

Everybody loves peas. East and west, it's the world's favourite vegetable. Peas were the first vegetable to be canned, the first to be frozen. They are the gourmet's delight—and the only green vegetable that most children will eat. As far away as Peking, boys and girls listen for the pea vendor's bell in early summer. They rush out with their bowls when he trundles his cart into the street, watch their ladle of peas being cooked, then run home picking at them as they go.

The peas of long antiquity were prized as an important part of winter's diet, not as summer's delight. Dried and grey, they could not be compared, even in their youth, with our modern garden peas, green, sweet, succulent.

For this we have to thank Italian gardeners of the late Renaissance, who developed better varieties of peas. No longer a case of cottager's pease pudding, lenten fare, but the courtier's pleasure. At Versailles the new *piselli*, or *petits pois*, the little peas from Italy, became an object of secret gluttony. Ladies who had eaten with Louis XIV—and eaten some of the best food in Europe—might be found gobbling peas last thing at night in the seclusion of their bedrooms.

No such orgies are recorded at the English court, when marrowfat peas were first developed at the beginning of the nineteenth century (the name describes the tenderness of these peas, which are wrinkled with sweetness). But they had their little drama. Do you remember the conflict between peas and politesse at Mr. Holbrook's party, in Mrs. Gaskell's *Cranford*? Mary, the young narrator, recalls that:

When the duck and green peas came, we looked at each other in dismay; we had only two-pronged, black-handled forks. . . . Miss Matty picked up her peas one by one, on the point of the prongs. . . . Miss Pole sighed over her delicate young peas as she left them on one side of her plate untasted, for they *would* drop between the prongs. I looked at my host; the peas were going wholesale into his capacious mouth, shovelled up by his large, round-ended knife. I saw, I imitated, I survived!

Would she, I wonder, have imitated Mr. Holbrook if he'd chosen another way—

I eat my peas with honey,
I've done it all my life.
It may taste kind of funny,
But it keeps them on the knife.

In these more relaxed days, our problem is not how to eat peas, but how to find good peas in the first place. People with gardens are able to pick them at just the right moment, and cook them within a couple of hours. This is perfection. The rest of us have to chase round greengrocers' shops, trying to find peas which haven't been picked too large, or kept too long.

Often one is driven back ineluctably to frozen peas, even in June. Professional eaters-out may scoff, but if they lived in the country and had to endure their neighbours' podded bullets, they would conclude that frozen peas are sometimes the only honest choice. They can be delicious, particularly the *petits pois*, if cooked with care. I reflect that we have been trying to beat winter starvation for centuries and centuries. I think we should be grateful, and not guilty, when we buy frozen peas—particularly in December—reflecting that a hundred years ago one subsisted for six or seven months of the year on root and dried vegetables.

I refuse, though, to feel any gratitude for canned peas, British style.[1]

[1] *In America many cooks consider canned Le Sueur brand tiny green peas quite desirable.*

Why can't our manufacturers lose their dye-bags, and study the methods of European firms? The tiny French peas stewed with onion and carrots are a vegetable no one need be ashamed of putting on the table.

Peas in cream   (for 6)

Do you ever try cooking peas with any other flavouring than mint? With savory, for instance, or young green fennel leaves? Or with spices? This old recipe using nutmeg and mace is a good starting point for experiment.

> 1 lb. shelled peas
> ½ cup water
> 4 tablespoons butter (plus extra for frying bread)
> 2 teaspoons chopped parsley
> 1 teaspoon sugar
> salt, black pepper
> ¼ teaspoon nutmeg & mace
> 1 heaping teaspoon flour
> ½–¾ cup heavy cream
> lemon juice
> 6 slices bread

Bring water and butter to the boil. Put in peas, parsley, sugar, salt and spices. Simmer until the peas are nearly tender. Put the flour into a bowl and stir in some of the cooking liquor, until you have a smooth paste. Stir in the cream and return to the pan. Cook gently until the liquor thickens and the peas are done. Taste and add more nutmeg and mace if necessary. Sharpen with a little lemon juice.

Serve as a separate course, with a dozen triangles of bread, fried in butter, tucked round the peas at the last moment before serving.

As a variation, cook a bunch of tiny young carrots separately, and add them to the peas before turning them into the serving dish.

Peas and lamb Stroganoff   (for 6)

Every cook hopes, perhaps against reason, to find dishes which are particularly good to eat, quick to prepare, and if not cheap, at least not outrageously expensive. There aren't many. An obvious one is boeuf Stroganoff (rapidly becoming Britain's national dish, to judge by reports in the *Good Food Guide*). It's a recipe which is easily adapted to other lean, i.e., expensive, cuts of meat—veal, for instance, or lamb chops:

> peas in cream, as in preceding recipe
> 4 inch-thick lamb chops
> 8 tablespoons [1 stick] butter
> salt, pepper, lemon juice
> 6 slices bread for toast

Strip the lean meat from the chops, discarding fat and bone. Cut into small slices about one-eighth inch thick; season them well with salt and pepper. Next prepare the peas in cream, and keep them hot. Also prepare 6 slices of toast, cut the crusts off, and divide each piece into two triangles. Last of all, when everything else is ready, fry the lamb quickly in foaming butter for 4 or 5 minutes. Mix meat and pan juices with the peas. Correct the seasoning with more salt, pepper and lemon juice if necessary. The flavour should be both rich and piquant. Serve immediately, not giving the lamb a chance to become tough, with the toast round the edge of the dish.

The amah's peas   (for 6)

When a friend of mine was a little girl in Peking, her *amah* used to cook peas this way as a special treat. It's a messy dish, but not as messy as asparagus. There are people who might think it a little noisy (the

Chinese are less inhibited than we are over good food), so choose your guests with care. Be sure to provide them with large cloth napkins; paper ones disintegrate.

> about 3 lbs. tender peas (in their pods)
> salted water

Peas of early middle-age benefit most from this method of cooking. Pick them over, discarding leaves, stalks, and any pods which are broken or blemished. Rinse and then cook them in a large pan of boiling salted water; try a pod after 15 minutes to see if the peas are ready; when they're done drain them well and serve in individual bowls as a first course (or as a separate vegetable course). The idea is to put a pod into your mouth, and suck out the steamed peas and the small amount of delicious juice inside the pod. The outer green part of the pod tastes good too (see pea pod soup, p. 230).

Eggs & peas in the Jewish style   (for 4)

I've slightly adapted this recipe from the 1758 edition of Hannah Glasse's *Art of Cookery*. It sounds very simple, even ordinary, but in fact the combination of peas, eggs and spices tastes delicious. An excellent first course for a dinner party. Be sure that the peas are young and sweet, the eggs very fresh.

> 2 lbs. peas, or 2 cups shelled peas
> ¼ cup water
> ¼ cup olive oil (or butter, melted)
> ¼ teaspoon each nutmeg, mace, black pepper
> salt, sugar
> 5 eggs
> 6 tablespoons light cream

Cook the peas with spices, water, oil and ¼ teaspoon salt, in a covered frying pan (use an enamelled cast iron pan, or a paella dish—something attractive enough to be put on the table). When they are half-cooked, season with more salt and a little sugar if necessary. With the back of a spoon, make four depressions in the peas and slip an egg into each one. Replace the cover of the pan, and continue to simmer for 5–10 minutes, until the peas are done and the eggs set, but not hard. Meanwhile break the fifth egg into a cup, beating it up with the cream. Pour over the eggs and peas, and put under a hot broiler for a moment or two to set. Serve immediately.

Pea and ham soup

Peas and smoked ham are a wonderful combination, either as a main course or cooked together in soup. This recipe solves the familiar summer problem of how to use up peas which looked fine in the shop, but turn out to be older and dryer than one thought.

> 1 cup shelled peas
> ⅓ cup chopped onion
> 3 oz. smoked gammon slices [or Canadian bacon
>   or ham slices] & 1 qt. water
>   or ⅓ cup diced potatoes & 1 qt. smoked ham stock
> 4 tablespoons butter
> 1 egg yolk
> 3 tablespoons heavy cream
> nutmeg, salt, black pepper

Soften the onion and gammon, or onion and potato, in the butter for 10 minutes over a low heat. Add water, or stock, and peas and seasoning. Simmer until the peas are cooked, then put through food mill or blender. Return to the cooking pan through a strainer and reheat. When the soup is just under the boil, pour a ladleful onto the egg yolk and cream, beaten together in a bowl. Put back into the pan and stir over a low heat, without boiling, for 5 minutes until the soup thickens a little more. Correct the seasoning.

Pea pod soup

A recipe for people who grow their own peas, and can't bear to waste the least result of their hard work. Only fresh, juicy pods should be used.

> pea pods from 2 lbs. peas
> 1 bunch spring onions, chopped
> 4 tablespoons butter
> 1 good sprig savory [or, if you must, ½ teaspoon dry savory]
> 6 tablespoons heavy cream
> 1 egg yolk
> salt, pepper
> 1 small bunch chives

Put pea pods into a large pan, and cover them generously with at least 1 quart of water. Boil until the green part of the pods is soft. Put pea pods and the liquid through the food mill (the rough white part will be left behind). Meanwhile, in another pan, melt the spring onions in the butter without browning them. Add the pea pod liquid, and the savory; season well and simmer until the onions are cooked. Purée in the blender or put the soup through a food mill and return to the pan to reheat. Pour a little of the hot, almost boiling soup into a bowl, in which you have beaten together the cream and egg yolk. Whisk well and return to the pan. Stir over a low heat until the soup thickens a little, but don't let it boil or the egg will curdle. Correct the seasoning. Serve with the chives snipped over the soup.

NOTE: If a few peas can be spared, add them when the strained pea pod liquor is amalgamated with onions and savory. The flavour will be even more delicious.

Peas in the French style   (for 6)

A marvellous way of cooking, or rather stewing, peas, whether they are young or not quite so young. It's surprising what a smooth texture the lettuce gives to the sauce, and how well the peas taste after their slow simmering with onion and carrot. (Incidentally, it's the use of this type of recipe which makes French canned peas so superior to any other kind.)

Quantities and timing are for middling peas. Small (or frozen) ones will need less time to cook, and half the amount of water. Keep an eye on the peas, to see how things are going; it's a mistake to overcook them.

> 1 lb. shelled peas
> 6 spring onions, roughly chopped
> 8 large lettuce leaves
> 1 tablespoon chopped parsley
> ½ teaspoon salt
> 4 tablespoons butter
> 5 tablespoons water
> 2 very young carrots, finely chopped
> sugar

Cut the lettuce into strips, and put with all the other ingredients, except the sugar, into a heavy pan. Cover tightly and simmer for about 20 minutes, or until the peas are cooked. There should not be much juice left in the pan. Taste and season with extra salt, and sugar if necessary (don't make the dish too sweet).

Artichokes Clamart   (for 6)

By a happy arrangement of nature, since their flavours go so well together, artichokes and peas are in season at the same time. This is a special dish, for a special meal.

The name Clamart is a souvenir of the days when Paris, like London, was ringed with market gardens. Different areas specialized in different vegetables, Clamart, to the southwest of Paris, being famous for peas. Every morning before sunrise carts from the suburbs would clatter into Paris with produce for the central markets, until in the nineteenth century the monstrous belly of the capital was no longer satisfied with young vegetables, and swallowed the gardens as well. It was the same with London—have you ever seen asparagus growing in twentieth-century Battersea? Most of the *petits pois* in Clamart these days are, I am sure, to be found in cans. But the name survives piously on menus and in cookery books; it still means "garnished with the best young peas."

> 6 *large artichokes*
> 2 *tablespoons wine vinegar*
> 1 *lb. shelled peas cooked in the French style (preceding recipe)*
> 8 *tablespoons* [1 *stick*] *butter*
> 1 *heaping tablespoon chopped parsley*
> *lemon juice*

Cut the artichoke stalks off close to their heads, and put them into a large pan of boiling salted water. Add the vinegar, cover the pan and cook for about 40 minutes, until a skewer goes easily into the base of the artichokes. Rinse them quickly under the cold tap, so that the leaves can be stripped off (keep them for another meal, to eat with vinaigrette sauce) and the hairy "choke" removed. You will be left with 6 saucer shapes of greyish-green artichoke—the best part, the *fond* or heart.

Cook the peas in the French style, adding the artichoke hearts for a few moments at the end to reheat. Mash the parsley and butter together, seasoning with lemon juice. Arrange the vegetables in a hot serving dish, with a knob of parsley butter in the hollow of each artichoke heart.

If you grow your own artichokes, you may find it more convenient to use 18 of the very young ones. Slice ¼ inch from the pointed leafy end of the artichokes, and boil them quickly in salted water until tender. Drain, and mix into the cooked peas. Stir the parsley butter into the pan before turning out onto a serving dish.

Risi e bisi, or rice & peas

Driving along between the arcaded, de Chirico-like Italian towns of Cuneo and Turin, one may round a corner to find that life has shifted suddenly to the Far East. Rows of girls, with skirts kilted up and low conical straw hats on the back of their necks, paddle along pushing rice plants into flooded fields. The extra-large grains that these paddy fields produce give the rice dishes of northern Italy a special succulence. For this dish of *risi e piselli,* or *risi e bisi* to Venetians, who make it a great deal, try to buy some of this delicious rice from an Italian food store.

¼–½ cup chopped onion
3 tablespoons olive oil
1 cup Italian rice
1 lb. shelled peas
sugar, salt, black pepper
grated Parmesan cheese

Brown the onion lightly in the oil. Add the rice and stir it over the heat until transparent—about 5 minutes. Add 2 cups water, and leave to simmer with the lid on the pan, until the rice is tender and the water absorbed. You may need to add more water, so watch the rice as it cooks. Meanwhile cook the peas in boiling water, seasoned with salt, pepper and a little sugar. Drain and mix with the cooked rice. Stir in 2 tablespoons Parmesan cheese, and serve extra grated cheese in a separate bowl.

By adding hot chicken stock at the end, this dish can be turned into a hearty soup.

SPINACH

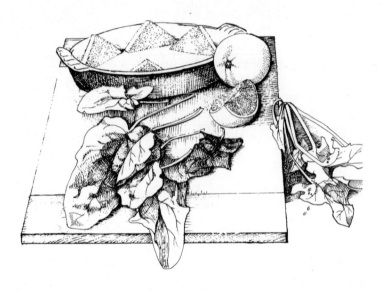

Don't be put off by either of two thoughts about spinach. First that it's baby food, and good for you. Second, that it's so often turned into a green slick, without taste or joy.

Perhaps when you stuff its unhairy plain leaves into your stringbag, or saucepan, you might reflect that spinach has a long and most respectable history. It has an Arab name (spinach: *isfināj* according to my dictionary), though it only came to Europe by way of the Arab world. They had eaten spinach in Greece and Rome, and earlier still. It is one of those plants of ancient cultivation whose wild forms and place of origin are unknown. Over the centuries it has driven out less worthy competitors in the line of a soft-leafed vegetable, annual, easy and quick to grow, easy and quick to prepare.

A soothing veg. There was a Frenchman who once said (according to the gardener and epicure Edmund Bunyard) that you have only to eat a few spoonfuls of spinach to increase in gentleness, benevolence and amiability. "You will be loving to your children and your wife: your home will be ruled by peace and harmony."

Perhaps so. But only if your spinach has been allowed to absorb plenty of butter or plenty of cream—not to say salt, pepper and nutmeg.

Our dampish British climate certainly gives us some of the most succulent spinach in the world.[1] Our subsidising government certainly gives us some of the cheapest butter in the world. Put the two together. (If you've never cooked, let's say, in France, where butter costs between 9s and 10s a pound, you don't know how lucky we are in this country).

Spinach has its own flavour, but the point is that it marries so well—with eggs, fish, ham, cheese, carrots, lemon juice, orange juice. And as a rule it's improved by the opposite accompaniment of something crisp. It always strikes me that, in cooking, far too many people fail to see how appetising it is to provide contrasts in texture. A few triangles of bread, fried in butter or olive oil, can turn spinach into a course on its own, instead of spoonfuls on the side of a plate.

Basic spinach

For six people, allow about 4 pounds of spinach. Pick off the tougher bits of stalk; discard brown, and alien, leaves. Wash in two or three changes of water, turning the spinach over and over to free it of earth—spinach can be very dirty. Drain in a colander.

Take a large, heavy saucepan and stuff in the spinach—or as much of it as you can. *Do not add any water.* Put the lid on, with a weight if necessary, and set over a low heat. There will soon be a bubbling noise, as the spinach exudes its moisture. Prod with a wooden spoon, adding the rest of the spinach as soon as the spinach in the pan begins to cook down. Raise the heat and cook with the lid off, stirring from time to time to make sure that the underneath leaves aren't sticking to the pan.

This sounds a long business, but the total cooking time will be about 20 minutes. Put the cooked spinach into a large sieve to drain, cutting it gently with a dull knife to help the liquid run away.

Just before the meal, melt a large knob of butter [1 *stick*] in a clean pan, and put the drained spinach back to absorb the butter. Season with salt, pepper and nutmeg.

[1] *Many varieties are available in the U.S. as the result of breeding experiments—color varies from yellow-green to very dark green, and spinach is one of the most satisfactory of America's abundance of frozen vegetables.*

This is the minimum of effort required to produce edible spinach. You may think I've been pedantic, and made the recipe—really very simple—sound complicated. But it's important that three principles about cooking spinach should be absolutely clear—it must be well washed, well dried out in the cooking, and well buttered.

Now you can have some fun with this delicious vegetable.

Creamed spinach with orange   (for 6)

4 lbs. spinach, cooked as above
3 large slices of bread
6 tablespoons butter
½ cup heavy cream
1½ large oranges, quartered

Remove crusts from the bread, cut into triangles and fry in the butter. Meanwhile add the cream to the cooked spinach instead of the knob of butter mentioned in the basic preparation, and cook until the cream is absorbed. Serve in a shallow oval or round dish, with the orange quarters in the middle, peel side up (to be squeezed over the spinach), and the croutons of bread tucked round the edge. If it's the right time of year, the flavour of the spinach is improved by squeezing the juice of a large Seville orange into it before arranging on the dish; include the quarters of sweet orange as well.

The unusual idea of orange with spinach comes from an eighteenth-century cookery book. It's an excellent combination of flavours—and colours.

Spinach and carrots   (for 6)

Another dish which is beautiful to look at. Like the creamed spinach and orange above, it should be served as a course on its own.

4 *lbs. spinach, cooked as in basic recipe, p. 235*
1 *lb. young carrots*
12 *tablespoons butter* [1½ *sticks*]
3 *large slices of bread, fried*
    in butter as in preceding recipe
salt, pepper, lemon juice, sugar

Wash and scrape the carrots. Melt 6 tablespoons butter in a heavy pan, remove from the heat and grate the carrots into it, using a fine shredder. Cover and simmer gently until the carrots are cooked, but not overcooked— about 5–10 minutes. Season with salt, pepper and lemon juice, with a little sugar if the carrots are not as full of flavour as they should be. Keep warm.

Add the other 6 tablespoons of butter to the well-drained spinach. Stir over a good heat until it's been absorbed.

Arrange the carrots in a border round the edge of a hot serving dish, and put the spinach in the middle with the croutons stuck into it. Serve immediately.

Four-day spinach   (for 6 to 8)

This recipe of unusual deliciousness shows the ability of spinach to absorb butter. I believe one can go on adding butter to it for seven days, but by the end of four days it looks and tastes so good that it has to be eaten.

3–4 *lbs. spinach*
1 *lb. unsalted butter*
salt, pepper, nutmeg, lemon juice

Day 1: cook the spinach and drain it in the usual way. Chop it roughly before adding 8 tablespoons of butter; keep the pan over a good heat until the butter's absorbed. Leave to cool in a clean bowl. Store in the refrigerator.

Day 2: reheat the spinach with another 8 tablespoons of butter. Leave to cool.

Days 3 *and* 4: repeat day two, except that on the fourth day the spinach will be served hot and not be left to cool. Season to taste.

You will have a rich, dark green purée, a cream or sauce rather than a vegetable. Spinach for adults, decidedly. Serve with boiled gammon [ham or Canadian bacon], or roast beef, or with grilled steak or grilled salmon.

Should there be any spinach left over, use it to stuff an omelette. Or to make individual eggs Florentine.

Terrine aux herbes

A reader living in the department of Essonne in northern France has sent me this delicious recipe for an herb pâté. As with all the other pâtés—game, hare, lark, chicken, duck—the basis and background is pork.

2 lbs. pork throat meat
½ lb. pig's liver
6 oz. gammon, or smoked lean bacon
6 oz. green streaky bacon [see footnote, p. 33]
1½ lbs. spinach (include some sorrel if possible)
2 medium onions, chopped very finely
2 large cloves garlic, chopped
2 eggs, beaten

seasonings: rosemary, thyme, basil, marjoram, nutmeg,
        salt & freshly ground black pepper

Grind the meat (or, preferably, chop it). Cook the spinach, drain it well and chop it up. Mix everything together, adding the seasonings to taste; if you are not prepared to chop onions very finely, they must be sautéed in some butter, without browning them, until soft and golden—they should disappear into the pâté.

Put into a well-greased terrine (or more conveniently into two) and bake for about an hour at a very moderate heat, 325–350°. Cover with a lid of foil, which should be removed about 15 minutes before the end of cooking time to allow the top to brown.

Although this pâté is best made with fresh green herbs and spinach, dried herbs and frozen leaf spinach may be substituted. The inclusion of sorrel is to be recommended, for its sharp pungency.

Serve it with hearty whole-grain bread (in lieu of *pain de campagne*) and anchovy butter.

Eggs Florentine *(for 6)*

The Italians love spinach, and make more use of it than we English do. All those varieties of green pasta, the *pasta verde*, are not coloured and flavoured by drops from a bottle, but by the addition of spinach and spinach juice. Sometimes ravioli and tortellini are filled with a mixture of spinach and cream cheese and Parmesan (a variation of the delicious little Middle Eastern spinach pasties on p. 241). When eggs, fish and ham are cooked and served with spinach and cheese sauce, we describe them as Florentine, in the style of Florence.

> 3–4 lbs. spinach, cooked as in basic recipe, p. 235
> 2 tablespoons butter
> 2 tablespoons flour
> 1 cup hot milk
> ½ cup light cream
> 1 heaping tablespoon Parmesan cheese,
>   or Cheddar to taste
> 6 medium eggs
> 2 crumbled rusks or biscottes
> salt, pepper, nutmeg

As the spinach cooks, make the sauce. Melt the butter in a heavy pan, and stir in the flour with a wooden spoon. Cook gently for 2 minutes, then gradually, to avoid lumps, incorporate the hot milk and the cream. Season with half the cheese or a little more to taste, with salt, pepper and nutmeg, and leave to simmer over a low heat for at least 15 minutes.

Meanwhile, having drained the spinach, put it into a buttered oven-proof dish, and prepare the eggs. They can be poached, but if, like me, you're not an admirer of poached eggs, try cooking them this way—put them into a pan of fast-boiling water *for exactly five minutes*. Then plunge them into a pan of cold water, set under a gently running cold tap. The moment they're cool enough to handle, tap them all over carefully and peel them (remember that the yolks will not be hard-boiled, so do this gently).

Make six depressions in the spinach with the back of a tablespoon, and set the eggs well down in them. Pour the hot sauce over the dish. Mix the rest of the cheese with the rusk crumbs, and sprinkle over the top. Bake in a hot oven for about 10 minutes, until the sauce bubbles and the top turns golden brown.

For sole or plaice fillets Florentine: roll up the fillets and secure them with a toothpick. Put them on the spinach instead of the eggs. Finish the dish as above, but bake for 30 minutes in a moderate oven to cook the sole or plaice. The top can be browned under the broiler, if necessary.

For ham Florentine: roll up slices of cooked ham, spear with a toothpick, and lay on the spinach. Pour the sauce over and finish as for eggs Florentine. If uncooked gammon [or country ham] is used, pour boiling water over the slices and leave for 5 minutes to remove excess saltiness. Lay them, overlapping each other, on top of the spinach, and finish as for eggs Florentine.

For individual eggs Florentine: put a spoonful of spinach (four-day spinach, p. 237, is ideal for this dish) into a buttered ramekin. Break an egg and slide it on top of the spinach. Bake in an oven (or cook in a pan of simmering water) until the white just starts to look opaque. Pour in a tablespoon of heavy cream; sprinkle with cheese, salt, pepper and rusk crumbs; brown quickly under the grill. Don't overcook. Serve with toast fingers.

Middle Eastern spinach pasties

A Lebanese reader sent me this recipe for some delicious tiny pasties, of a kind which are popular all over the Middle East. Variety of filling and of dough is enormous, depending on the resources and ingenuity of the cook. Bread dough may be used, or flaky pastry, or shortcrust pastry, or that papery-fine pastry called *fila* which is sold in Greek delicatessen shops.

Dough made with 1 lb. [about 3½ cups] flour—the
other ingredients in proportion

filling: 2 lbs. spinach
1 very large onion, chopped
3–4 tablespoons olive oil or butter
salt, pepper
3 oz. pine nuts or other nuts, chopped,
or 6–8 oz. Gruyère or crumbly cheese

plus: 1 egg yolk beaten with 1 tablespoon water

Cook the onion gently in the oil or butter until it's golden and transparent. Cook and drain the spinach very well. Mix with the onion, and season. Fry the chopped nuts, if used, in the liquid remaining from the onion cooking. Stir into the spinach. Alternatively grate the cheese and stir that in instead.

Roll out the dough as thinly as possible. Cut into squares and circles about 3 inches wide. Put a knob of filling in the middle, moisten the pastry edges and fold the pastry to enclose the spinach mixture. Press the edges firmly together.

Brush with egg and water (leave to rise, if bread dough is used), and bake at the appropriate temperature until the pasties are light and golden. Puff pastry needs a very high temperature; the other ones need something between 375 and 400°.

An alternative method, a very good one, is to deep-fry the pasties. They will puff up to golden brown lightness very much more quickly than they will in the oven.

But whichever method of cooking you choose, they should be eaten very hot as a first course. Or as part of a buffet table at a party. Meat can also be included in the filling; spices can be used as flavouring too. The main thing is to make a really piquant filling; otherwise these tiny mouthfuls are not worth the bother of making—or eating.

TOMATOES

Millions of us eat tomatoes; few of us ever eat a good one; and few of our great-great-grandparents ever ate a tomato at all.

Odd? Well, perhaps not. The tomato needs sun. It's a native of the hot lands of Central and South America ("tomato" from the Mexican *tomatl*). Early sixteenth-century travellers brought it to Europe, where it soon flourished in the warmth of Spain and Italy. Can you imagine Italian cooking without the tomato?

Italians called the new fruit *pomo d'oro*, golden apple. They still do. The name refers to its shining brilliance; it was not intended as a prognostic of our Moneymaker, the variety most of us have to endure if we are to eat tomatoes at all. Another early name, *pomo dei Mori*, Moors' apple, is reputed to be the origin of the French *pomme d'amour*. And so of our British "love apple." But "its supposed power of exciting tender feelings" did not weaken English suspicions of the tomato. Tomatoes were still regarded as medicine in the eighteenth century. Even the most advanced gardeners were shocked at Italians and Spaniards, who "eat these Apples as we do Cucumbers, with Pepper, Oil and Salt; and some eat them stewed in Sauces, etc, but considering their great Moisture and Coldness, the Nourishment they afford must be bad."

It was not until after the 1850's that the love apple commonly became the tomato. Its popularity increased but slowly. People still needed re-assurance that it didn't cause gout or cancer.[1] Perhaps the tale that Fijians enjoyed tomatoes as a side dish to Cold Missionary had some effect on its slow progress in the national diet.

Now we know that tomatoes are a valuable source of vitamin C. Twice as valuable if grown out of doors. Hybrids have been developed for northern industrial conditions and climate. We buy nice-looking, glossy, even-sized, perfectly spherical, perfectly red, perfectly tasteless tomatoes all the year round; they are the growers' and grocers' delight, "moneymakers" to the last pip. In their *Guides to the Grades No. 4. Tomatoes*, the Min-istry of Argiculture describe this perfectly desirable object, classifying it elaborately, down to the last millimetre, into Extra Class, Class 1, 2 and 3. Advice is handed out on packing and labelling. The only word missing is "flavour." In the 24 pages there is little indication of the fact that tomatoes are for eating; they're just for buying and selling, like the tins of sardines in a favourite Jewish story.

The ideal tomato is firm to the knife all through, sun-ripened out of doors to a rich but refreshing flavour, often a "large, irregularly-shaped furrowed fruit," as a nineteenth-century botanical dictionary described it, a glorious red, not only furrowed but scarred and split in a way that would horrify a supermarket manager ("unattractive in appearance," Min. of Ag., *op. cit.*). You'll have to grow tomatoes yourself, choosing a variety recom-mended for its flavour by a good nurseryman, unless you can afford a day-trip to France once a week. So the problem is how to make the best of the poor commercial tomato we're left with.

Sugar first, then freshly ground black pepper and unadulterated sea salt. These are the three great flavour enhancers; our tomato needs them all. Essential accompaniments are parsley, and the onion family from garlic to shallots, onions and chives.

In Italy the great herbs for tomato dishes are sweet basil and sweet or

---

[1] "We raised our first tomatoes about 1832 as a curiosity," wrote the secretary of the Connecticut Board of Agriculture, "but made no use of them, though we had heard that the French ate them. By about 1835 culinary use had become more general, although many people still considered them poisonous. . . ."

wild marjoram (*origano volgare*). Such herbs need sun. In England we can grow them (they are annuals), but out of doors they are chancy, needing a warm summer. On the window sill, or in a greenhouse, they have a better chance of success. Oregano (as the wild marjoram is known in U.S.) dries quite successfully, but to my mind basil loses its essential freshness, its magical flavour of the sun, and becomes too strong when dried.

Tomato salad

The simplest and best way of serving good tomatoes. But don't make the salad too long before eating it, or it will lose freshness and become nasty.

Pour boiling water over 1 lb. tomatoes and leave for 15–20 seconds. Run the tomatoes under a cold tap. The skin will peel off easily. Slice into a serving dish. Sprinkle evenly with about a tablespoon of sugar (depending on the tomatoes), a few turns of the black pepper mill, and a teaspoon of sea salt crystals. Drip a teaspoon of vinegar, wine vinegar, over the salad—malt vinegar is too brutish—and a tablespoon of olive oil. Just before serving, scatter with finely chopped garlic, or chives, or raw onion, and parsley. Sweet basil alone, if you have it. For vinegar and oil, you could substitute 3 tablespoons of thick cream and lemon juice to taste.

A salad which goes well with hot or cold roast duck and pork, if you add two peeled, sliced oranges.

Egg & tomato salads

A build-up of egg and tomato slices and chopped chives or shallots, dressed with oil, vinegar, salt and pepper, is a favourite French hors d'oeuvre. Bowls of it provide a refreshing start to midday picnics during the grape harvest in Touraine. You must use first-class fresh eggs, and season each layer of the salad as you build it up, using a little sugar on the tomatoes only. Serve immediately.

In French middle-class homes and small hotels, presentation is a little more elegant. And in the wonderful cooked-food shops to be found in every French community above a village. Slice the tomatoes almost, but not quite through. They will fan out, so that you can slip a slice, or half a slice of hard-boiled egg and a sliver of anchovy fillet into each cut. Garnish with chopped parsley and the chopped whites from the ends of the hard-boiled eggs. Serve with a bowl of mayonnaise (p. 158). Add black olives, salami, crisp green salad (p. 208), some unsalted butter and a good loaf of bread, and you have a fine lunch for a hot day.

Stuffed tomatoes

I am no believer in tomato water-lilies and tomato baskets: there are better uses for one's time. But there is no denying that stuffed tomatoes are a useful way of stretching delicious and expensive mixtures, such as crab or lobster mayonnaise. A small can of tuna fish (preferably canned *without oil*), broken up and mixed with chopped anchovies, parsley, 2 or 3 hard-boiled eggs, and mayonnaise, makes a cheaper but excellent filling. Peel each tomato first, cut off a lid, scoop out the inside and leave upside down to drain. Season with salt, pepper and a little sugar before filling.

For baked stuffed tomatoes, there are many simple fillings, with variations depending on what you may happen to have in larder or store cupboard. I think that garlic in fair quantity is a good idea: crush a couple of large cloves and fry them gently in butter with a chopped medium to large onion, then mix in bread crumbs and parsley, the chopped firm inside part of the tomatoes, salt, pepper and perhaps some nutmeg. A rasher of lean smoked bacon [see *footnote*, p. 33] can be chopped up and fried with onions and garlic. Remember not to peel the tomatoes, or they will collapse as they cook. Bake at 400° in a buttered dish for 20–30 minutes (the temperature may be altered to suit your convenience of course, when other things are being cooked at the same time). With large tomatoes, an egg may be baked in the centre instead of stuffing.

Basic tomato sauce

When we return from staying in France or Italy, I spend a despairing fortnight trying to re-create hot and vivid noonday flavours. A hopeless pastime. It's bound to be. But I persevere with this tomato sauce, made from canned tomatoes, which produce a better-flavoured result than fresh ones sold in shops. As you will see, this sauce has many uses.

    1 cup chopped onion
    1 outer stalk celery, chopped
    ⅓ cup chopped carrot
    2 large cloves garlic, finely chopped
    1 tablespoon butter
    1 tablespoon olive oil
    1 lb. 14 oz. can Italian tomatoes
    1 heaping tablespoon sugar
    2 teaspoons wine vinegar
    ½ cup red wine
    1 good teaspoon sea salt
    black pepper, dried oregano, basil, fresh parsley

  optional: 2 rashers bacon, diced [see footnote, p. 33]

Cook over very low heat the onion, celery, carrot, bacon if used, and garlic in the butter and oil for 10 minutes, then turn the heat up so that they brown lightly. Add the rest of the ingredients, and bring to the boil. Don't cover the pan, but keep the sauce bubbling and busy for at least 15 minutes. It will reduce to a rich stew. No need to stir.

This sauce can be stored in the fridge for a day or two, and used in the following ways:

Pizzaiola sauce. Sieve or put through the coarse plate of a food mill. Don't purée in the blender. Serve with steak, and spaghetti or other kinds of pasta.

Tomato soup. Purée in the blender 1 cup of the sauce with 1 cup of beef or veal stock. Add a pinch of baking soda and reheat, adding more stock if you like a thinner consistency. When the soup is just under the boil, add ½ cup of boiling light cream and serve immediately, sprinkled with parsley, without allowing it to come to the boil. Small cubes of bread fried in olive oil or butter are a good accompaniment.

Peperonata and ratatouille. Italian and French vegetable stews, eaten hot or cold. The main fault of the English when making them is wateriness, but this can be avoided if you use about 1 cup of the tomato sauce and cook the other vegetables in it. For peperonata take two or three red and yellow peppers. Cut them into strips—remove stalks and seeds first—and simmer in the sauce for half an hour. For ratatouille, slice one or two aubergines [eggplant] and half a pound of courgettes [zucchini] and cook in the same way. Don't peel the vegetables. Quantities depend on taste, supply and pocket.

If you feel that these mixtures (particularly ratatouille) are becoming too liquid, turn up the heat and boil hard without a lid on the pan.

Cod, fresh or dried, in tomato sauce. When you can get fresh cod, cut it into cubes of 1 inch, discarding skin and bones. Add to the tomato sauce and simmer for 15 minutes (never overcook fish—remember that it will continue to cook a little in the hot sauce as it's dished up and brought to table). Add 16 black, stoned [pitted] olives to the stew for the last 5 minutes.

With dried salt cod, soak it for 24 hours first, changing the water several times. Drain and put into a pan of cold water and bring slowly to the boil. The moment the water bubbles, remove the cod and cut it into pieces. Discard skin and bones. Add it to the tomato sauce and cook for about 10 minutes, or until cooked but not disintegrating. Olives to be put in as above.

Roasting chicken with tomato sauce. Cut chicken in pieces, roll in seasoned flour and brown in olive oil. Add to the tomato sauce and simmer until cooked (40–60 minutes). A good recipe for battery chicken [tired, old cold-storage chickens].

Soufflé aux tomates

Prepare a soufflé dish with a greased collar of foil. Whirl 1¼ cups of the basic tomato sauce (p. 247) in blender, or put through a fine sieve. Melt 2 tablespoons butter in a heavy pan, stir in 2 tablespoons all-purpose flour, then ½ cup warmed milk. Cook to a thick sauce, which will leave the sides of the pan. Add puréed tomato sauce, then 3 egg yolks one by one, off the heat. Beat 4 egg whites to a stiff foam, and fold into tomato mixture gently with a metal spoon. Add ⅓ cup Gruyère cheese, diced. Pour into the collared soufflé dish, sprinkle 2 tablespoons of grated Parmesan cheese on top. Lay a buttered paper across the collar, and bake for 25 minutes at 375–400°. Timing is always a little difficult with a soufflé, as it can be altered by the size of dish used, and naturally the amount of mixture. When the top has risen and is nicely browned, it's usually a good indication that the soufflé is done. Serve immediately, having first removed the buttered paper and the foil collar. The centre will be creamy as the serving spoon dips into it; the outside will be a deliciously crusty brown.

Veal with tomato sauce (ossi buchi)

Find an intelligent butcher who will cut 1½-inch-thick slices across a veal shin. These are *ossi buchi*, hollow (marrow) bones, a favourite Milanese dish. Season and brown the bones and their meat carefully, so that the marrow doesn't fall out, in olive oil. For 8–10 pieces of veal bone add about ¾ cup of dry white wine. Boil hard to reduce, for about 5 minutes. Transfer the bones to a casserole, where they can lie flat in a single layer. Add 2 cups or a little more of tomato sauce to the pan juices, bring to the boil and pour over the veal. Simmer gently in a low oven until tender [about 1½ hours]. This can be done in advance, and the dish reheated just before the meal.

Serve sprinkled with 2 tablespoons chopped parsley, mixed with the grated rind of half a large lemon, 1 chopped fillet of anchovy, and 1 chopped clove of garlic. Boiled rice is usually served with this excellent dish.

Fruit

APPLE & QUINCE

We have rather betrayed the apple. It's the most important fruit in our eating and cooking. It's the foundation fruit of our Western culture. It's the fruit of Aphrodite and the Virgin, of earthly and heavenly love, and so on. What a pity, and what a betrayal, that commercial growers have now concentrated on the look of fruit at the expense of flavour and texture (and scent).

Apple history or prehistory provides a clue for cooking. The sour crab in the copse or hedge may descend from orchard apples, but orchard apples don't descend from the crab: if botanists are right, they descend from an apple tree native to southwest Asia and the Balkans, with fruit sizable and often sweet.

Sweetness is the clue, or the cue. In the kitchen avoid most of the cooking apples (unless you have space to keep them until they are mellow) and cook with good eating apples. Experiment with the eaters you can buy or the ones in your orchard. Don't use just any apple, or the ones which happen to have fallen most and soonest, for applesauce, to give an example. Among the best for that purpose[1]—and for apple dishes in general—sweet but not too sweet and not needing so much sugar, is the delicious eating apple, Cox's Orange Pippin (which Mr. Cox, retired Buckinghamshire brewer, raised in his garden near Slough, about 1830), and the Reinette d'Orléans, favourite apple of the French, which was first recorded in 1776.

We British have no difficulty with the Coxes, and our grocers may sometimes have Reinettes (in England a Reinette tree is easily bought for the garden). The Reinettes last well into the summer, and in applesauce their clear, concentrated flavour goes especially well with summer veal, and with chicken.

In apple dishes the rule is: avoid water. For flavour, the apple's best allies are butter and cream. Expensive, but I prefer eating a little of something delicious to eating quantities of acid-mush-cum-sugar.

The apple has another cooking ally, its relative the quince, altogether more Oriental, original home Central Asia: apple tart with quince, baked quince, quince and apple jelly, etc. And the scent and the look of a bowl of ripe quinces in the house in the autumn are enough to make you believe that the golden fruit Earth gave to Hera and Zeus when they were married was quince and not apple. Here in England quinces seem to be coming back. Good greengrocers have them in a good quince year, and a quince tree in a damp corner doesn't have to be very big before it bears. You will have the bonus, too, of the most beautiful of the blossoms of spring, the quince's soft pink globes, with their falling ruff of silver green leaves.

Bircher muesli

This raw fruit porridge, more appetisingly known as Bircher muesli, makes a luxurious breakfast dish. It was invented by Dr.

---

[1] Good New England cooks consider Gravensteins especially good for applesauce; also Greenings, Baldwins and russets. American baking apples include Rome Beauty, Northern Spy, and Winesaps. Newtown Pippin, York Imperial, and Jersey Red are among many from which U.S. pies are made.

Bircher-Benner, pioneer of food reform, for patients at his Zürich clinic.

He explained that he felt muesli "corresponds with the laws of the human organism," its composition, i.e., its proportions of protein, fat and carbohydrate calories, being identical with mother's milk. This may be so (but is mother's milk a suitable food for mature adults, one wonders). The fact is that Bircher muesli tastes delicious: it's the one great contribution of the vegetarian movement to the pleasures of European eating.

Raisins, blackberries and peaches make fine additions to the basic recipe given below. Soaked, dried fruit such as apricots and peaches may also be added, but I think that a proportion at least of grated apple is essential to the texture of the dish. I think, too, that the dish is better made immediately before breakfast, even if the coarsest oatmeal is used, as this gives a drier, more appetising mixture. Soaking the oats overnight makes muesli uncomfortably close to cold porridge.

Here, though, is the true original recipe, with ingredients for one person.

> 1 *level tablespoon coarse oatmeal,*
>   *or rolled oats*
> 3 *tablespoons water*
> 1 *tablespoon condensed, sweetened milk*
>   *(or honey & light cream)*
> *juice of half a lemon*
> 1 *medium apple, or apple & other*
>   *fruit mixed*
> 1 *tablespoon chopped nuts*

Put oats and water into a bowl and soak for 12 hours (overnight). Just before eating, stir in the sweetened condensed milk (or honey and cream) and the lemon juice, which sharpens the flavour agreeably and helps to keep the apple from turning brown. Put a flat grater over the bowl and grate in the apple, peel, core and all, but no stalk. Stir the apple into the oatmeal mixture every so often, to prevent its discolouring. Add the nuts and serve.

Blackberries are surprisingly good with muesli, and peaches and strawberries make it into a luxurious dish. More of a pudding than a breakfast food.

Pheasant
à la Normande

Pork with applesauce, duck with applesauce, are often eaten in England. The apple tartness is used to cut the richness of the meat. Apples, however, can be combined with cream to make very successful sauces for dryer things such as pheasant or veal or chicken; and this and the following recipe show how it's done with both large and small pieces. The apples I use are always eating apples of the Reinette or Cox type, which provide a slightly acid flavour and enough natural sweetness to need no sugar.

> 1 large pheasant
> 6 medium-sized Reinettes or Coxes
>   [or Newtown Pippins]
> 6 tablespoons butter
> ½ cup heavy cream
> salt, pepper, cinnamon

Brown the pheasant all over in half the butter. Peel, core and slice the apples; fry them lightly in the rest of the butter, sprinkling them with cinnamon as they cook. Put a thin layer of apples into a deep casserole, and arrange the pheasant on top, breast down. Tuck the rest of the apples round the sides, so that the bird is embedded in them. Pour in half the cream. Cover and cook in the oven, 350°, for about an hour. Turn the bird breast side up at half time, seasoning it with salt and pepper. Cover again and complete the cooking. Stir the rest of the cream into the apples when the pheasant is cooked, giving it a few moments to heat through.

Serve in the casserole, or carve the pheasant and put it on a bed of apple and cream sauce on a clean serving dish. The pheasant juices make the sauce particularly good. (Chicken can be cooked in the same way.)

Apple sauce   (for 4)

Reinettes, Coxes or Sturmers are best for this useful sauce.[2] Try it with veal escalopes, or thin slices of pork tenderloin, dipped in egg and bread crumbs and fried in butter. Or with boiled chicken, or sweetbreads. Apart from some boiled potatoes, accompanying vegetables are unnecessary, indeed undesirable.

> 3 good-sized apples
> 4 tablespoons butter
> ½ cup dry white wine, cider or light stock
> ⅓–½ cup heavy cream
> 1 tablespoon Calvados, brandy, or applejack
> sugar, lemon juice, salt, pepper to taste

Peel, core and cut the apples into ¼-inch dice. Cook gently in the butter in a covered frying pan, stirring from time to time. When they are golden, remove to a serving dish and keep warm. Add wine to pan juices, boiling down by half to a rich sauce. Pour in the cream. When the sauce is amalgamated, flavour with Calvados or brandy and seasonings, and pour over the apples.

Arrange the meat on top. As with all cream sauces, make sure that serving plate and dinner plates are really hot.

Apple meringue pudding   (for 6)

A delicious Sunday pudding.

---

[2] Vermont apples are excellent in sauce; so are New York greenings, Southern Imperials, Midwest Baldwins and Wealthies, Yellow Pippins from Washington.

2 lbs. eating apples
  or 1¾ lbs. cooking apples & ¼ lb. quinces
4 tablespoons butter
apricot jam, or cinnamon, or cloves
sugar to taste

meringue: 3 egg whites
          ¾ cup sugar
          1 heaping teaspoon cornstarch
          1 teaspoon vinegar
          2 oz. blanched & split almonds

for serving: cream

Melt the butter in a large pan. Wash the apples (and quinces), cut into rough quarters and add to butter. Cover and simmer gently until there is about an inch of juice in the pan, then turn up the heat until the apples are cooked. They won't burn if the heat is low enough to start with: water is to be avoided. Push the fruit through a sieve and season with sugar and apricot jam (if you use Golden Delicious), or cinnamon or cloves (if you use cooking apples). With cookers, quince provides the best flavouring of all. Spread the purée into a shallow serving dish, ovenproof, and leave to cool.

To make the meringue, beat the egg whites stiff. Fold in sugar and cornstarch sifted together, and last of all the vinegar. Pile up on top of the apple, keeping the meringue thin at the edges, as it will spread a little while cooking. Stick the almonds all over the meringue. Bake at 250°, for 1–1¼ hours. If the meringue could be browner at the end of this time, turn the heat up a little. Remove from the oven, and serve warm or cold with cream.

Evreux apple tarts

At the Vieille Gabelle restaurant in Evreux, 63 miles to the west of Paris, they serve these tarts made with Golden Delicious apples.

Do not be tempted to cook the tarts before the meal, or the juices will soak away into the pastry. Put them into a hot oven as you serve the first course, and baste once or twice with the apricot mixture.

shortcrust: 1½ cups all-purpose flour
               10 tablespoons butter and lard mixed
               2 level tablespoons confectioners' sugar
               1 egg

crème pâtissière: 2 tablespoons flour
               2 egg yolks
               1 egg
               4 tablespoons sugar
               1¼ cups milk

apricot mixture: 6 tablespoons apricot jam
               2 tablespoons water
     plus: 1½ lbs. Golden Delicious apples
               1 cup heavy cream

Make the pastry and use it to line four straight-sided patty pans, of about 4½ inches diameter (from the dime store). Make the *crème pâtissière* next: mix in a bowl the flour, egg yolks, egg and sugar, and stir in the milk, which should first be brought to just under boiling point. Cook over a low heat until the custard is thick. Cool, then pour a ¼-inch layer of it into the pastry cases.

Peel, core and cut the apples into ⅛-inch slices. Halve the slices and arrange curved side up in the *crème pâtissière*, so that they resemble records nicely graded in a rack.

Melt the apricot jam and water together, and strain. Pour a little over the tarts. Cook in a hot oven (425–450°), basting from time to time with the rest of the apricot mixture. The top edges of the apple slices should catch the heat and turn dark brown. Golden Delicious apples will not lose their shape or disintegrate to white fluff as cooking apples do. When you cut into the tarts, a delicious aromatic juice bursts out. Serve plenty of cream with them.

This recipe sounds like a lot of trouble, but it's worth it for the blend and contrast of flavours.

Moroccan meat stew
with quince

One of the interesting things about Middle Eastern and Arab cooking, from an Englishman's point of view, is its similarity to our own medieval food. The abundant use of sweet substances with meat, the strong seasonings of ginger and various peppers, remind us that once dishes and courses were not so separately conceived as they are now (the well-defined three- or four-course dinner is really a nineteenth-century institution, soup, fish, meat, dessert and so on). To jump from reading a modern Middle Eastern cookery book to a fifteenth-century English one is much less of a change than going from the fifteenth-century one to Mrs. Beeton.[3] It may seem obvious to say "Crusaders!" but I'm reluctant to believe such romantic notions, remembering that Marco Polo didn't bring back from Cathay half the things he's credited with. Let's be cautious, and say that such dishes, whatever their origin, came to us via France and our medieval French court (like the recipe following, for quince pies).

1 large chicken, jointed [cut in pieces], plus 2 tablespoons
  butter or 2½ lbs. cubed mutton or lamb
2 large onions, finely chopped
½ cup chopped parsley
about ½ teaspoon ground ginger
salt; black, cayenne & paprika pepper
1 lb. quinces (or more to taste)[4]
6 tablespoons butter

[3] Vide The Book of Household Management, by Isabella Beeton, London, 1861.

[4] Luther Burbank did considerable good for quinces when he developed a hybrid of Cydonia oblonga to be eaten out of the hand, like an apple, which he called the pineapple quince. In the autumn both the pineapple and the pear quinces can be bought at luxury fruit markets. But quinces that make wonderful custard pies, jellies, marmalades and win blue ribbons when baked with honey are to be found from Maine to Minnesota and westward to the Pacific. Maybe confusion with the flowering Japonica quince has persuaded some that no quinces are edible; actually many New Englanders and fruit enthusiasts of the Northwest consider the flavor of the greenish-yellow quince to be somewhat exotic, especially when baked. Early colonists brought quinces to these shores, and The Cook's Own Book, published in Boston in 1845, offers ten recipes, including an ice tart made with preserved quinces.

Put meat (and, in the case of the chicken, butter with it) into a large pan with onions and parsley. Just cover with cold water and season with ginger, salt, and the three kinds of pepper. Bring to the boil and simmer for about an hour, until cooked. Slice and core the quinces (leave peel on), brown them very lightly in butter, and add to the stew half an hour before the end of cooking time.

NOTE: The meat is not browned before cooking, and lamb has enough fat of its own to do without the butter.

Quinces in paste

This fifteenth-century recipe for a corporate quince dumpling is delicious. It should be made with the usual shortcrust paste in a deep pie dish or cake tin, according to the size of the quinces.

"Take and make fair round coffins of fair paste; then take fair raw quinces and pare them with a knife, and take fair out the core thereof; then take enough sugar and a little powdered ginger, and stop the hole full; and couch two or three quinces in a coffin and cover them and let them bake; and for default of sugar, take honey; but then put powdered pepper thereon and ginger, in the manner aforesaid."

Cover the "coffins" of quinces over with a lid of pastry, brush over with beaten egg, and bake for at least an hour and a quarter in a moderate oven. The time depends on the size of the quinces.

Quince pie

Here's a pie from three centuries later, this time with a flavouring of orange, or of mulberries.

Quince pie

Line a pie dish with shortcrust pastry, then fill it with peeled, cored and sliced quinces; add sugar, cinnamon and strips of candied orange peel to the layers of fruit. Pour ½ cup of orange juice or mulberry syrup over fruit. Put on a pastry lid and bake in the usual way in a moderate oven.

Mulberry syrup

Put ripe mulberries[5] into a large jar, and stand in a pan of boiling water. As the fruit gives up its juice, pour it off into a measuring cup. To each 2 cups, add 1 lb. sugar and boil to the consistency of cream. Skim well and bottle when cold. (To make a preserve, boil 2 cups of the juice with 1½ lbs. sugar. Add 2 lbs. ripe mulberries, ripe but not soft, and simmer for 15 minutes. Leave until next day. Strain the juice into a pan and boil again until thick, add the mulberries and simmer for a further 15 minutes. Good with cream cheese, junket and so on.)

Pears with quinces   (for 6)

Apples and quinces are a famous—and ancient—combination. Pears too are enhanced by the flavour of quinces, which one does not quite expect.

> 3 medium quinces
> 6 large pears
> 1 vanilla pod [or bean]
> 1¼ cups water
> ½–¾ cup sugar

for serving: 1 cup heavy cream

Peel and quarter the quinces, removing their cores, then put them quickly into a bowl of cold water to prevent their turning brown. Peel, quarter and core the pears. Split the vanilla pod (vanilla essence won't do at all) and put it in a large pan with the water and ½ cup of sugar. Bring to the boil, stirring to dissolve the sugar, then add pears and quinces. Simmer, covered, for an hour—or until the fruit is tender. Taste the syrupy juice at half time, and add more sugar if necessary, but be careful not to over-sweeten the dish. Leave to cool, and serve well chilled with cream.

Pears and juice take on a deep coral red colour from the quinces, which is accented by the black vanilla pod. A most beautiful dish in every way.

[5] America's native mulberry is called *Morus rubra* by botanists and it's indigenous from New England to the Rockies and south to Florida. When fully ripe these berries are dark purple. Other varieties are called white, red, and black, and in Florida some of these bear fruit through a period of several months. Rural U.S. cooks especially make good use of mulberries, putting up jams and jellies and sometimes baking pies.

Sir Isaac Newton's baked quinces

This favourite pudding of Newton's is a recipe for the fortunate with a supply of good quinces. If three or four are likely to be your annual total, it's better to distribute them among apple pies and puddings, applesauce and apple jelly as a spicing ingredient.

Choose one fine quince for each person. Gently rub off the whitish-grey fluff, wash and core them. Stand in a baking dish respectable enough for the table (oval yellow and brown gratin dishes are ideal for baked fruit). Add ¼ inch of water. Stuff superfine (not confectioners') sugar into the cavities and top with a good lump of butter. Bake in a moderately hot oven, 375–400°, for about an hour (timing depends on the size and state of the fruit—they're done when a skewer easily pierces the fruit round the centre cavity). Serve hot or warm with cream.

NOTE: When baking apples by this method, sprinkle them generously with sesame seeds, and a little superfine sugar, about half an hour before the end of cooking time.

An eighteenth-century quince pudding

2–3 quinces (just over ½ lb.)
sugar
ground ginger
1¼ cups heavy cream
2 egg yolks
2 tablespoons butter

Cook the fruit whole in boiling water to cover. Cut them in pieces and push through a sieve. To a generous half cup of purée, add sugar and ginger to taste, 1 cup of cream and 2 egg yolks. Add the butter cut up into small knobs.

Butter a baking dish, pour in the quince mixture and bake at about 375°, or less, until set. Eat hot. As this pudding is a kind of fruit custard, don't cook it so fast that the mixture boils—this will curdle the eggs. The proportion of fruit purée to custard may be varied to taste. It's important that the purée should be on the dry side, before mixing in the other ingredients.

Membrilo, or quince paste

This deep red Spanish quince paste is delicious eaten with cream cheese and sugar as dessert. Some people like slices of it with grilled pork and lamb. It could also be used—but discreetly, on account of the sugar—to flavour a chicken or lamb stew, when quinces are not in season (see recipe, p. 260).

Wash 4 lbs. of quinces. The weight can be made up with apples, but too many will spoil the flavour; south of Paris in the Orléanais, where a more elaborate quince paste is made, oranges are used sometimes in the proportion of 1 part orange to 3 parts quince by weight.

Quarter the quinces and stew them with 1 cup of water until they're soft. Drain, weigh [or *measure*] and put into a clean pan with an equal amount of sugar. Boil slowly until the mixture leaves the sides of the pan. *Don't burn the mixture, keep stirring* (wrap your hand in a tea towel and use a wooden spoon). Pour into greaseproof-lined metal trays, for instance a jelly roll or other oblong tin. Dry for 3–4 days in an airing cupboard, or on top of a solid-fuel stove—protect it from dust with a light muslin cloth. Cut into small pieces or oblong slabs, roll in superfine sugar and store in airtight boxes between sheets of greaseproof paper. The sugar can be spiced with ginger and cinnamon.

Quince paste was once thought to be particularly good for the stomach.

Pickled Siberian crab apples

In our Wiltshire village Siberian crab apples go to waste. The tiny perfect yellow and red fruit fall to the ground, and are crushed by cars and passersby. Even the children don't bother with their sharp sweetness. But just as the tree is a great embellishment to any garden, so jars of pickled Siberian crabs (or of Siberian crab apple jelly) are a great embellishment to winter supplies.

> 3–4 lbs. crab apples
> 1-inch stick of cinnamon
> 15 cloves
> 15 allspice berries
> 5 cups wine vinegar
> 2 cups white sugar

Tie the spices in a little bag. Put them into a pan with the vinegar and sugar and bring to the boil, stirring so that the sugar dissolves. The crab apples should be washed and their stalks trimmed to ¼ inch with scissors. Put them into something such as a deep-fry basket and lower them into the boiling vinegar. Leave for 5 minutes: they should be removed before the skins start to crack. Put the apples into small bottling jars or jam pots. Meanwhile boil down the vinegar and sugar until it's syrupy, then cover the apples with it, and seal immediately. Leave for 2 months.

In time the apples lose more and more of their red colour to the liquid, which makes a beautiful-looking pickle. Serve with pork or ham.

Soft fruit, e.g., peaches, may be dealt with in the same way, but use 2 cups sugar to 1¼ cups vinegar, and vary the spices according to the fruit.

Apple or quince or medlar jelly

A simple method which can be used for windfall apples, for Siberian and wild crab apples, for quinces on their own or mixed with apples. For medlars[6] too. Ordinary windfalls may be flavoured with cloves or cinnamon stick (don't use powdered cinnamon: it's inferior in quality

---

[6] In Latin the tree which bears this interesting fruit is called *Mespilus germanica*; it is not to be confused, as do some dictionaries, with the New World's naseberry or sapodilla.

and will make a sediment in the jelly), or just a few quinces. Crab apples are best left alone with their wonderful flavour.

Such jellies may be eaten instead of applesauce with pork, or with bread and butter, or as a dessert with *coeur à la crème* and the cream cheese mousse described on pages 304 and 305. A versatile addition to the storecupboard.

Cut the fruit into rough pieces (medlars may be left as they are, but use while still firm. Put into a large preserving pan and cover with water. Bring to the boil and simmer until the fruit is soft. Lay a large white cloth over a colander, set the colander across a large bowl and pour into it the fruit pulp. Make a bag of the cloth, and leave to drip overnight.

Measure the juice next day (don't squeeze the jelly bag, or the final results will be cloudy). Allow 2 cups of sugar to 2 cups of juice and boil until setting point is reached; spices such as cinnamon or cloves should be tied in a little bag and removed when the flavour is not too strong. Bottle in sterilized jars and cover immediately in the usual way.

GOOSEBERRIES

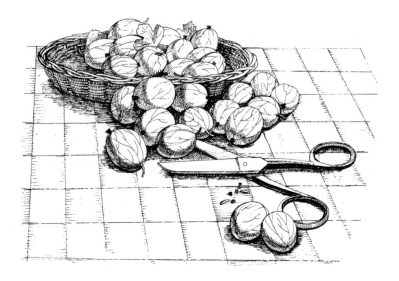

Gooseberries which are northern and condescend to grow up to the Arctic Circle provide the first fruit of the English year.[1] Unless you count strawberries flown in from Kenya. I don't.

Edward Bunyard, the fruit gourmet and grower, wrote in the 1920's very nicely of gooseberries as "the fruit *par excellence* for ambulant consumption. The freedom of the bush should be given to all visitors

[1] Music critic and gourmand Henry T. Finck wrote: "I have read in a London journal that 'American visitors are highly appreciative of the flavor of English gooseberries, as those of their own country are not nearly so good. . . . As judges of fruit Americans are proverbially keen, and their selections are usually worth following.'" In New England, according to one regional authority, gooseberry preserves were a Sunday night staple with cold meat and also "nice with soft cream cheese and surprisingly good with a sweet cake." Because of their susceptibility to various fungus diseases, however, gooseberries are little cultivated in the U.S. In some communities cultivation is, in fact, prohibited because the plant is host to the white pine blister blight. Don't pass up gooseberries, though, when you find them on the market. Gooseberry fool (see p. 273), according to James Beard, is "one of the wonderful old-fashioned dishes that is neglected these days."

. . . and the exercise of gathering, too, is beneficial to the middle-aged and also stimulates their absorptive capacity"—i.e., for lunch; he was describing that sociable summer hour which ambles along—or used to —between Matins and Sunday lunch.

From the cook's point of view the best gooseberries aren't entirely the fattest, sweetest, ripest, and yellowest. Gooseberries small, green, primitive and hairy—early gooseberries—make the best pies, jams, jellies and fools. And the best sauce for mackerel. That's a habit we seem to have lost, gooseberries with mackerel, let alone with pork, veal, lamb, goose or duck. We've forgotten how well the sweet-sour astringency of young gooseberry purée goes with such rich flavours.

A word about picking gooseberries. A blacksmith in our village years ago—so the legend goes—used to pull his hand firmly down the gooseberry branches, when he wanted his Whitsun pie. Off sprang the fruit (and leaves) at high speed without that carapaced hand receiving one scratch. This method is said to be painless, even if you haven't spent a lifetime at the anvil. It may be true. I've never had the nerve to find out, preferring to shield hands and wrists with solid leather gloves.

Incidentally it's quicker to top and tail gooseberries with a pair of scissors, rather than a knife.

Gooseberry sauce for mackerel

By tradition, gooseberry sauce is the Maytime companion of boiled or grilled mackerel. The French honour this antique alliance by naming the gooseberry *groseille à maquereau*: in practice they usually serve a purée of sorrel instead—the two acidities have a similar taste—as gooseberries are not widely grown in France. Make the most of the early green fruit (the later, mellow gooseberries will not do at all) and serve one or other variation of this sweet-sour sauce with roast duck, pork, goose or lamb, or with roast and grilled veal.

Here are four recipes for a sauce which has been eaten for centuries in Germany, France, Holland and Great Britain:

1. Top and tail 1 lb. gooseberries. Put into a heavy pan with butter the size of a walnut, and cook gently, with the lid on the pan, until the fruit is soft enough to put through a strainer. Add either an egg or 4 tablespoonfuls of béchamel sauce. Season with a teaspoon of sugar, and ginger or nutmeg to taste.

2. Top and tail 1 lb. gooseberries. Cover with cold water and bring gently to the boil. By this time or very soon after, a gooseberry taken from the pan will give a little between the fingers, without collapsing to a mush. Drain and mix into a béchamel sauce made with 2 tablespoons butter, 2 tablespoons flour and a generous cup of hot milk (the gooseberries can either be strained or left whole). Reheat and season with a heaping tablespoon of chopped new fennel leaves, a little nutmeg and some salt, pepper and lemon juice. A teaspoon of sugar may also be an improvement if the gooseberries are very young.

3. Prepare and blanch 1 lb. gooseberries as in recipe 2. Drain them well. Put 2½ tablespoons water and ½ cup sugar into a frying pan and bring to a spanking boil. Turn the gooseberries over in the syrup, shaking the pan very gently. Pour round the meat or fish as a garnish. This recipe, which depends for seasoning solely on the sharpness of the gooseberries, and the sweetness of the sugar, was very popular with Germans at the beginning of the nineteenth century.

4. Put ½ lb. gooseberries in a pan with 2 tablespoons butter. Cover and cook gently until they are soft enough to go through a strainer. Add ½ cup boiled cream and 2½ tablespoons of fish or meat juices from the dish the sauce is intended for. I like sauces of this kind, which are linked in flavour with the food they accompany. They have a rightness and succulence that are more agreeable, and they are never quite the same twice running. This gooseberry sauce comes from *French Provincial Cooking*, by Elizabeth David (Penguin. 7s.6d., U.S. 95¢); it's a very good one.

Robert Southey's
gooseberry pie   (for 6 to 8)

Do you follow the country tradition of eating the first gooseberry pie of the season at Whitsunday lunch? If you do, here's a nice
proposition of the poet Robert Southey's to stimulate some quiet post-
prandial reflection: "Two gooseberry pies being supposed, their paste made
at the same time, and indeed of one mass, the gooseberries gathered from
the same bushes and of equal age, the sugar in just proportion, and clotted
cream to eat with both, it follows that the largest is preferable. I love
gooseberry pie . . . and I think the case is plain."

2 lbs. gooseberries, young & green
½–¾ cup sugar
2 tablespoons butter
8 oz. shortcrust pastry made with 1½ cups flour
1 egg white
extra sugar (superfine)

for serving: heavy cream

Grease a 1-quart pie dish with the butter. Roll out the pastry; moisten
the edges of the pie dish and fasten a strip of pastry round it. Top and
tail the gooseberries, put them into the pie dish with sugar between the
layers (very sharp gooseberries will need a full cup) and mound them up
in the centre above the rim of the dish. Brush the pastry edge with egg
white before laying on the pastry lid; knock up [see note, p. 51] or crimp.
the edges, brush the pastry with egg white and sprinkle it with an even
layer of superfine sugar. Bake at 400°, for 30–40 minutes. Serve with plenty
of cream.

Raised gooseberry pie

In some parts of England, from Gloucestershire up to the
Midlands, a raised gooseberry pie is made around Whitsun. It looks just
like a pork pie.

hot-water crust: 1 lb. plain [all-purpose] flour*
               (about 3½ cups)
               ½ teaspoon salt
               3 tablespoons confectioners' sugar
               ¾ cup water
               12 tablespoons [¾ cup] lard
               1 egg, beaten, for glaze

filling: gooseberries
          sugar (½ cup to each lb. of fruit)

Sift flour, salt and sugar into a bowl. Make a well in the middle. Bring water and lard to the boil and pour immediately into the well, mixing the flour in gradually with a wooden spoon, until a smooth ball of dough is formed. Leave in a warm place until the paste is just cool enough to handle and keep its shape.

Using greased jam jars, upside down, mould the pastry round the outside of the jars to make a casing of dough, and tie a piece of brown paper outside the pastry to hold it in shape when the jar is removed. Cool and chill in the refrigerator until the pastry is set, then remove the jars and turn the cases right way up. Fill with gooseberries and sugar, moisten the rims and fix on a lid. Brush with beaten egg. Bake for 1–1¼ hours, 300–350°. Let the pies cool before removing the paper.

One can occasionally buy wooden pie moulds to shape the pastry round. The easy way out is to use a cake tin with a removable base, and bake the pie inside it. For raised meat pies, see page 49.

Gooseberry tart   *(for 6)*

As gooseberries become larger and sweeter, tarts like this are a better way of using them:

shortcrust pastry: 1½ cups flour
                  8 tablespoons [1 stick] butter
                  2½ tablespoons confectioners' sugar
                  1 egg or water

---

* More flour or more hot water may be required; different brands of flour absorb different amounts of water.

filling: 1½ lbs. prepared gooseberries
    1 cup light cream
    2 egg yolks
    1 cup sugar

Make the pastry. Line small tart tins (or one large flan tin with a removable base) with the pastry. Arrange the gooseberries close together in a single layer, tail end down, on the pastry. Mix cream and egg yolks and sugar and pour over them. Bake in a moderately hot oven, 400°, for 15 minutes (30 minutes for one large tart). Serve warm or cold.

GOOSEBERRIES, FRONTIGNAN & ELDERFLOWERS

"I was very well brought up," wrote Colette. "As a first proof of so categorical a statement, I shall simply say that I was no more than three years old when my father poured out my first full liqueur glass of an amber-coloured wine which was sent up to him from the Midi, where he was born; the muscat of Frontignan." This lovely dessert wine made from muscat grapes grown on the slopes outside the small town of Frontignan on the Languedoc coast was drunk in quantity in Britain during the eighteenth and early nineteenth centuries—one of the great periods of gooseberry enjoyment and cultivation. It was so popular that homemade elderflower wine, which does have a muscat flavour, became known as English Frontignan. It was perhaps when drinking such wines with summer fruit and puddings that people discovered how perfectly the fragrance of muscat goes with gooseberries.

Gooseberry & elderflower jelly

4 lbs. gooseberries, young & green
sugar
2 large elderflower heads
cup muscat de Frontignan

Put the gooseberries in a large pan and barely cover with water. Simmer until they are soft and mushy. Strain through a jelly bag without squeezing the pulp. Measure the juice and put into a clean pan with 2 cups sugar to every 2½ cups of juice. Boil until setting point is reached. Tie the elder-flowers in muslin and stir them round in the hot jelly until the right balance of flavours is achieved. The muscat should not be too dominant. Pour into sterilized jars and cover.

Gooseberry salad

A wonderfully fresh dessert:

1½ lbs. large sweet gooseberries
½ cup sugar
1¼ cups muscat de Frontignan

Three hours before the meal, top and tail the gooseberries. Put them into a deep bowl with sugar and wine, and leave in a cool place (but not the refrigerator, which is too cold). Serve in individual glasses.

Gooseberry fool   (for 4 to 6)

Every Briton knows that gooseberry fool, like steak and kidney pudding or junket, is a truly national dish. What many people don't know is that "fool" comes from the French verb *fouler*, to crush; it is not a description of someone prepared to pay 24p for half a pint of cream. In France grapes, not gooseberries, are *foulés*, crushed, or rather mangled, quite literally, on their way to the winepress. This, I think, gives a good idea of how a gooseberry fool should be made. Too often goose-berries are overcooked, then sieved or blended to a smooth slop. Ideally they should be very lightly cooked, then crushed with a fork, before being folded into whipped cream. Egg custard is an honourable and an ancient alternative to cream; commercial powder custard is not. Don't spoil this springtime luxury. It's better to halve the quantities than to serve a great floury bowlful.

> ¾ lb. young gooseberries, topped & tailed
> 4 tablespoons butter
> sugar
> 1 cup heavy cream, whipped
>   or ½ cup each heavy & light cream, whipped
>   or 1 cup light cream & 3 egg yolks

Stew the gooseberries slowly in a covered pan, with the butter, until they are yellow and just cooked. Crush with a fork, sweeten to taste and mix them carefully and lightly into the whipped cream.

If you prefer custard to whipped cream, make the custard by bringing light cream (or rich milk) to the boil, and pour onto the egg yolks, whisking all the time. Set the bowl over a pan of hot water and stir steadily until the custard thickens to heavy cream consistency. Strain into a bowl, and leave to cool before folding in the gooseberries.

Serve in custard glasses or plain white cups, with some homemade almond biscuits or macaroons. It's said (and reported in *Kettner's Book of the Table*)[2] that the young folk of Northamptonshire, "after eating as much as they possibly can of this gooseberry fool," used frequently to roll down a hill and begin eating again. Cream must have been cheaper in those days.

Gooseberry fools can be frozen and served as cream ice: in this case, sieve the fruit, as the pieces of gooseberry produced by mashing would spoil the texture of the ice. Later in the year other fruit may be substituted for gooseberries, uncooked raspberries and strawberries and peaches for instance, and in the autumn cooked purée of apple flavoured with apricot jam, and of quinces. Use just over a cup of purée to a cup of cream or custard.

---

[2] *A gastronomical compendium first published in 1877 and reprinted in 1968 by the Centaur Press; written by a London journalist, E. S. Dallas, it contained advice, recipes, and the inspiration resulting from free meals provided by August Kettner, the Soho restaurateur—a splendid partnership.*

Gooseberry cream   (for 6 to 8)

Here is a gooseberry dish—not so rich as gooseberry fool—
which was popular during the eighteenth century. One person who enjoyed it was that Norfolk glutton, Parson Woodforde, who left his rectory
at Weston Longeville one summer day of 1784 to visit a friend at Matti-
shall. The small party of nine ate for dinner: boiled beef, roast and boiled
chicken, part of a fine ham, a couple of ducks roasted and peas, puddings,
tarts and cheesecakes. In the evening there was a "cold collation" of lamb
steaks, green peas, and—finally—gooseberry cream, etc. No doubt the etc.
included wine, which would have helped the company to clear the last
dish of the day, and to keep merry until four in the morning.

That gooseberry cream was very likely made from Hannah Glasse's best-
selling *Art of Cookery*;[3] there was a big reprint that year, 1784, backed by
twenty-six publishers.

1½ lbs. gooseberries, topped & tailed
½ cup water
sugar
4 tablespoons unsalted butter
3 eggs, beaten
orange flower water, Malaga or Frontignan fortified wine
    or 1 head of elderflowers

Put the gooseberries in a pan with the water and cook slowly until they
can be put through a sieve. Measure the purée—2½ cups are required.
Sweeten to taste and reheat. Stir in butter and eggs, and keep stirring over
a low heat until the gooseberry cream is thick. *Don't let it boil,* or the
eggs will curdle. Leave to cool and flavour with orange flower water, Malaga
or Frontignan. Alternatively put a head of elderflowers, tied in muslin,
into the cream after adding eggs and butter; remove as soon as the flavour
is right—it should not be too strong.

[3] *The Art of Cookery, Made Plain and Easy was first published in London in 1747,
and it caused Samuel Johnson to complain that "Women can spin very well, but they
cannot write a good book of cookery." Mrs. Glasse could, and did, however, protest "the
blind folly of this age, that would rather be imposed upon by a French booby (in the
kitchen), than give encouragement to a good English cook!"*

LEMONS

I think it's just worth remembering that lemons don't originate in boxes or grocers' shops, but on trees—trees which filtered through from the Far East to Spain and Italy.

Italy is England's lemon land (smaller supplies reach us from Cyprus, Israel, the United States and Spain) and I suppose the nearest place where you can taste lemon juice, fresh, real ripe lemon juice, in its purest form, from freshly picked lemons, is at Limone on Lake Garda, where you are hardly clear of the Italian Alps—*limone spremuta*, lemon juices squeezed into a glass and served with iced water and small packets of sugar; down below the blue of Garda, up above snow on the mountains—and a German sketching at an easel at every corner.

D. H. Lawrence, when he was on Garda after running off with his Frieda Weekley, was taken round the lemon gardens in November when they were under their winter roofs of wood. The *padrone's* wife told him lemons had been brought there by St. Francis of Assisi, and that one lemon from a Garda lemon house was worth two from an entirely open-air tree in Sicily (which is the source of most of our Italian lemons). Lawrence, in turn, thought of St. Francis wandering about with a lemon in his pocket, or making lemonade—*limone spremuta*—in the hot summer; and then remarking to himself that "Bacchus had been before him in the drink trade."

In the food trade, in cooking, lemons came into their own far north of the Alps before and especially after Mrs. Beeton's day. Italian lemons rolled into Britain (no longer possible to be "12 miles from a lemon," as Sydney Smith had once complained when he began living in a North Riding rectory).[1] British cooks diversified and improved on old recipes for such things as "lemoned honeycomb" (which was in the edition of Hannah Glasse's cookery book of 1767) or lemon cheese cake; they borrowed, they invented new lemon puddings, new lemon desserts and ices, preserves, and drinks.

What I think is about the tastiest of all northern lemony sweets I have taken from Mrs. Beeton's first edition of 1861—neatly reproduced in facsimile by Jonathan Cape in 1968. In it Wales's Snowdon pudding represents the solid tradition of British puds, and there is also a cold lemon soufflé in the modern American style of light but rich desserts. The most surprising recipe, surprising in its exquisite finality rather than in its ingredients, is for lemon rice, taken from the Portuguese.

By the way, if a lemon is a bit green, don't reject it. It is artificial ripening with ethylene gas which gives trade lemons their smart uniformity of yellow.

Avgolemono soup (for 6)

The name means egg and lemon, which are the two important finishing ingredients of this soup. In Greek restaurants here, it's usually made with a basis of chicken stock—but try using fish stock as they

[1] It would be hard, if not impossible, to find a food store that does not sell lemon juice in some form, but more and more it appears separated from the fruit and processed in one way or another—canned, frozen, or in plastic facsimiles of the fruit. And although California and Arizona alone (lemons prefer summers dryer than those of Florida) produce more lemons than Italy and Spain, it is a regrettable fact that the fruit is too often picked before it is completely ripe, to facilitate shipping. A way to get 50 per cent more juice from a lemon that is not fully ripe is to drop it in boiling water for a couple of minutes and squeeze it when it cools.

often do in Greece. Here in England most fishmongers are delighted to hand over free plaice bones, or cheap fish pieces, left over from filleting, which gives you a luxurious soup at a low price. Avgolemono has a light foamy texture, which tastes particularly agreeable on warm days.

For the stock:

>1½–2 lbs. fish bones & pieces
>6 cups water
>½ cup wine vinegar
>1 medium onion, stuck with 4 cloves
>1 medium carrot, sliced
>8 peppercorns
>½ bay leaf, sprig of thyme & parsley

Simmer together for 1 hour. Strain and reduce to about 5 cups. Correct the seasoning.

To finish the soup:

>¼–⅓ cup rice
>3 eggs
>1–2 lemons

Simmer the rice in the stock until cooked. Have ready in a bowl the eggs beaten up with the juice of 1 lemon. Add a ladleful of hot soup, whisking all the time. Return to the pan and, *without boiling*, cook until slightly thickened. Keep whisking. Add more lemon juice to taste. Serve at once.

Lemon & chervil sauce for chicken

The combination of lemon with meat does not come quite so naturally to us as it does to an Italian, a Viennese or a Frenchman. Parsley and lemon butter are often served with grilled steak, it's true, but very rarely with grilled lamb—which is a pity. Stews of chicken or veal, with tomato or pale sauces, could be much improved by the last-minute Italian addition of chopped parsley, lemon peel, garlic and an anchovy fillet. Mayonnaise and vinaigrette sauces often go better with cold meats if lemon juice has been substituted for vinegar.

Here's a lemon and herb sauce for roast or boiled chicken, written down by the great Frenchman Carême. Never forgetting the pride he took in the *grosses pièces* he invented for the tables of Napoleon, the Prince Regent, Talleyrand and the Rothschilds, he also appreciated (and improved on) the recipes of homelier kitchens.

> 1 *tablespoon unsalted butter*
> 1 *tablespoon flour*
> 1 *cup (or a little more) chicken stock*
> *salt, pepper, nutmeg to taste*
> *juice of half a lemon*
> *extra unsalted butter*
> 1 *tablespoon fresh chopped chervil*

Melt 1 tablespoon of butter in a heavy pan. Stir in the flour, and then, gradually, the hot chicken stock. This can be from the boiled-chicken pot, or made from giblets and neck of any chicken.

When the sauce is smooth and thick, season with salt, pepper and nutmeg. Simmer gently for at least 15 minutes, giving an occasional stir; the most trouble-free way of doing this is to place the pan over another pan of simmering water—the sauce can then be virtually ignored until dishing-up time.

Just before serving, add lemon juice, extra butter and chopped chervil (an equal quantity of parsley can be substituted, or half the quantity of tarragon). If the sauce has thickened too much, add more chicken stock or a little water.

Honeycomb mould   (for 6)

This delicious pudding of childhood should not be relegated to the nursery. Its clear, true flavour (not to be found in packet-mix versions) is a luxury these days. The mixture plops into a jelly mould— choose one with an elaborate pattern—and several hours later it comes out as an elegant three-layered pudding.

3 large eggs
juice & rind of two lemons
½ oz. gelatin [2 packages]
⅓ cup sugar
6 tablespoons [⅓ cup] cream
generous 2 cups Channel Islands² milk

Separate the yolks and whites of the eggs. Put the yolks in a large bowl or top of a double boiler. Add the thinly pared lemon rind, gelatin, sugar and cream. Heat the milk to just under boiling point and whisk into the egg yolk mixture (creamy Channel Islands milk gives the best results). Set the bowl over a pan of simmering water, and stir until you have a custard the consistency of heavy cream more or less. Taste and add more sugar if you like, but this pudding should not be very sweet. Mix in the lemon juice and strain. Beat the egg whites until stiff, then fold in the strained custard with a metal spoon: turn and lift the mixture gently. Pour into a quart jelly mould, and chill. When it's firmly set, slip a knife round the edge of the pudding, which will then turn out easily (no need to dip the mould into hot water). It will have a cap of clear lemon jelly, then a thin band of opaque cream jelly shading off into a honeycombed spongy base which makes a slight crinkling noise as it's eaten.

Mrs. Beeton's baked lemon pudding   (for 6 to 8)

I've halved most of the quantities for this richest and best of lemon-curd tarts (or, as they often used to be called, lemon cheese cakes), in the interests of modern digestion. Double the amount was described by Mrs. Beeton as being right for 6 to 7 people—the Victorians certainly ate with stamina and capacity. She used a puff pastry crust, but most of us these days would, I think, prefer a crisp, sweet shortcrust.

² Where both Jersey and Guernsey cows originally were bred.

pastry: 6 tablespoons butter
1 heaping tablespoon confectioners' sugar
pinch of salt
1 egg
1¼ cups flour

filling: juice of 2 lemons
grated rind of 1 lemon
½ cup superfine sugar
6 tablespoons (⅓ cup) heavy cream
4 egg yolks
2 oz. [about ⅓ cup] ground almonds
8 tablespoons [1 stick] unsalted butter,
melted

for serving: light cream

To make the pastry, cream together butter, sugar and salt. Add the egg and then the flour, until a dough is formed. Leave it to rest for an hour or so, then roll it out and line an 8½- or 9-inch tart tin with a removable base.

Beat the filling ingredients together until smooth. Pour into the pastry case, and decorate with a lattice made from the pastry trimmings. Bake for 30–40 minutes in a slow oven, 325°, until risen and nicely browned. Serve hot, warm or cold, with some light cream (on the whole, I think it's best warm).

Lemon soufflé   *(for 6 to 8)*

As we're not Christmas pudding eaters in our family, finding it too bulky, too unrefreshing after the turkey course, we've made our own tradition of this cold lemon soufflé. I've tried to vary the recipe by adding orange juice and peel, by altering the amount of eggs and cream, but it's no good. Everyone says, "Yes, this is nice, but please next year may we have our proper lemon soufflé again?"

3 egg yolks
¾ cup superfine sugar
grated rind & juice of 2 large or 3 small lemons
½ oz. gelatin [2 packages]
¼ cup hot water
1¼ cups heavy cream
    or ¾ cup heavy & ½ cup light cream
3 egg whites
2 oz. almonds [about ⅓ cup], blanched & split

Put egg yolks, sugar, grated rind and juice of the lemons into a large bowl or top of a double boiler. Stand it over a pan of simmering water and whisk with a rotary beater until the mixture is a thick liquid, about 5 minutes. Take the bowl from the pan, stand it on a table and beat for another 5 minutes. By now it will be pale yellow, and thick and billowy. Dissolve the gelatin in the hot water, and add it to the lemon custard. Whisk the cream until it begins to hold its shape, and fold that into the custard. Last of all, whisk the egg whites until they are stiff. Fold in the cream and custard mixture with light movements until everything is amalgamated. Pour into a collared soufflé dish [see *footnote, p. 223*], and leave in the refrigerator to set. Toast the split almonds in the oven until they're golden brown. When cool, use them to decorate the soufflé. Remove the paper collar before serving, so that the cold soufflé rising above its dish has the appearance of a well-risen hot soufflé. Light cream may be served with it.

Lemon rice pudding   (for 6)

This beautiful lemon pudding is based on the Portuguese *arroz doce*, sweet rice. Guaranteed to convert the most ardent rice-pudding-hater.

¼ cup rice
rind & juice of 1 lemon
1½ tablespoons sugar
2 tablespoons butter

1¼ cups creamy milk & 1¼ cups light cream
   or 2½ cups light cream
cinnamon
extra cream

Wash the rice, and peel the lemon thinly, taking off strips about ¼ inch
wide and 1 to 2 inches long. Put rice, lemon peel, sugar, butter and light
cream and milk into a Pyrex or other ovenproof dish. Cook in a very slow
oven, 250°, for 2 to 3 hours until the rice is cooked. Stir it every 45 minutes.
About half an hour before the pudding is cooked, add about a teaspoon of
cinnamon or less, depending on your taste. When the pudding is done,
stir it up well, adding the lemon juice and some more cream if it's too
solid. Put a light sprinkling of cinnamon on top and place under a medium
hot broiler to brown the top lightly. Serve well chilled. You will find that
the lemon peel has almost dissolved, and so has the rice, although it still
feels gently grainy to the tongue.

Snowdon pudding   (for 8)

"This pudding," wrote Eliza Acton in Modern Cookery,[3]
published in 1845, "is constantly served to travellers at the hotel at the foot
of the mountain from which it derives its name." I don't think that this is
so any longer. I notice that the Wales Gas Board in the excellent booklet
Croeso Cymreig, A Welsh Welcome, uses her recipe.

First, though, you will need some lemon marmalade. If you find it difficult to buy, make it this way:

1½ lbs. lemons
7½ cups water
6 cups sugar

Halve the lemons and squeeze out the juice. Divide the halves again in two
and remove with a sharp knife as much as you can of the ragged insides

[3] The Best of Eliza Acton, recipes from her classic Modern Cooking for Private
Families, first published in 1845, selected and edited by Elisabeth Ray, introduction by
Elizabeth David, Longmans, London, 1968.

and pith. Put all this into a muslin bag and suspend it by string from the handle of a heavy pan. Add water, lemon juice and the peel shredded. Simmer until the peel is soft. Add the sugar and boil fast until setting point is reached.

For the pudding:

> butter for greasing the mold
> 6 eggs
> ½ lb. beef suet
> 3 cups bread crumbs
> ¼ cup ground rice [rice flour]
> ¾ cup dark brown sugar
> ¾ cup lemon marmalade
> grated rind of 2 lemons
> pinch of salt
> ½ cup seedless raisins

Butter a 6-cup pudding basin or mould liberally. Ornament it with some of the raisins, cut in half but not separated, placing the cut side to the buttered mould. Beat the eggs and mix in the rest of the ingredients. Scrape into the mould. Cover with a double layer of greaseproof paper or foil, making a pleat across the middle in case extra expanding room is needed. Tie on with string and make a handle across. Stand the basin on a small grid in a large saucepan, pour boiling water into the pan to come half way up the basin, and put the lid on. Set over the heat and keep the water simmering for 1½ hours (top it up as required with more boiling water). Lift the pudding from the pan by means of the string handle, remove the paper or foil and turn the pudding out on to a hot serving dish.

  Serve with this wine sauce of Miss Acton's:

> thinly pared rind of half a lemon
> 3 tablespoons sugar
> wineglass of water (about ½ cup)
> 2 tablespoons butter
> generous ½ teaspoon flour
> 1 cup sherry, Madeira, or good white wine

Simmer lemon rind and sugar in the water for 15 minutes. Mash together butter and flour, and add to the strained lemon water over a gentle heat,

TO COOK A STEAMED PUDDING

1. Fill the buttered basin

2. Cover with a cloth and tie with string

3. Place in pan of water on a rack

4. Cover and boil the required time

until it thickens. Stir in the wine, reheat to just below boiling point and serve immediately.

Or with this:

Lemon & gin sauce (for 4)

This simply made aromatic sauce is an excellent complement to our robust steamed puddings. Try it, too, with bananas rolled in cinnamon and sugar, then baked, like apple dumplings, in a rich, sweet shortcrust pastry. The recipe comes from that lively and erudite dictionary, *Kettner's Book of the Table.*

"Put the thin rind of a lemon with three tablespoonfuls of sugar to simmer for 20 minutes in a tumblerful of water. Some persons think it enough to grate the lemon with lumps of sugar—but this detracts from the clearness of the sauce. When the simmering is ended take out the lemon-peel and add the strained juice of the lemon. This is extremely simple, but it is nicer than many a much more laboured sauce. Perhaps it is not quite fair to add that it is sometimes supplemented with gin. To be used with sweet entremets."

In other words, the gin is what matters. Add a jigger to the above quantity of sauce. Reheat gently, without boiling.

Lemonade & milk lemonade

In the early, dark months of the year, it was the habit in South Shields (and no doubt in places outside of Durham County, too) to brew lemonade in quantity. My grandmother called it Spring Medicine. She felt that her children's blood needed a "springclean" just as much as her china from China or the huge antipodean shells her husband had brought home from voyages in the Far East. Perhaps she shared his sea-man's fear of scurvy.

Our winter diet today may not be as stodgy as it was then for struggling widows on crowded, coaly Tyne, but memories of that river and the sharp clarity of lemonade come gratefully, all the same, in early spring and summer.

The method used was the one given for Kettner's lemon sauce in the preceding recipe, adding more water and a pinch of cream of tartar, but stopping short at gin. Unless you're making lemonade for children (who tend, unflatteringly, to prefer squash and pop), don't follow her example in this respect: the flavour of juniper goes particularly well with lemon.

Milk lemonade belongs to the prosperous Tennysonian nineteenth century we prefer, not to the north of England and its whitened doorsteps. Its light, interesting flavour was popular on vicarage lawns, under the cedars, on hot days of middle-class leisure. In our more strenuous lives, it makes an excellent long drink—very refreshing.

> 3 lemons
> 2 cups dry white wine
> 1 lb. superfine sugar
> 6 cups milk

Peel the lemons thinly and put the peel into a large bowl. Pour ½ cup boiling water over peel. Leave overnight. Next day add the juice of 2 of the lemons, the wine and the sugar. Bring the milk to boiling point—unpasteurized milk is best, if you can get it—and add quickly to the other ingredients. Leave to cool. As the milk will have turned to curds and whey, the lemonade must now be strained through cheesecloth or muslin two or three times until it's perfectly clear.

Taste and add the juice from the third lemon, if required. Serve well chilled.

Some versions of this recipe substitute ½ cup of sherry for the white wine, but I find the flavour of sherry too obtrusive.

PRUNES

Many people dislike prunes. With good reason, as anyone who has done time in a boarding school, a boardinghouse or a prison knows. Such prune-haters should be converted, they should be purged of their stewed prune memories, the prune being an essential to some of the best meat and fish recipes ever devised.

The prune is a dried plum, full of sunshine and sweetness (for instance, when added to a bottle of rough marc, prunes soften the taste and make a classy drink out of a merely alcoholic one). The finest prunes have come for centuries from the plum orchards of the Agenais district of southwest France. Monks of the abbey of Clairac, between Agen and Bordeaux, are said to have had their prune industry well organized by the sixteenth century. And by the sixteenth century the prunes of Tours were famous, and on sale in Paris.

Owing, I suppose, to a less reliable sun, the prune industry of Touraine has given way to the Agenais producers. And the housewives no longer dry their own plums for the winter storecupboard. One may walk along a sunken lane in the harmonious land between Loire and Loir, and come to a hamlet of old cave houses warrening an exposed rock face. There will be a walnut tree or two as a token of past living, a bay tree, some apples, a quince, and a medlar, but the plum trees will have disappeared. Chimneys poke through the slopes of the clifftop above, but there's no smoke. The only other sign of past existence, of life before the First World War, is a blackened flare of rock above a gaping hole at waist height, beside one of the cave doors. A child could crawl into this miniscule cave, this horseshoe-shaped oven cut into the rock and lined with bricks or wedge-shaped stones. One imagines the wives of the hamlet baking their bread, then quickly laying the wicker trays of plums in the dying heat. Next day the process would be repeated, and the day after that. When the plums had wrinkled from purple to black, they'd be stored away—with bay leaves tucked sometimes between the layers.

Modern methods have regularized but not changed this old process. Plums stay on the trees as long as possible to acquire as much sweetness as they can from the sun. Then they are dried out of doors, or in tunnels warmed by controlled blasts of hot air. In California, where more prunes are produced than anywhere else in the world, it's still a French plum, the *prune d'Agen*, that provides 90 per cent of the crop (the industry was started by a Frenchman, Louis Pellier, in 1856).[1] Now the Californians, particularly those of the Santa Clara valley, produce about 340,000,000 pounds of prunes a year, far more than the Agenais growers with their average of 11,250,000. No wonder the packages of prunes in the grocery shops of Tours itself are more often than not marked "Santa Clara" (in a discreet corner).

If these American prunes are not quite so rich, or so delicate in flavour as the French ones, they are almost as good. It would, I think, be unwise to claim to tell the difference between Agen prunes from Agen and Agen prunes from California, when eating a matelote of eel. Both yield their excellence with generosity.

One must ignore what modern puritans of the last century or two have done to prunes, the dreadful alliances they have made between prunes and rice, or prunes and custard powder. These recipes I've chosen go back to a medieval tradition abandoned in English cooking: the tradition of mixing

[1] Cuttings of the famous French prune were stuck into raw potatoes, then in sawdust, and packed in two leather trunks to make the long trip around Cape Horn to Pellier's orchard at San Jose; he grafted them to stocks of native wild plum.

sweet and savoury in such things as genuine mincemeat (ox tongue, beef or mutton with suet and dried fruits) or plum (i.e., prune) porridge, the original of the plum pudding, which was made with tongue, raisins, prunes, spices, wine, meat stock and bread crumbs. Prunes add a succulence to meat and fish, a blandness as well as an always welcome contrast—or anyway a slight change of texture. Moreover, using prunes this way saves you the need of providing a green vegetable. A few boiled or mashed potatoes, or fried croutons, are all that's required, though a green salad should follow, preferably chilled, as buffer and refreshment before you come to cheese or pudding.

When it comes to puddings or desserts made with prunes, remember the Middle Eastern origin of the cultivated plum, and concentrate on richness. Walnuts, almonds, rum, wine, cream—they are the key to success.

Giant prunes are the best (25–35 to the pound). If your grocer doesn't have them, try a health food store. They don't need long soaking: often an hour or two is all that's necessary to start them off—final plumpness comes with the cooking.

Matelote of eel in the Anjou style

Fresh-water eels stewed in wine are very popular in France. Different regions make their own variations, and naturally along the Loire prunes are included to increase the richness of the sauce. Strangely enough, the gentle flavour of the eel is enhanced.

Some London fish shops sell eels. Out of London you may have to persuade an angler to catch, kill and skin one for you. This is worth some determination, as eels are luxuries. They can sometimes even be acquired for nothing. Medium-sized ones are best. Very large, they become a little oily.

Ideally, eels should be killed immediately before cooking. To remove the skin, suspend the eel by a slip knot just below the neck from a strong hook. Slit the skin round with a sharp knife—it's very tough and was used in the past to hold the two parts of a flail together, and by small boys for whipping their tops. Now pull the skin down as if you were pulling off a glove. Some people find this quite easy, but I resort to pliers in one hand and a cloth in the other. Wash and clean the eel, and cut into 3-inch pieces.

2–3 lbs. eel
½–1 lb. prunes soaked in tea
1 lemon
8 tablespoons [1 stick] butter
¼ cup brandy
½ lb. button mushrooms
2 cups white wine, preferably from Saumur
1 bay leaf
salt, pepper to taste
1 egg yolk
3 tablespoons heavy cream
parsley

Squeeze the lemon and soak the eel in the juice for 15 minutes. Drain the pieces, then brown them lightly in 4 tablespoons of butter. Pour in the brandy, warmed, and set alight. When the flames have gone out, add the mushrooms to the pan; cover and cook gently for 10 minutes.

Pour in the wine. Add prunes and bay leaf, and season. Boil hard until the eel begins to part from its bones—about 15 minutes. Arrange eel, prunes and mushrooms on a hot serving dish. Discard the bay leaf, and attend to the sauce.

Beat egg yolk and cream together. Stir into the cooking liquid with the heat very low, so that the sauce thickens *without boiling*, or the egg yolk will curdle. Correct the seasoning. Add the rest of the butter in small knobs to the sauce, without any further cooking: this gives the sauce a specially good flavour and a shiny appearance. Pour over the eel, etc., sprinkle with parsley and serve immediately.

Variation: In Touraine red wine might be used, and there would be salt pork and onions instead of the mushrooms:

2–3 lbs. eel, cut in pieces
½ lb. prunes, soaked
½ lb. salt pork or unsmoked streaky
    bacon, diced [see footnote, p. 33]
15 pickling [small white] onions
1 tablespoon lard
2 teaspoons flour
1 cup red wine (or dry white)
½ cup water
bouquet garni
salt, pepper
3 tablespoons oil
2 tablespoons marc or brandy
triangles of fried bread
parsley

Brown pork and onions in lard. Stir in flour and brown lightly; incorporate wine and water to make a smooth sauce. Add bouquet garni and seasoning. Cook for half an hour. Brown eel pieces in oil, flame them with marc or brandy, and add with prunes to the sauce. Simmer until eel is cooked. Serve with triangles of fried bread and a sprinkling of parsley.

NOTE: It is important to flame eel with brandy or spirits. It reduces its oiliness.

Beef (or hare) with prunes

2-lb. piece of chuck steak
    or 1 hare, jointed [cut in pieces]
1 lb. giant prunes
½ lb. piece uncured streaky bacon [see footnote, p. 33]
3 large onions, chopped
3 large carrots, sliced
8 tablespoons [1 stick] butter
1 heaping tablespoon flour
bouquet garni
24 pickling [small white] onions
2 teaspoons sugar
½–1 cup beef stock

½ *lb. button mushrooms*
nutmeg, ginger, pepper, cinnamon, salt

Marinade: 1 *bottle red wine*
1½ *tablespoons* brandy
2 *onions, sliced*
1 *large carrot, sliced*
3 *cloves*
bay leaf
1 *sprig thyme*
1 *sprig rosemary*
12 *peppercorns*
½ *teaspoon salt*

Put the steak, cut into 2-inch pieces, or the hare into a bowl with the marinade ingredients, and leave overnight. An hour before cooking preparations are started, add the prunes, with some cinnamon.

Cut the rind from the bacon and chop it into small cubes. Brown it, with the chopped onions and carrot, in 4 tablespoons of the butter. Transfer to a casserole, and add the drained meat to the frying pan. When it's lightly browned, stir in the flour and leave it to colour. Pour in the strained marinade gradually (keep the prunes to one side); when it thickens transfer meat and sauce to the casserole, season with bouquet garni, spices, and salt and simmer until nearly done. The hare may take 2½ hours, whereas the beef will be cooked in just over an hour and a half.

Meanwhile peel the pickling onions. Put them whole into a heavy pan with 2 tablespoons butter, a pinch of salt and the sugar. Put over a low heat until the butter's melted, then add enough stock barely to cover the onions. Boil steadily until the stock, etc., reduces to a rich brown caramel, and the onions are cooked, and well glazed (shake them about from time to time). Use the last ounce of butter to cook the button mushrooms.

When the beef or hare is almost ready, add the prunes and finish the cooking (10–20 minutes). Arrange the onions and mushrooms on top of the casseroled meat, and bring up a prune or two to make an appetising contrast. Serve very hot.

If you have the hare's blood, mix it with 2 tablespoons of cream and a little of the hot sauce from the meat. Pour it into the casserole (before adding onions and mushrooms), which should be just off the boil. Stir over a very low heat for a few moments—if the sauce boils again, the blood will curdle.

Turkey or capon stuffed with prunes & chestnuts

This Breton recipe adds a moist richness to turkey or capon. For a chicken of more moderate size reduce the quantity of prunes by one-third, and of the other ingredients by a half.

40 chestnuts
30 prunes soaked overnight in tea
1½ lbs. pork, ⅓ fat, ⅔ lean
3 rashers lean unsmoked bacon [see footnote, p. 33]
2 heaping tablespoons parsley
3 heaping tablespoons bread crumbs
½ teaspoon each nutmeg, cinnamon, ground cloves
salt, freshly ground black pepper
sprinkling of flour
butter
½ cup port
8–10 lb. turkey or good-sized capon

Slice the hard skin of the chestnuts round the middle on both sides. Boil for 20 minutes. Remove a few at a time from the pan, and take off the two skins. Chop half the chestnuts into nuggets, leave the rest whole. Remove pits from the prunes. Chop half of them roughly, leave the rest whole.

Mince pork and bacon. Mix with parsley, bread crumbs, spices and seasoning. Make sure the seasoning is strong enough. Stuff the bird not too tightly.

To roast, butter the bird lavishly all over. Lay it on one side of the breast in a roasting pan. Put on a lid of double foil. Cook at 375° for 2–3 hours according to the weight of the bird, turning it onto the other side of the breast at half time. When the bird is almost done, remove the foil and pour off as much fat as you can, leaving the meat juices behind. Turn the bird onto its back. Sprinkle with salt and a little flour, then put back in the oven to brown surrounded by the whole chestnuts and whole prunes (about 20 minutes).

Transfer bird to warm serving dish. Arrange chestnuts and prunes round it. Skim surplus fat from the pan juices, then boil up with the port to make the sauce. Correct the seasoning and pour over the chestnuts and prunes.

Tripe de Gourin aux pruneaux

Gourin, a market town in the Breton Black Mountains, is the centre of an important stock-raising district. So you would expect tripe (a favourite market-day dish in Brittany) to be a particular speciality.

> 2 lbs. tripe [honeycomb, which has been previously soaked,
>   blanched, and is ready to use] cut into small squares
> 15 large soaked prunes
> 6 tablespoons butter
> 3 medium-sized carrots, sliced
> 10 shallots, chopped
>   or 1¼ cups chopped mild onion
> bouquet garni, 3 cloves
> beef stock
> ¼ cup brandy

Fry the tripe to golden brown quickly in the butter. Remove it to a casserole (or small *tripière*, if you have one), and fry the carrots and shallots. Add to the tripe with all the other ingredients, including enough beef stock just to cover. Fasten on the lid with a strip of flour and water paste, or a double layer of foil, and simmer for 2 hours.

Rabbit with prunes

This excellent recipe adds flavour to the insipid domestic rabbit (or cold-storage chicken). Made with wild rabbit, it's a recipe for a special occasion.

    1 rabbit, jointed [cut in pieces]
    seasoned flour
    6 tablespoons butter
    4 medium-sized carrots, sliced
    12 small onions (pickling)
    1 cup beef stock
    1 cup red or white wine
    12 oz. [1½ cups] prunes, soaked
    bouquet garni
    salt, pepper

and to finish:

    ⅓ cup port
    ⅓ cup currants
    ⅓ cup sultanas
    chopped parsley
    triangles of bread fried in butter

Turn the rabbit pieces in the flour, and cook the stew as in preceding recipe. Adjust the cooking time to the age and tenderness of the rabbit. Finally add port, currants and sultanas, and keep just under the boil for 10 minutes. Before serving, sprinkle chopped parsley over the dish, and tuck the croutons round the side of the casserole.

Noisettes de porc aux pruneaux de Tours

This classic dish of French provincial cooking combined originally the prunes of Huisnes, downstream from Tours, and the white wine of Vouvray, upstream from Tours on the opposite bank of the Loire. The prunes may nowadays come from California, but at least the Vouvray wine is still with us.[2] The vineyards there are on the top slopes of the

---

[2] Coming also from California are vintage Napa Valley White Pinot wines, from the same grapes which produce Vouvray and Saumur, and well worth trying when you can get vintage bottlings.

cliff, with the wine, as so often in Touraine, stored beneath them in caves. A neat arrangement. Above all the white wine producer needs nerve: he has to wait, before picking his grapes, through the red wine and rosé vendage of October, past All Saints' Day and into November with its trickier weather. This is because the grapes need to be *pourri*, almost rotting, if they are to produce a good white wine.

This recipe comes from *Recettes des Provinces de France*, chosen by Curnonsky.[3]

> 50 giant prunes (about 1½ lbs.)
> ½ bottle Vouvray
> 8 slices fillet of pork (or boned loin chops)
> 2 tablespoons flour seasoned with salt and pepper
> 4 tablespoons butter
> 1 tablespoon red currant jelly
> 1–1½ cups heavy cream

Soak the prunes 6 hours or overnight in the Vouvray. Turn the pork slices in the seasoned flour and fry in butter on both sides until golden. Cook gently with a lid on the pan until the meat is done. Meanwhile simmer the prunes for half an hour in the Vouvray. Drain them and arrange on a serving dish with the pork. Add the prune liquor to the meat juices, reduce, add the red currant jelly and bind with the cream. Season well and pour over the pork and prunes, and serve very hot.

Prunes stewed in Vouvray

This combination of prunes and Vouvray produces almost as good a result as the more famous *porc aux pruneaux de Tours* on page 296. Almost, but not quite—the pork recipe is one of the best I know; few dishes come up to it.

[3] Famous in twentieth-century France as the Prince of Gourmets, his real name was Maurice Edmond Sailland and he devised his pseudonym from the Latin *cur non* (why not?). With Marcel Rouff he produced the 28-volume *La France gastronomique*, which encompassed all the best of French food and where to go to eat it.

> 1 lb. giant prunes
> 1 bottle Vouvray wine
> ⅓ cup sugar
> 1 vanilla pod [the bean], split lengthways
> grating of nutmeg
> 3 curls of lemon peel

for serving: whipped cream

Put the prunes to soak for an hour. Simmer the rest of the ingredients for 20 minutes, strain into a clean pan and bring back to the boil when the prunes have finished soaking. Boil the prunes gently for 4 *minutes only.* Pour the whole panful into a bowl and leave in the refrigerator for 3 days. The prunes will have absorbed a lot of the wine, and taste delicious. Serve with a separate bowl of whipped, slightly sweetened cream.

Prune tart

Another dish from Tours. For success, the prune purée must be rich and well flavoured, not in the least watery.

> 8 oz. shortcrust pastry [see p. 57]
> 1 lb. giant prunes, soaked
> sugar
> rum
> 1 egg, beaten

for serving: heavy cream

Line a tart tin with a removable base with pastry (save the trimmings). Prick all over with a fork and bake blind [unfilled] until cooked, but not very brown, about 10 minutes at 425–450°.

Simmer the prunes in just enough water to cover them. Drain and sieve. Flavour the purée with sugar and rum, and put into the pastry case. Using the pastry trimmings, make a criss-cross lattice over it, with strips about ¼ inch wide. Brush the pastry with beaten egg, and bake until golden brown. Serve with cream.

NOTE: Mix the prune purée above with double its weight in homemade vanilla ice cream. Refreeze. Serve with almond biscuits (p. 254). I know this sounds unpromising, but try it.

Pruneaux fourrés de Tours

Walking along the main street of Tours, one is attracted again and again by the cake and confectionery shops. And of all these shops, the finest is the Maison Sabat. There in the ravishing window display, among the other specialities of the Sabat family, are charming little baskets, miniature hampers, filled with rows of stuffed prunes. These *pruneaux fourrés* are one of the great specialities of Tours. Each house makes its own (no sweets factory to vulgarize the old recipes). What I like about them is that they are not too sweet, that their flavour is rich but subtle, with just a hint of kirsch or rum. Discerning natives of Tours prefer the original *pruneaux noirs* which go back, I think, to the eighteenth century—they are stuffed with a prune and rum purée. I find it difficult to choose between them and the ones filled with pale green almond paste or an orange apricot purée, flavoured in both cases with a little kirsch.

Mlle. Madeleine Sabat finds it more and more difficult to get traditional baskets for prunes. They are made now only by the old women of Vilaine, a village in Balzac country near Chinon which once relied on supplying baskets to local prune packers at Huismes. (With the decline of the prune trade, the young people of Vilaine concentrate on fashionable and profitable wicker furniture.) Soon the *pruneaux fourrés* will all be packed in paper boxes. Soon, too, the prunes may come from California—at the moment they come from Agen.

> 2 lbs. giant prunes, soaked, stoned [pitted] & dried
>
> *almond filling:* 1 cup sugar
>   ¼ cup water
>   4 oz. (about ½ cup) ground almonds
>   kirsch
>   few drops green coloring
>   confectioners' sugar

prune or apricot filling: 4 oz. (¼ lb.) prunes or apricots, soaked
                        sugar
                        rum or kirsch

coating syrup: 1 cup sugar
                ¼ cup water

Leave the soaked and pitted prunes to dry on a rack in a warm kitchen.

To make the almond filling, bring sugar and water to the soft-ball stage. Pour in the almonds, remove from heat and beat until cold (use an electric beater), adding kirsch to taste, and just enough green colouring to produce a delicate tone. Knead the paste on confectioners' sugar spread over a Formica or marble surface, until the marzipan is coherent and firm.

To make the fruit filling, stew prunes or apricots with a very little water until they begin to be soft. Drain and weigh (discard prune pits first). Add about half the weight of fruit in sugar and sieve, or purée in a blender, using a little of the cooking liquor if the fruit sticks. Put the purée into a heavy pan and cook slowly over a steady heat until it dries to a thick mass. Extra sugar may be added, but these purées should not be oversweet. Remove from heat, flavour with rum (prunes) or kirsch (apricots) and leave to cool.

To fill the prunes, roll the paste or purée into fat nuggets and slip them into the prunes. The filling should show an almond-shaped bulge through the split in the prune. Make two or three light indentations across the filling at a slant, for decoration.

At the Maison Sabat, the fruit purées are piped into the prunes with a forcing bag before they have set. I think it's easier to shape the mixtures with a teaspoon, rolling them in superfine sugar if they are a little sticky.

Bring sugar and water to the hard-ball stage to make the coating syrup, and have ready an oiled rack. Quickly dip the prunes into the syrup (use a larding needle or knitting needle), and transfer them to the draining rack. This makes them shiny. It also makes them sticky, so put them into tiny paper cases before handing them round or packing them into a small basket.

More stuffed prunes

Prunes and haddock: pour boiling water over ½ lb. smoked haddock. Leave for 10 minutes, then drain and mash with 3 tablespoons of heavy cream. Season well with salt and black and cayenne pepper. Stuff 1 lb. prunes, soaked and stoned. Heat in the oven and serve on croutons of bread fried in butter.

Devils on horseback: replace the pit in each soaked prune with a salted almond. Wrap the prunes in pieces of bacon, fastened in place by a cocktail stick, and broil.

Prunes for a goose: this delicious recipe of New York chef Louis P. de Gouy demands 1½ lbs. prunes soaked and simmered in ½ water, ½ red wine, plus a sliced lemon. Chop ¾ lb. pork (⅔ lean, ⅓ fat), and fry in 4 tablespoons butter with 4 tablespoons chopped onion and 18 small green olives (or 12 large), pitted and chopped. Season with salt, pepper, nutmeg, mace, marjoram and thyme. When the mixture is cooked, put into a bowl and leave to cool. When it's just warm beat in 2 eggs. When it's cold, stuff the prunes. Leave in the refrigerator 24 hours, and put into the goose 2 hours before it is roasted.

Prunes and cheese: stuff soaked and pitted prunes with a knob of high-fat cream cheese. Put a toasted almond down the middle of each prune.

STRAWBERRIES

A rich man whose teeth, constitution and heart were all stainless steel might reasonably look back to life in the mid-eighteenth century with longing. But not if he liked strawberries. Strawberries are one of the fruits of modernity which are better as well as bigger.

The fruit our ancestors knew was one species or other of small European strawberry—fruit sacred to the Northern fertility goddess, Frigg, and then to the Virgin. Bulgy modern strawberries would hardly be recognized by a medieval miniature painter, who ran hautboys—or wood strawberries—round the margins of his Book of Hours.

The grand improvement came from a happy conjunction of the Virginian and Chilean strawberries in a French market garden at the end of the eighteenth century. The two species, one with good colour and flavour, one with size, had the same number of chromosomes, but had been separated by the expanse of the Americas.

Since then directed variation has never ceased. Experiments are now assailing the chief disability of the strawberry—that it will grow only low on the ground, out of doors, in summer rain and sun. This keeps up the price. Strawberries have to be picked by hand (fruits ripen on the same plant at different times).

In the strawberry field, women of the village pick along the rows of plants, on their hands and knees. They have to be knowing to select the right strawberries, careful in handling the delicate fruit. It's a sweaty, muddy, skilful job, for women, not for unthinking girls. And not for the sort of people who joined that strawberry-picking party in Jane Austen's *Emma*: large bonnets, little baskets with pink ribbons, a gypsy party under the trees, a table in the shade, everything as "natural" and "simple" as a wealthy landowner and employer of labour could make it. Listen to the conversation: "Morning decidedly the best time—never tired—every sort good—hautboy definitely superior—Chili preferred—white wood finest flavour of all . . . only objection . . . the stooping—glaring sun—tired to death—could bear it no longer—must go and sit in the shade."

After half an hour. How modern pickers would have laughed.

So did Jane Austen. She knew all about the realities of strawberry picking. But it was a good scene for the central moments of a love story ("sweet to the eye and mind. English verdure, English culture, English comfort, seen under a bright sun, without being oppressive"). Against a background of strawberries, misunderstandings knot to an intricate tangle. And suddenly we are back four centuries with Hieronymus Bosch and his great painting of the *Garden of Delights*, which wheels round a naked man presenting a strawberry of delight to a naked girl—the theme of all love stories. "You shall be Queen . . . and feast upon strawberries, sugar and cream."[1]

Strawberries, sugar, cream. The combination allows no improvement, you think? But certainly the cream of today can be improved, and occasionally the strawberries.

Strawberries & cream

When you find a greengrocer selling proper weights of strawberries in openwork baskets, stick to him. If you live near a strawberry

---

[1] *They had to make do without sugar and cream, but the Pilgrims were mightily solaced by the strawberries they found at Plymouth soon after the landing. Modern varieties, abundant in U.S. stores, are largely derived from Fragaria chiloensis, native to the West Coast.*

field, you'll be able to buy the best strawberries available, freshly picked at the best moment. Beware of roadside strawberry sellers, unless they are unmistakably attached to a nearby strawberry field. Don't neglect cheaper "jam" strawberries: they sometimes excel in flavour, with a sharper sweetness than the more perfect-looking specimens.

Preparation

Strawberries are easily bruised, do not keep well, and *should always be washed quickly in the minimum of water, before removing the stems.*

If you have to keep them overnight, wash and stem them, then leave in a dish in a cool place with a good sprinkling of sugar. If the refrigerator is the only cool place, cover the dish closely (or you will find the smell difficult to get rid of) and leave in the salad crisper drawer. If your strawberries are not as ripe as they should be, leave the dish two or three hours in the sunshine if you can, with a good sprinkling of sugar.

Serve straightaway, washed but not stemmed, in individual bowls, with individual bowls of sugar and cream. Each person dips his strawberries by their leaves first into sugar and then into cream. Flavour the cream with a few drops of lemon juice. Or beat equal quantities of soured and heavy cream together until they are thick, not stiff. Modern pasteurized cream is too bland. It lacks the sourish tang of French cream, which brings out so well the flavour of fruit.

Coeur à la crème

Cream is cheap in France, compared with the price of other food, but frugal housewives stretch it most successfully by the addition of fresh cheese (*fromage frais, fromage blanc*) and beaten egg white. Usually it's served in a large bowl, but for special occasions heart shapes of this delectable mixture appear surrounded by strawberries. Few of us are able to buy drippingly fresh cheese, but cottage cheese, farmer's cheese, Petit Suisse or Gervais will do. And it's no good making your own in a muslin drip bag, from sour pasteurized milk; the result is a rubbery, bitter curd. If you can buy unpasteurized milk, it's another matter.

One used to buy heart-shaped metal moulds, pierced with draining holes, from Madame Cadec at her Soho shop. Now Elizabeth David, on London's Bourne Street [*see p. 367 for U.S. sources*], sells little white china hearts, and so do some of the better kitchen suppliers on both sides of the Atlantic. They make a good summer birthday present.

> ½ cup heavy cream, whipped
> ½ lb. cottage cheese, or farmer's cheese[2]
> 1 egg white, whipped stiff
> sugar to taste

Mix the cream into the cheese, and fold in the egg white with a metal spoon. Add sugar—don't overdo it. Line the moulds with buttered muslin and pile in the cheese mixture, smoothing the top. Leave to drain overnight in a cool place, or the refrigerator.

To serve, turn out and surround with strawberries. Additional sugar, light cream and thin homemade almond biscuits (p. 354) are good accompaniments.

In France, this cheese mixture is often served with apricot jam, the kind with large pieces of fruit in it, or strawberry jam from Plougastel in Brittany. Quince jelly or crab apple jelly goes well with it too. An ideal way of using up runny jams.

Cream cheese mousse

A simple delicious mousse, one of the delights of summer when served with strawberries (or other soft fruit, but particularly strawberries). It's really a more elaborate form of *coeur à la crème,* made with the low-fat cheese on sale in most grocers' shops.

[2] *In most such recipes as this, farmer's cheese, cottage cheese, pot cheese, Neufchâtel, and the domestic version of ricotta are interchangeable, dependent on the use of some discretion. To Mrs. Grigson's taste, most commercial so-called cream cheese "seems too caramelized, like eating solid evaporated milk—too denatured for this kind of recipe, though of course it can be used."*

½ lb. low-fat cottage cheese
2 egg yolks
¼ cup sugar, vanilla sugar for preference
½ oz. gelatin (2 packages)
6 tablespoons very hot water
½ cup heavy cream
½ cup light cream

for serving: strawberries
orange juice or orange liqueur

Sieve the cottage cheese to get rid of the large-grained texture (if home-made cheese is used, make sure it's well drained before weighing). Beat in egg yolks and sugar—for quick vanilla sugar, see page 347. Dissolve the gelatin in the hot water, add the two creams and whisk until stiff. Fold in the cheese carefully, so that the mixture is well blended, but still light and fluffy. Brush a 3-cup mould (or little heart-shaped moulds) with a thin film of nontasting oil and sprinkle with superfine sugar. Pour in the mousse and leave to set. Serve chilled, with unchilled strawberries dressed with a little orange juice or orange liqueur.

Strawberry brulée

Adapted from an American recipe, strawberry brulée sounds complicated, but it's really worth the trouble. You need a round, sightly, ovenproof dish (Pyrex is ideal) at least 1 inch deep and about 8½ inches across.

sweet shortcrust: 1½ cups flour
2 tablespoons confectioners' sugar
8 tablespoons [1 stick] butter
1 egg

filling: 1 cup light cream
½ cup heavy cream
3 egg yolks

15–20 *large strawberries*
1 *tablespoon orange liqueur*
1 *tablespoon sugar*
extra superfine sugar

Make the pastry in the usual way and line the Pyrex dish (keep what is left over for the next recipe). Prick all over with a fork, and bake blind [unfilled] until light brown and cooked. A sheet of foil and haricot beans may be used as well to keep the pastry from rising, but the fork treatment is usually enough.

Boil the cream, both kinds together, for one minute exactly. Stir into the egg yolks, beating with a fork. Set over a pan of simmering water for five minutes, stirring all the time to avoid lumps. Pour through a sieve into a clean bowl and leave to cool.

Meanwhile halve the strawberries. Sprinkle with sugar and liqueur and set aside for an hour.

Assemble the tart about 2½ hours before the meal. Arrange the strawberries in a single close layer, flat side down on the pastry case. Mix their juice into the custard and pour over the fruit. Chill for 2 hours. Sprinkle the top with a bare ¼-inch layer of superfine sugar. Set under a hot broiler, revolving the pie from time to time, so that the sugar melts into an even golden-brown marbled sheet of caramel. Chill for half an hour (while serving and eating the first course or courses).

Barquettes aux fraises

Use boat-shaped tartlet tins, though, of course, round ones will do. Line with pastry, the sweet shortcrust left over from strawberry brulée, rolled thinly. Bake blind [unfilled]. Cool, then store for a day or two in an airtight tin until required.

Arrange a nicely graded line of ripe, firm red strawberries in each *barquette*. Melt 2 tablespoons each red currant jelly and raspberry (or apricot) jam together in a pan, and sieve. Spoon carefully over the strawberries while just warm and still runny.

Large strawberry tarts can be made in the same way, but they are most successful if the strawberries are arranged on a bed of *crème pâtissière*, as the apples are in the Evreux tart on page 258. Pour the jam over just before serving.

Strawberries & sharpness

In Venice, in the season of Alpine strawberries, they are served with lemon juice, or red or white wine, and sugar. No cream. In France, in the Vendômois, one friend sprinkles large Quatre Saisons berries from his garden with a few drops of red wine vinegar to bring out the juice. This really works very well, though it may require an act of faith to try it the first time. They are then eaten with cream and sugar in the usual way, or with his own red wine.

In England, we've eaten strawberries in claret for centuries. Try orange juice and orange liqueurs, fortified wines, or champagne, or Asti Spumante. Purées of fresh ripe raspberries and black currants bring out the sharpness and sweetness of the strawberry.

These seasonings must be added at the last possible moment, mostly at table, but never more than half an hour before eating.

WALNUTS

After the grape harvest comes the harvest of walnuts, in such districts as the Corrèze and the Vaucluse in France, and the peninsula of Sorrento below Naples.[1] Poles move along sunken lanes like lances in Velázquez's *Surrender of Breda*, heads appear, like Green Men in church carving, above the tops of the trees or right in the middle of the high foliage, walnuts patter to the dry ground, the new season's supply, much of which will end up in our shops and on our sideboards.

In cooking with walnuts, it's a good idea to use them early in the season before the kernels shrink and lose their finest flavour. In October and November, early November, one may see in London greengrocers' shops netted sacks labelled "fresh walnuts from France." They are very juicy,

---

[1] The *juglans Californica* is the walnut that grew wild on the West Coast, and the Madeira walnut was introduced soon after the arrival of the white man. Now California-grown walnuts are shipped all over the world and furnish most of the U.S. supply. The black walnut is native to the East and the Middle West and is a great favorite in, among many other localities, eastern Tennessee, where it is used in making cakes, ice cream, pie, salads, catsups, and "old-timey walnut pancakes" made with rice.

the ones to go for if you want to make walnut and onion bread from Burgundy, or a walnut cake, or soup.

A little later on, English shoppers find the kiln-dried Sorrento walnuts, from the same place as the ones which were found under the dust of Pompeii, lying in their bowl beside eggs and cereal, still waiting for the priests of Isis. One year I was tempted by the perfect appearance of some enormous walnuts from Turkey—walnuts the size of golf balls, but they were tasteless compared with the smaller French and Italian nuts in neighbouring boxes.

English walnut trees produce good fruit, but they are not very certain croppers, as you might expect of an introduced tree whose native home stretches from southeastern Europe to the Far East. In walnut you have the same word as in Wales and the Welsh—the country of foreigners, the foreign nut. Farther south, in France, Italy, Spain, Portugal, where it's found a second home and been thriving for centuries, the walnut is called simply "the nut."

Perhaps it is this uncertain status of walnuts in our island that explains why traditional uses of them are almost confined to walnut catsup, to pickled walnuts, and to walnuts as dessert, walnuts with wine, walnuts with raisins. The last is an old medieval combination (like the four mendicants or friars—dried figs, raisins, hazelnuts and blanched almonds, whose colours resembled the habits of the Dominicans, the Franciscans, the Austin friars and the Carmelites) from the time when fresh fruit was hard to come by in winter. Walnut layer cakes, tea breads and salads, now so familiar to us, arrived in Britain from America at the beginning of this century. It's to that country and to France, to the Middle East and to China that we must turn for recipes which show the walnut to be as versatile in cookery as the more popular almond.

Walnuts can replace or augment almonds in mincemeat, or in biscuits. If you use an American cookery book, you will find them a good—and cheaper—substitute for pecans.

Walnut soup   (for 6)

This French soup—which I first came across in Elizabeth David's *Summer Cooking*—is one of the most delicious and unusual ones

I know. Particularly when made with fresh walnuts. The garlic is not optional, but essential to the flavour (without being identifiable by people who may think they don't like it).

> 6 oz. shelled walnuts
> large clove garlic
> up to 1 qt. light stock* (see recipe)
> ½ cup heavy cream
> salt, freshly ground black pepper

Crush walnuts and garlic to a paste with a little of the stock (use a blender, a mortar and pestle, or the end of a wooden rolling pin and a bowl). Incorporate the rest of the stock slowly until the mixture is the consistency of light cream. If the walnuts have been puréed in the blender, they will probably take up most of the quart*; if they've been pounded by hand, they'll take about 3 cups. Pour the soup through a sieve into a saucepan, and bring to the boil. Add the cream and correct the seasoning with salt and pepper. Serve straightaway.

Walnut bread from southern Burgundy

John Evelyn, in exile, seems to have loved especially the walnut trees of France. "Burgundy abounds with them," he wrote in 1658, "where they stand in the midst of goodly wheat-lands, at sixty and an 100 feet distance, and so far are they from hurting the crop, that they are looked upon as great preservers by keeping the ground warm, nor do the roots hinder the plow." I expect this bread was made then, real farmer's food, filling but tasty. (Farther north, where walnut trees begin to thin out, in Touraine for instance, fresh walnuts are eaten with bread hot from the baker's oven, salt, and a glass of white wine.)

> 5 cups all-purpose flour
>   (preferably unbleached)
> 1 tablespoon salt

> 2 tablespoons sugar
> 2 envelopes yeast
> 2 cups warm milk
> ½ cup walnut oil
>   or 8 tablespoons [1 stick] melted but cool butter
> ½ cup walnuts, roughly chopped
> ¾ cup onion, finely chopped

Sift flour, salt and sugar into a warm bowl. Dissolve the yeast in ½ cup of warm milk, and pour it into the middle of the flour, together with the walnut oil (or butter) and the rest of the milk. Knead well until the dough is firm and blended into a smooth, springy ball (about 10 mins). Leave in a warm place to rise for 2 hours (or in a cool place overnight). Punch down the dough, mix in the walnuts and onion, shape into four rounds and leave on a greased baking tray to rise for 45 minutes. Bake at 400° for 45 minutes, or until the loaves sound hollow when tapped underneath.

Cerneaux, or walnuts pickled in the French style

John Evelyn again, this time on green walnuts: "In France they eat them blanched and fresh, with wine and salt, having first cut them out of their shells before they are hardened, with a short brass knife, because iron rusts; and these they call Cernois, from their manner of scooping them out." *Cerner* means to cut away or cut round.

Three hundred and eleven years later, the same recipe given in more detail in *La Vraie Cuisine de l'Anjou et de la Touraine*, by Roger Lallemand: "Take walnuts which are not ripe. Halve them and remove the soft kernels from the shells without breaking them. Blanch in water acidulated with a little vinegar. Leave them for several days to soak in good white wine vinegar, with tarragon and tiny onions. Drain and serve them as an hors d'oeuvre, dressed with oil and other seasonings, preferably verjuice." For the verjuice, the acid juice of unripe grapes, we must today substitute lemon juice or vinegar.

Eliza Acton records a simpler version of this salad. She had spent a year in France as a girl, a century and a half after Evelyn[2] wrote *Sylva . . . a Discourse of Forest Trees,* and had become engaged briefly to a Frenchman. Her memories of dishes eaten there are gently coloured with romantic gourmandise, an unembittered nostalgia.

She writes that "this is a common summer salad in France, where the growth of walnuts is generally abundant, but is not much served in England; though the sweet flavour of the just-formed nut is very agreeable. Take the walnuts when a pin will pierce them *easily,* pare them down to the kernels, and toss them gently, just before they are served, in a French or English salad-dressing (the former would generally be preferred we think), and turn them into the salad-bowl for table."

Pickled walnuts in the English style

This wonderful black pickle, a favourite in England, has changed as little over the centuries as the preceding Cerneaux recipe. Hannah Glasse, Eliza Acton and the flock of lesser cookery writers disagree only about the blend of aromatics. The method has never changed. For clarity, I've chosen Mrs. Beeton's instructions:

> *100 walnuts*
> *salt and water*
> *to each quart of vinegar:*
> > *4 tablespoons whole black peppercorns*
> > *2 tablespoons allspice*
> > *2 tablespoons bruised ginger*

"Procure the walnuts while young"—from the beginning to the middle of July, before they harden—"be careful they are not woody, and prick them well with a fork; prepare a strong brine of salt and water (4 lbs. salt to each gallon of water), into which put the walnuts, letting them remain 9 days, and changing the brine every third day; drain them off, put them on a dish, place it in the sun until they become perfectly black, which

[2] Also author of *The French Gardener: Instructing How to Cultivate All Sorts of Fruit-trees,* Evelyn had anticipated urban ecological problems by suggesting that "sweet-smelling trees" be planted in London to purify the smoky seventeenth-century air.

will be in 2 or 3 days; have ready dry jars, into which place the walnuts, and do not quite fill the jars. Boil sufficient vinegar to cover them for 10 minutes, with spices in the above proportion, and pour it hot over the walnuts, which must be quite covered with the pickle; tie down with bladder"—use small bottling jars, which fasten tight with a rubber ring— "and keep in a dry place. They will be fit for use in a month, and will keep good 2 or 3 years."

NOTE: For best results use sea salt and wine vinegar. You could also insert an onion or two, stuck with cloves, in the middle of the nuts, as Hannah Glasse and Eliza Acton did, and augment the spices with mustard seed and mace. Eat with cheese and salads; add 10 or 12 to a beef stew as a cheap piquant substitute for oysters.

Pheasant in the Georgian style   (for 4 to 5)

This lovely and unusual dish takes time to prepare, but it's worth the trouble. Make it above all in autumn, in November, when walnuts are still fresh and juicy and when, in England, the first good grapes and oranges arrive. Here is a modernized version of a recipe, given in *La Gastronomiten Russie,* by A. Petir, published in Paris in 1860, which came originally from that Caucasian land where walnuts, oranges, grapes and tea all flourish—and pheasants too.

Keep any vegetables you may think of serving as a separate course. This is a dish on its own.

> 1 *pheasant*
> 30 *walnuts, or 8 oz. shelled walnuts*
> 2 *lbs. grapes*
> 4 *oranges, preferably blood oranges*
> ½ *cup sweet muscatel wine, e.g., Frontignan*
> 1 *tea bag, preferably containing green tea*
> 6 *tablespoons butter*
> *salt, pepper*
> 2 *tablespoons flour*

Pour boiling water over the shelled walnuts, leave for three or four minutes and then remove the skin surrounding the nuts themselves (a pointed knife helps). This removes the bitter part of the walnuts. Put the grapes through a vegetable mill (or in the blender and then sieve), to obtain a thick juice. Squeeze the oranges. Pour ½ cup boiling water over the tea bag, brew for 5 minutes, then strain off the tea. Put all these ingredients, including the walnuts, with the pheasant, the wine and half the butter, into a casserole; ideally, it should be of a size only a little larger than the bird, so that the mixture and the walnuts almost cover the pheasant. Season with salt and pepper, and cover. Bake in a moderate oven, 375–400°, for 50 minutes or until the pheasant is just cooked. Cut it into four, or carve it as appropriate; arrange the pieces on a hot serving dish, and put the strained walnuts around them.

Measure the cooking juices (there will be about 3–4 cups) and reduce the quantity to half by boiling hard. Meanwhile keep the pheasant warm in the oven (protect with buttered paper), and fork the flour into the remaining butter. When the reducing is completed, add the flour and butter to the sauce in little pieces, stirring them in well. The sauce will thicken, and acquire an appetising glaze. Pour a little of it over the pheasant, and serve the rest in a sauceboat.

Two walnut stuffings

For boned loin, breast or shoulder of lamb

4 oz. dried apricots, soaked overnight
2 cups bread crumbs
1 tablespoon chopped parsley
4 tablespoons butter, melted
2 oz. walnuts, roughly chopped
1 large egg
salt, pepper

Chop the apricots, and mix all the ingredients together.

For duck or goose (halve the quantities for duck)

½ cup chopped onion
1 large clove garlic, crushed
2 large eating apples, peeled, cored & diced
¾ lb. belly of pork, minced
4 tablespoons butter
2 cups bread crumbs
2 oz. walnuts, chopped
2 teaspoons honey
1 large egg
1 tablespoon chopped parsley
salt, pepper

Fry onion, garlic, apples and pork in the butter gently for about 15 minutes. Mix with the other ingredients. The chopped liver of the bird may also be added.

Prunes stuffed with walnuts

A Book of Middle Eastern Food, by Claudia Roden (Nelson, £3·50),* is the kind of cookery book I like, even at that price. It's not just a collection of recipes, but recipes explained, recipes plus information—poems, stories about that holy wit and gourmet, the Hodija, bits of social and religious history—which help one to understand this cookery so basic to our own in western Europe. I was interested to find a walnut sweetmeat identical to one made in Périgord (a nugget of almond paste sandwiched between walnut halves, topped with a blob of brittle caramel), and this rich-tasting but light confection of prunes and walnuts and cream.

1 lb. prunes
1 pint freshly made tea
as many shelled walnut halves as there are prunes
2–3 tablespoons sugar
1 tablespoon lemon juice

* Now available in Penguin edition for 6op and to be published in hard cover by Alfred A. Knopf in 1972.

1 cup water
½ cup each heavy and light cream, mixed
2 tablespoons superfine sugar (optional)

"Wash the prunes if necessary. Pour strained boiling hot tea over them and let them soak overnight. Drain. Remove the stones, replacing them with half a shelled walnut. If you find this difficult, boil the prunes in the tea until nearly tender, then cool, remove their stones and stuff them.

"Bring the water, sugar and lemon juice to the boil and simmer for a few minutes. Drop in the stuffed prunes and simmer gently, covered, for 30 minutes, adding more water if necessary. The walnuts will become impregnated with the rich syrup. Allow to cool and serve chilled with cream, whipped and sweetened with superfine sugar if you wish; or allow to cool, smother with the whipped cream and chill together for a few hours. This last method is particularly delicious.

"Modern variations which add to the aroma of the prunes include cooking them in sweet red wine (in this case using less sugar or none at all) or in the tea in which they have been soaked, flavoured with a few drops of vanilla or a packet of vanilla sugar."

NOTE: Hesitating to drop the prunes into the syrup for fear the walnuts would come out, I arranged them in a single layer in a large pan, fitting them closely together, and poured the boiling syrup over them.

Lavardin cakes

A year or two ago a new pastry cook arrived in Montoire, a small market town in the department of Loir et Cher. Everyone watched his window—Montoire is careful of its gastronomic reputation—to see what sort of show he'd put on (and how he'd compare with his two rivals). Very soon, among the evanescent stars of the usual repertoire, the éclairs, the *barquettes aux fraises*, the amandines, the *présidents*, rows of plain, white-iced discs appeared. They were labelled *Lavardins, notre spécialité*. Now Lavardin castle, or its remains, on one side of Montoire, together with Trôo church on the other, dominates our valley landscape of the Bas-Vendômois. Could these cakes be a local speciality we'd all missed? We bought some—feeling a little piqued—and they were so delectable that I asked for the recipe.

I learnt, in the simple, beautiful kitchen behind the shop, that lavardin cakes had nothing to do with Lavardin at all, that they came from the southwest of France, via an old pastry cook in Normandy who had specialized, against the dominant French tradition, in cakes which keep. And these do. They are also very much to the English taste. In fact of all the recipes in this chapter, I think that lavardins show off best the flavour and texture of walnuts.

filling: 1¼ cups sugar
3 tablespoons water
6-oz. can evaporated milk
scant 4 tablespoons unsalted butter
generous ¼ cup heavy cream
pinch baking soda
10 oz. walnuts, roughly chopped

sweet pastry: 2 cups flour
¼ lb. [1 stick] butter
½ cup superfine sugar
3 medium eggs

icing: 2 egg whites
½ cup confectioners' sugar

First make the filling: bring sugar and water to the hard-crack stage (310°—when it snaps between the fingers) over a brisk heat, stirring with a wooden spoon from time to time. Remove from heat and quickly stir in the evaporated milk, butter, cream and baking soda. Cook until the mixture reaches the soft-ball stage, add the walnuts and pour out onto a marble slab or a sheet of greased paper. It will cool to a soft nut toffee.

While the filling cools, make the pastry in the usual way. Roll it out thinly and line 3–4-inch flan rings laid on a greased baking sheet (or smooth-sided tart tins), leaving a little frill of pastry overlapping the edge. Fill slightly over half full with the walnut mixture. Brush the pastry edges with water and fit on lids of pastry, which have been pricked half a dozen times with a fork. Take off the surplus pastry by running a rolling pin across the tins. Bake at 350°, or a little less, until the pastry is cooked but not brown—about 15 minutes. As with mince pies, the point is to bake these little cakes so that the pastry cooks without the filling bursting through.

Remove the lavardins from their rings or tins, and cool upside down on a wire rack.

Set a bowl over a pan of boiling water, put in the egg whites and confectioners' sugar, and whisk until they blow up to a fairly stiff meringue, which feels hot but not uncomfortably so. Spread thinly over the top and sides of the cooled and inverted cakes with a palette knife, leaving the pricked surface exposed. Dry overnight in a cool place, or in the refrigerator, and store in an airtight tin.

If time is short, there is no reason why you shouldn't make 2 or 3 large lavardins, instead of the 20–30 small ones. Use a French flan ring, a tart tin with a removable base, or a straight-sided tart tin.

Chinese walnut brittle

I sometimes think that the charm of a country's cookery lies not so much in its classic dishes as in its quirks and fancies. Take this recipe, for instance—the universal (and boring) nut brittle, transformed by a little salt and a lot of freshly ground black pepper into a delicacy entirely Chinese. The surprising thing is that it tastes spicy rather than peppery. It leaves one's mouth feeling fresh and clear.

> ¾ cup sugar
> 1 level teaspoon salt
> 4 oz. shelled walnuts
> black pepper in a pepper mill

The shelled walnuts may be left as halves, or split again into quarters. In a small heavy saucepan dissolve the sugar in 3 tablespoons water, brushing down any sugar that clings to the side of the pan. Stir over a good heat until it reaches the softball stage—a saucepan thermometer for measuring the heat of sugar, jam or fat is a good investment, which I recommend to any cook. Add salt and walnuts. Bring the mixture to the hard-crack stage, turning the pepper mill about 20 to 25 times over the pan between stirs. The nuts will take up the sugar until they are lightly coated and sticking together in a cluster. Pour out onto a greased baking tray. As the mixture cools, which it does quite rapidly, pull it apart into pieces with a couple of forks. Eat the same day.

NOTE: Don't use powdered black pepper, or any kind of white pepper, which is less aromatic than the black and more fiercely hot.

Walnut biscuits

Almonds are so often used to make biscuits, and so successfully, that walnuts are overlooked. They produce a stronger flavour than almonds, which goes well with coffee, and a delightfully chewy texture. A good accompaniment too, to coffee, walnut or chocolate ice cream (see pp. 346, 349).

4 egg whites
4 oz. grated walnuts
2 oz. chopped walnuts
½ cup brown sugar
2 heaping teaspoons plain [all-purpose] flour

for baking: 4 sheets rice paper

Whisk the egg whites until they are stiff. Fold in the other ingredients carefully. Arrange the rice paper on two baking trays and spread spoonfuls of the walnut mixture on it (it does not run much in the baking, so the spoonfuls can be set fairly close together).

Bake at 300° for about 20 minutes, until lightly browned and firm. Tear away from the uncovered rice paper, and cool the biscuits on a wire rack.

Walnut pie   (for 6 to 8)

Anyone who has a weakness for English treacle tart will like this version of American pecan pie. In fact they'll probably prefer it: the nuts cut the sweetness of the filling much more deliciously than bread crumbs, in our traditional recipe.

shortcrust pastry: 2 cups flour

8 tablespoons [1 stick] butter

2 tablespoons confectioners' sugar

1 large egg

about 1 tablespoon water

filling: 8 tablespoons [1 stick] unsalted butter

½ cup soft brown sugar

3 eggs

¾ cup dark corn syrup

8 oz. shelled walnuts

juice and grated rind of 1 lemon

pinch salt

for serving: light cream

Make the pastry in the usual way, and line an 8½- or 9½-inch tart tin, with a removable base. For the filling, cream together butter and sugar until light and smooth. Beat in the eggs one at a time. Warm the syrup very slightly until it's runny and mix into the butter and sugar, etc., with the walnuts, lemon juice and rind and salt. Turn into the pastry case. Bake for about 45 minutes at 375° until the filling is lightly browned and risen. Eat warm or cold, and serve with light cream.

Cheese & walnuts

A walnut cheese from France is on sale in many British groceries these days. The walnuts are fine, but the cheese is soapy, processed and unrewarding. This recipe, from a pamphlet on potting meat, fish and cheese by Cyril Connolly's father (Wine and Food Society, 1946), is a great improvement.

½ lb. Cheddar cheese

6 tablespoons fresh butter

¼ teaspoon prepared mustard

1 tablespoon wine vinegar—with cayenne pepper to taste

12 chopped walnuts (24 halves)

Rub the cheese through a wire sieve, mix in butter smoothly, stir mustard with vinegar and mix again; add walnuts chopped very finely. Press mixture into small jars and cover very thinly with butter.

For variety a little paprika may be mixed in.

Walnut oil

Walnut oil may once have been popular all over Europe with painters, for mixing "white and other delicate colours, also for gold size and varnish," but its use in cookery has been confined to kitchens of the walnut districts of France. In other words, one will not find it mentioned in manuals of bourgeois and haute cuisine. Turn instead to the regional cookery books of Périgord, Burgundy and Touraine.

It may be that there has never been a great deal of walnut oil to spare—certainly it holds no place in the fat-consumption statistics of France—but we are able to buy it in one or two places in England (Louis Roche, 14 Old Compton Street, Soho, London W1; Elizabeth David Ltd, 46 Bourne Street, London SW1).[3] It's worth making an effort to find some, as the delicious flavour adds variety to many salads we take for granted.

Dressing: 2 teaspoons wine vinegar, 8 teaspoons walnut oil; season with salt, freshly ground black pepper, French mustard, sugar and garlic to taste.

Chapon: a good addition to green salads and soups. Cut a slice of white bread per person. Rub it over lightly with crushed garlic, and cut into cubes or triangles. Fry to golden brown in walnut oil.

Green salads: lettuce, batavia, lambs' tongues, endive, chicory, with walnut oil dressing and chapons. Garnish with hard-boiled egg, or a few shelled walnuts.

[3] *For U.S. sources, see page 367.*

Touraine salad: diced cooked potatoes, cooked green beans sliced, and small haricot beans soaked and cooked. Bind with mayonnaise made with walnut oil. Sprinkle with chopped tarragon and parsley.

Anjou salad: vegetables as for Touraine salad, with walnut oil dressing.

Potato salad: slice boiled waxy potatoes while hot. Put into the salad bowl with 2 or 3 tablespoons white wine. Leave for half an hour, turning over after 10 and 20 minutes. Add walnut oil dressing, plus 2 teaspoons chopped mild onion or shallots. Garnish with slices of hard-boiled egg and pickled gherkins.

Tomato salad: peel and slice 1 lb. tomatoes. Leave for several hours with salt, pepper, a dusting of sugar and a generous teaspoon brandy. Drain and dress with walnut oil dressing. Garnish with thinly cut rings of mild onion. (Brandy and sugar are great improvers of our tasteless, commercially grown tomatoes.)

Leek salad: in other words, "poor man's asparagus," and asparagus itself, are delicious with walnut oil dressing and chopped hard-boiled egg mixed with some chopped parsley.

Cress and walnut salad: 1 bunch water cress, 2 oz. Gruyère, diced, 1 eating apple, cored and diced, 4 oz. shelled walnuts, 1 tablespoon chopped onion, 3–4 hard-boiled eggs, quartered. Walnut oil dressing.

And . . .

FIVE FRENCH CAKES

Pâtisserie need not be left to professional pastry cooks. One's first attempt at a *Villesalem* or a *gâteau St. Honoré* may lack style, but there is no reason, given the right ingredients, why they should not be extremely edible. Slimmers [i.e., weight watchers] may call such things the works of the devil: the particular devil was in fact the great chef Carême, who turned his intellect and incorruptible skill to reviving French cookery after the Revolution.

He began with pâtisserie; he considered it a branch of architecture, making up the designs from rococo and neoclassical engravings (later nineteenth century elaborate plaster ceilings are referred to, slightly disparagingly, as pâtisserie). His masters were the masters of Europe. Europe's diplomacy in fact revolved round his original *pièces montées*. As for the content of his confections, rather more important, Carême improved old recipes and invented new ones; and so inspired a magnificent century of inventive pastry cooks. If I go into English cake shops, homemade genteel ones, alongside cathedrals, I reflect sadly that Carême *might* have reformed our confectionery too (how about a Decorated or Perpendicular *pièce montée*?). He did come to England to work for the Prince Regent, but went home when the Prince became concerned about the weight of the Royal Belly. "My job," he remarked, "is to stimulate Your Highness's appetite, not to curb it."

It is Carême's spirit which survives in the pâtisseries of most small towns in France[1] where intricate delicacies are prepared for the Sunday lunch, the First Communion and weddings to appease and gratify the discerning French appetite.

The main essential in French cake making is not so much cream as unsalted butter, liqueurs, almonds (don't buy ready-blanched, ready-flaked packages—with half the flavour gone), farm eggs, finely flavoured plain chocolate and superfine sugar which has been imbibing flavour in its screwtop jar from a vanilla bean. It helps if you have an electric mixer and a sugar thermometer.

The following four cakes, and many other recipes in the French repertoire, involve the simple making of six subsidiaries: three containers, two fillers and a flavouring. The containers are puff pastry, choux pastry and sweet shortcrust pastry. For the first two kinds, follow any good general cookery manual. For the sweet shortcrust, follow the usual method but with these ingredients: 2 cups flour sifted with 1 tablespoon each of superfine and confectioners' sugar, a pinch of salt, ¼ pound unsalted butter, and 1 medium egg to bind the mixture together.

The two fillings are *crème pâtissiére* and butter cream; the flavouring is praline powder.

> **Crème pâtissière,** or confectioners' custard, is widely used
> in France where we might use cream. Bring to the boil 2½
cups milk containing a short piece of vanilla pod. Pour onto 4 egg yolks

---

[1] Thirty years after his death, the *New York Tribune,* taking note of the opening in 1862 of one of America's most famous restaraunts, said: "Who would know Carême must be an habitué of Delmonico. Carême was in his glory on the inauguration of the new Fourteenth Street and Fifth Avenue house . . ." Triumphant *pièces montées* were featured on many of the menus of Delmonico's Union Square establishment. Emulators of Carême embellished a dinner there in honor of President Andrew Johnson with 10 such creations, including a miniature Washington monument. In honor of Charles Dickens in 1868 Chef Ranhofer's confectioners created a "Temple de la Litterature," "Le Monument de Washington," and "The Stars and Stripes," among others. Nowadays, however, ornamental cakes have all but disappeared—except, perhaps, on nuptial occasions.

and 1 whole egg, beaten together in a large bowl. Whisk in 1 cup vanilla sugar [see p. 347] and 4 tablespoons flour. Set the bowl over a pan of simmering water and stir until custard is thick and cooked (about 25 minutes). Keep tasting, and remove the vanilla pod when the flavour is strong enough. Strain into a clean bowl, fold in ½ oz. gelatin [2 packages] dissolved in 2 tablespoons hot water and the stiffly beaten whites of the 4 eggs. Cool. The egg whites are sometimes left out.

Butter cream. Put ½ cup of superfine sugar and 1 tablespoon of water into a heavy pan and heat to the soft-ball stage (240° on the sugar thermometer, or when a little of the syrup dropped into a mug of cold water forms a *firm* soft ball). Pour quickly onto 2 well-beaten egg yolks, stirring with a fork or a whisk. When this mixture is nearly cold, beat in 10 tablespoons unsalted butter. This is much more satisfactory and subtle in flavour than the slaphappy English system of beating confectioners' sugar and ordinary salted butter together.

Butter cream à l'anglaise. A very super French recipe—in spite of the name. Bring ¾ cup of milk to the boil. Meanwhile put the yolks of 6 eggs into a bowl with ½ cup of sugar and beat them to a thick foam. Pour in the boiling milk, stirring well. Return to the fire (over a pan of simmering water, if you want to be safe) and stir with a wooden spoon until the custard thickly coats the spoon. Strain it into a clean bowl and leave this custard—*crème anglaise*—to cool. Put 1¾ cups of unsalted butter into a bowl over a pan of hot water. Beat with a wooden spoon until it turns to a cream; don't let it melt. Stir in the cooled custard (take the butter off its pan of hot water first).

These creams can be flavoured in various ways. With 4 oz. of plain chocolate, melted, to 8 oz. of butter cream. Or with 1 tablespoon of powdered coffee, mixed to a paste with a teaspoon of boiling water. Or with 2 teaspoons of liqueur. Or with:

Praline powder. The best flavouring in confectionery apart from liqueurs. Take ½ lb. blanched, split almonds, and roast them to pale golden brown in the oven. Melt 1½ cups sugar in a heavy pan with 2 tablespoons of water. As it becomes a thick syrup, add the almonds, cooking until the whole thing is toffee-coloured. Pour out onto a sheet of buttered greaseproof paper. Break into pieces when cold, store in an airtight jar and powder in an electric coffee mill or blender, or with a wooden rolling pin, as required. Use about ½ cup of this praline powder to 1 cup of butter cream.

And now the five cake recipes:

Paris-Brest

choux pastry: ¼ cup butter
½ cup boiling water
½ cup all-purpose flour
2 eggs

2 oz. blanched almonds
1 cup cream, whipped,
  or 1 cup butter cream
½ cup praline powder
confectioners' sugar

First make the pastry. Heat butter and water in a saucepan until the butter's dissolved. Pour in flour all at once and stir hard with a wooden spoon until the paste comes away from the sides of the pan. Leave to cool down for 4 minutes, then beat in the eggs one by one.

Using a pastry bag, pipe the choux paste into a circle on a greased baking tray, a circle about the size of a dinner plate. Sprinkle the top with split and slivered almonds—the pieces should not be too small. Bake for 30 minutes in a moderately hot oven, 400°. Slice across into two while still hot, and leave to cool. Just before the meal, sandwich the two pieces together with plenty of whipped cream or butter cream, flavoured with praline powder (see p. 329). Dredge with confectioners' sugar. Like all choux pastry, this cake will not appreciate standing around, or being kept until next day, with the filling in it.

Gâteau St.-Honoré

"One day when Honorius, Bishop of Amiens, was celebrating mass, a divine hand sent down a loaf of bread. Thereupon the bakers adopted him as their patron saint."

> shortcrust pastry made with ½ cup flour
>   (other ingredients in proportion)
> choux pastry with ½ cup flour (p. 330)
> 1 cup sugar
> 1 cup water
> crème pâtissière (p. 328)
>   or whipped & sweetened cream
> *optional:* glacé fruits & toasted almonds

Use a dinner plate to cut a circle of sweet shortcrust pastry. Lay it on a greased baking sheet and prick with a fork all over. Using pastry bag, pipe a smooth ring of choux pastry just inside the edge of the circle, then pipe 8 or 10 small balls of choux paste on a separate baking tray. Bake the circle in a moderately hot oven, 400° for 30 minutes, without opening the oven door. Then bake the tray of puffs at the same temperature for 15–20 minutes.

Bring sugar and water to the crack stage in a thick pan (310°, snaps between the fingers). Dip each small puff into the syrup, so that it acquires a transparent toffee cap. Dip the opposite end into the syrup and stick it on to the choux wall of the pastry circle. (The final effect of this cake is rather like Old King Cole's crown.) When the cake is cool, not too long before serving it, fill the centre with *crème pâtissière*, or with whipped cream. If you like, decorate with glacé fruits and toasted almonds.

Villesalem

The Villesalem monastery is a beautiful ruin of a place, a mile or two outside the Vienne town of Montmorillon, where the owner and master cook, Monsieur Mercier, of the Hôtel de France produces this exquisite delicacy at the end of a fine meal. He has sent me his recipe:

For 10 Villesalem:

> a little over 1 lb. semi-sweet chocolate (16¾ squares)
> butter cream (p. 329)
> 10 boudoir biscuits [or lady fingers]
> 2 tablespoons each Grand Marnier, cognac & marc
> crystallized fruit

You will also need 10 bucket-shaped paper cases about 2¾ inches high and 1½ inches across the top. (Or any other paper case for cakes that you can buy—the bucket shape is difficult to find.)

Melt the chocolate in a pan at the side of the stove or over hot water. Fill a paper case using a small ladle. Immediately pour the chocolate back into the pan. A layer of chocolate will have adhered to the paper. Turn it upside down on to a baking sheet and continue with the other 9 cases. Refrigerate. Keep the remaining chocolate to one side.

Make the butter cream. Soak the biscuits in the three alcohols (use extra brandy if you have no marc) until they are impregnated but not mushy. Chop the crystallized fruit. Warm the baking sheet very gently and remove the chocolate cases. Fill each one with a layer of butter cream, some fruit, a layer of biscuits and a final layer of butter cream. Refrigerate. Cover each cake with a lid of chocolate, remelted and smeared on with a palette knife. Refrigerate again, peel off the paper cases (a damp cloth makes this easier) and there are your ten *Villesalem*.

NOTE: It's sometimes difficult finding the right-shaped paper cases. One has to improvise. Buy some small fluted cake cases, the kind stocked by many grocers. Stand one in each hole of a small tartlet tin, preferably of the smooth-sided kind. This is essential, as the melted chocolate will flatten out the fluted paper if it's not supported. Put a good spoonful of melted chocolate into each paper case, and as it cools mould it up the sides to the top. Not a quick job, but a peaceful one. It doesn't matter if the inside looks a bit rugged, as it won't show when the cakes are filled, but try to get the chocolate as even as you can. Put into the refrigerator to set, and then follow the recipe as usual.

Naturally these chocolate cases can be made well in advance, and stored in airtight tins. Their shape will not be so *soigné* as the *Villesalem*, but they are still impressive by comparison with the cakes one can buy in Great Britain.

Gâteau de Pithiviers feuilleté

Having adopted this recipe from Carême, who published it a century and a half ago, I was delighted to find that an exactly similar almond mixture is still being used in the Peché Mignon restaurant, set among chestnut trees in the Beauce town of Pithiviers. When you have made the cake a few times, vary it by the addition of a roasted and ground pork kidney. The filling will taste interestingly granular—nobody will be able to guess why. Incidentally they no longer make this addition at Pithiviers, which is, I think, a pity.

> *puff pastry made with* 1 ¾ *cups flour &* ½ *lb. butter*

filling: ½ cup ground almonds
½ cup superfine sugar
3 tablespoons melted butter
2 egg yolks
2 tablespoons heavy cream
1 egg, beaten
confectioners' sugar
optional: 1 kidney, roasted & ground

glaze: 1 beaten egg
          confectioners' sugar

for serving: light cream

Roll out the pastry. Use half to line a greased enamel or tin pie plate (9½ inches diameter). Mix together almonds, superfine sugar, butter, egg yolks, cream and kidney (if used), preferably in a blender, until smooth. Put into the pastry-lined plate, leaving the flat rim free. Brush the rim with the beaten egg, fasten on the lid of puff pastry, pressing it down round the edges. Make a small central hole, brush over with beaten egg and leave for five minutes in a cool place.

Using a knife, nick the edge of the pastry twelve times at regular intervals. Push up the pastry on either side of each nick to form a scalloped, rose petal edge. Score light inner scallops, and then long curving lines from the central hole outwards to designate formal petals. Be careful not to cut through the pastry.

Bake for 10 minutes in a very hot oven (475°), then lower the heat (to 400°) and bake for 30 minutes. Dredge with confectioners' sugar and return to a very hot oven—the sugar will turn to a dark brown glaze. Serve warm with light cream.

Gâteau de Pithiviers fondant

The other Pithiviers cake is also an almond mixture, but this time without the pastry. It has a rich, moist texture inside and a crisp outer crust. I bake it as a fairly thin cake to serve with coffee at dessert. For more than six people the quantities should be doubled.

> *cake:* ½ cup ground almonds
> 1 cup confectioners' sugar
> ¼ lb. [1 stick] butter, melted
> 3 egg yolks
> ¾ cup flour
>
> *icing:* ¾ cup confectioners' sugar
> 1¾ tablespoons hot water
> glacé cherries and angelica

Mix the cake ingredients together. Line a shallow sponge tin or a flan tin with removable base, about 7 to 9½ inches diameter, with foil. Brush it lightly with corn oil, or melted butter. Put in the cake mixture and spread it out; it will need a little space to rise, but not much. Bake for 40 minutes, or until cooked, at 375°. (Should you be doubling the quantities and making a thicker cake, it would be prudent to bake it at 350° for about an hour. At a higher temperature the outside will become too crusty before the inside is cooked.)

Let the cake stand for 5 minutes when you take it out of the oven, then lift it out gently by means of the foil lining. Lay it on a wire rack to cool. Blend confectioners' sugar and hot water for icing. Then turn the cake over carefully, remove the foil, and ice it, using a knife blade dipped in hot water and dried to push the icing evenly about. Decorate with glacé cherries and angelica and leave to harden. This cake keeps well in an airtight tin.

WATER &
CREAM ICES

Both water and cream ices can be delicious. And they are easy to make, as long as you have an ordinary domestic refrigerator with a freezing compartment. In their simplicity they seem entirely the product of modern technology, serving our modern desire for convenience.

Most people, I think, would credit the first ices to the Italians (they do, after all, make the best in the world, and many of our refrigerators come from Italian factories these days), or to the Americans, who designed and manufactured the first household fridges at the beginning of the twentieth century.

Both guesses would be wrong. Water ices in particular have a much longer history. The business of refrigeration started with the Chinese. As early as the third century B.C., someone worked out that blocks of river ice could be stored underground, in a dry place, until the hot weather arrived. The miracle of ice in summer to cool food and drink.

By the T'ang dynasty, in the eighth century, magistrates in cold corners of the empire were well organized in supplying ice for the icepits and ice-houses of the great palace at Ch'ang-an, in east-central China and now called Sian. Royal refreshment included watermelons brought up from cold storage, and served in jade bowls on beds of ice (the nearest thing in nature to a water ice is the crisp, chill flesh of watermelon). There was iced tea, and, for one young emperor, milk mixed with snowlike flakes of camphor and frozen in an icebox—the first dairy ice cream?

A description of the ices of those times by a lady of the eleventh-century Japanese court, Sei Shonagon, makes one think of an Italian *granita*: "chips of ice mixed with fruit juice and served in a new silver bowl." How refreshing, how elegant that ice must have been, semiliquid, a little grainy to the tongue.

Ices did not arrive in Britain until centuries later. They had a long journey to make along the silk road to the Middle East—the words sorbet and sherbet derive from *shariba*, Arabic for a drink, a cool drink naturally— then to Renaissance Italy, and then to seventeenth-century France. It was Charles II who built the first icehouse in Britain in 1660, soon after his Restoration (no doubt he licked his first ice at the French court, in exile). He included it in his improvements to St. James's park:

> *Yonder the harvest of cold months laid up,*
> *Gives a fresh coolness to the royal cup,*
> *There ice, like crystal, firm and never lost,*
> *Tempers hot July with December's frost.**

No doubt the ice came from there to make the first ice cream known to have been eaten in England, at Windsor Castle in 1667.

Those who could afford this royal innovation soon followed suit, and in time most estates acquired an icehouse. A few of them have survived the invention of refrigerators—the icehouse at Rufford Abbey in Lancashire was still in use in the 1930's—but shabbily by comparison with more decorative souvenirs of China such as orangeries and grottoes.

Nowadays the water ices of the 1,100-year-old Jade Kingdom, and the cream ices of England's royal Stuarts, are within everyone's reach. This we owe to the development of commercial, then domestic, refrigeration in the nineteenth and early twentieth centuries. One thing, though, I do not understand. More and more people buy refrigerators. Ices, *granitas* and sorbets in particular are easy to make. Yet the sales of commercial ice creams are still enormous (would they be affected, I wonder, if ingredients

---

* From a poem written by Edmund Waller in 1661, *On St. James Park*, "as largely improved by His Majesty."

and their quantities were clearly printed on the wrappers?). This is such a pity. I've never bought an ice in England to match the ones made with so little trouble at home.

WATER ICES

Lemon granita & lemon sorbet

Two warnings first of all. Lemon ices must have a pure, direct flavour, so do not be tempted to use bottled lemon juice, and do not squeeze the lemons so thriftily that the juice is embittered by the pith of the fruit—a point to watch if you use an electric juicer.

> about 1 cup lemon juice
> 1 cup sugar
> 2 cups water
> *optional:* 2 egg whites

First, set the refrigerator to the lowest possible temperature, and leave it half an hour before putting the ice into the freezing compartment. Simmer sugar and water in a pan for 5 minutes. Cool, then flavour with the lemon juice: the full cup may not be necessary if the lemons were particularly good. Strain into ice trays and cover with foil (or use a plastic box with a lid). If you are using a *sorbétière,* follow its freezing instructions.

It's important to stir the frozen sides of the mixture into the more liquid middle part every so often. With shallow trays this needs to be done every half hour; deep boxes can be left for much longer.

In 2 to 3 hours—the time depends on the depth of the mixture—you will have a thick mush of iced granules. This is what the Italians call a *granita.* Serve it in tall glasses, with almond biscuits (see p. 354). I don't think that whipped cream goes well with citrus water ices, but this is a matter of personal taste.

In 3 to 4 hours, you will have a firm but not impenetrable block of water ice ready to be turned into a sorbet. Beat the egg whites in a large bowl until they're stiff (use an electric beater if possible), then add spoonfuls of the ice gradually. If this is done too fast, sploshes of ice fly about the kitchen. Properly done, the mixture blows up to a mass of white foam. Refreeze in a larger container until the sorbet has the consistency of firm snow; it is not necessary to stir this egg white mixture. Serve in biscuit flowers (p. 353), or in wide glasses.

Lime sorbet

Limes on sale in the better greengrocers' shops may seem expensive, but they are very juicy and make an exquisite ice. If you can afford only a couple of limes, add the cool syrup to their juice until it tastes very fresh and not too sweet.

> 5 limes
> 1 cup sugar
> 2 cups water
> *optional:* 2 egg whites

Follow the previous recipe for lemon *granita*, adding egg whites as directed to make sorbet.

Grape water ice

Most fruit can be turned into a good sorbet or *granita*, but black grapes provide a flavour which is rich and subtle compared to the straightforward flavours of orange or peach. Particularly when they are reinforced with a muscatel dessert wine, or brandy. White grapes produce a lighter-tasting ice of golden transparency—it will be improved by a white wine which has a pronounced grapey flavour.

      1 lb. grapes
      1 cup sugar
      ½–1 cup water
      4 tablespoons of dessert wine, or ⅓ cup of white wine,
        or ⅛ cup of brandy
      juice of 1 lemon
optional: 1 or 2 egg whites

The method is similar to the recipe for lemon *granita*, but one has first to produce a fruit purée. Cut the grapes in half and mangle them through a food mill, or put them in the blender for a few seconds. Make a syrup of the sugar and ½ cup water. When it is cool add the grape purée and strain. Flavour to taste with lemon juice. Dilute with the extra water if required.

Freeze according to directions on page 338, adding the wine or brandy at the end. For instance, with a *granita*, pour the wine in gradually at the last stirring; with a sorbet, add the wine when ice and beaten egg white are mixed together.

Serve with slightly sweetened whipped cream, and almond biscuits.

Strawberry or raspberry water ice

      1 lb. strawberries or raspberries
      1 cup sugar
      1–2 cups water
      juice of 1 lemon
      juice of 1 orange
      5 tablespoons orange liqueur, or kirsch
optional: 2 egg whites

These two excellent ices can be made with frozen fruit very successfully. Follow the method for grape water ice, previous recipe. Add the syrup gradually to the purée and stop before the mixture is too sweet—fruit varies so much in flavour that this is always a wise precaution.

Black currant sorbet

1 lb. black currants
1¼ cups sugar
1½–2 cups water
2 teaspoons lemon juice
optional: 5 tablespoons crème de cassis, 2 egg whites

Follow the method for grape water ice, page 339. There is no doubt that water ices particularly are improved by alcoholic additions. If you cannot buy crème de cassis, use kirsch instead.

Cherry water ice

This Victorian recipe takes time and patience, but if you grow your own cherries you will find it worthwhile.

1 lb. morello [sour] cherries
6 almonds, blanched & bruised
1¼ cups sugar
2 cups water
juice of 1 lemon
optional: 5 tablespoons kirsch, 2 egg whites

Pit the cherries and crush them. Extract kernels from cherry stones and bruise them. Make a syrup of the sugar and water, add while it's still hot the cherries, the kernels, and the almonds. Strain into the cherry pulp when cold, and freeze according to directions on pages 338–9, adding the kirsch, if used, at the end.

Iced oranges

Ice-filled oranges, arranged in a plain white dish with sprigs of bay leaves, make a refreshing and beautiful end to rich dinners. The orange containers can be prepared in advance, like the water ice, and are not too difficult to deal with.

Choose large brilliant oranges, one for each person. Slice a neat cap from the stem end, and just enough from the opposite end to prevent the orange from keeling over on the serving dish. With a sharp knife cut a little way down the cap end, between segments and pith. Then slide in a dessertspoon, pressing the flesh inwards so that it separates from the pith neatly and can be removed. This works well so long as the spoon moves outside the skin of the segments. Press the pulp in a sieve over a basin— the juice can be used in one of the following recipes, or for drinks.

(Lemons and good-sized eating apples can be scooped out and filled with ice in the same way as oranges.)

> 1½ cups orange juice
> 2 cups water
> ¾ cup sugar
> juice of 1 lemon
> 3½ tablespoons orange liqueur, or orange flower water
> *optional:* 2 egg whites

Follow the grape ice recipe, page 339. Chill the oranges before filling them with water ice. To store, wrap them in foil and leave in the icemaking compartment of the refrigerator (or in a freezer).

> Or: 6-oz. can concentrated frozen orange juice
> 2 heaping tablespoons sugar
> water
> *optional:* 2 tablespoons maraschino liqueur or
> brandy, 1 egg white

Make a syrup of the sugar and ½ cup of water, as for lemon *granita* on page 338, by boiling them together for 5 minutes. Pour into a 1-quart container and leave to cool. Stir in the orange juice and enough water to bring the mixture up to 2½ cups. Fill oranges as above. (Or you may freeze in trays in the usual way, see page 338, adding liqueur and beaten egg white if desired.)

Peach and orange ice

Don't despise this American recipe because the fruit is canned—the combination of flavours is most successful. Use white peaches if you can—they are more finely piquant than the yellow ones.

> 1 cup sieved canned peaches
> 1 cup orange juice
> ½ cup sugar
> 2 teaspoons lemon juice

Mix together until the sugar is dissolved. Freeze to a *granita*, stirring every half hour. Fresh strawberry pulp or canned apricot pulp may be substituted for peaches—they all combine well with orange juice.

Granita al caffè con panna

On holiday in Italy in the heat, one rapidly discovers two surprising things—that *caffè espresso* is far more refreshing than water, or even a pink slice of watermelon, and that bought ices can taste deliciously clear and subtle. (The second discovery can be quite a shock after experiences of raspberry ripple, choc bars and iced lollies.) These two bits of wisdom soon lead one to the finest of all water ices, *granita al caffè*, which combines the stimulus of black coffee with the refreshment of intense cold. And do not forget the important words *con panna*—with cream— because whipped cream sets off perfectly the bitter-sweet granules of blackish brown ice.

Use finely ground espresso coffee if you can buy it, otherwise a Continental, after-dinner roast coffee.

> 15 tablespoons coffee
> ¼–⅓ cup sugar
> 5 cups boiling water

Warm a stoneware jug [or use a *Melior French cafetière*], put in the coffee and then the water, which should be boiling. Stir well and leave in a warm place for 10 minutes to brew. Strain off and sweeten with ¼ cup sugar. When cold, pour twice through a piece of sheeting or doubled muslin. Add more sugar if required. Freeze, stirring every half hour until the mixture is a mush of granules. Serve in tall glasses with a generous swirl of whipped cream on top.

Wine sherbet

Here is another superb water ice. To me it's the judgement of Paris, trying to decide between *granita al caffè*, this sherbet made with *muscat de Frontignan* or the black-grape water ice above.

Champagne or sweet sparkling wine can be used as the flavouring for the syrup, but Frontignan, or a similar muscatel dessert wine, is a more economical choice, as such wines do not spoil with a little keeping once the bottle has been opened.

> 1¼ cups wine
> ½ cup sugar
> 1¼ cups water
> juice of 1 lemon
> juice of 1 orange
> *garnish:* sweetened whipped cream

Make a syrup of sugar and water by simmering for 5 minutes. Cool, then add the other ingredients and freeze to a *granita*. Serve in champagne glasses, with a topping of slightly sweetened whipped cream, and some almond or vanilla biscuits (see p. 354).

Grand Marnier water ice

Orange liqueurs make a very successful water ice, and so does crème de cassis. Here are the proportions for a liqueur ice:

1½ cups sugar
scant 3 cups water
juice of 1 lemon
generous ½ cup Grand Marnier

Make a syrup of the sugar and water by simmering for 5 minutes. Cool and add the lemon juice. Freeze in the usual way, and when almost at the *granita* stage stir in the liqueur. Freeze until almost solid. Serve in glasses, with a little more Grand Marnier poured over, or with whipped cream flavoured with Grand Marnier.

CREAM ICES

Although I like eating water ices better than cream ices, it's the latter I prefer to make. Their flavouring can be a most delicious exercise in ingenuity. The one thing not to forget is the word "cream"—milk is no substitute, as it turns to watery granules when frozen (unless it's combined with so many egg yolks that you might as well have bought cream in the first place).

There are four basic ways of making a good cream ice: one can add cream to a water ice mixture, or to a sweetened fruit purée, one can use cream alone with various flavourings, or—most successfully of all—one can mix a rich custard made with light cream and eggs with an equal quantity of heavy cream.

Water ice method

Ingredients for a water ice, minus egg whites:

½ cup heavy cream
plus: ½ cup light cream

Follow the water ice methods (pp. 338–40), but fold in whipped cream instead of beaten egg white.

This produces a light cream ice which is very refreshing in hot weather. The following recipes are all very much richer in texture and flavour. This sounds expensive, and indeed it's not cheap, but heavier ices are eaten in much smaller quantities, so the cost in the end is much the same.

Pure cream ices

This is the simplest, quickest way of making good ice cream. For perfect texture and flavour, it's true that you need a cream and custard mixture (see pp. 348–9); but this is a useful second best when unexpected visitors arrive for a meal. And on hot days when you don't want to spend time over a stove.

The flavouring can be nuggets of candied fruit or ginger, grated chocolate, toasted nuts, or a glass of orange, chocolate or coffee liqueur. Or more homely ingredients such as whole-wheat bread and oatmeal—the results do not taste homely at all.

1 cup heavy cream
1 cup light cream
¾ cup vanilla sugar (see below)
¾ cup bread crumbs made from good whole-grain bread
    or ⅓ cup oatmeal
¼ cup granulated sugar
⅓ cup water
optional: 1 egg white

Whip creams and vanilla sugar to a light thick mass. Freeze (in shallow trays for extra speed) at the lowest possible temperature, turning sides to middle when they begin to harden. Toast the bread crumbs in the oven to a crisp golden brown (for brown-bread ice cream); or dry rather than toast the oatmeal until it's hard and crunchy and slightly brown (Caledonian ice cream). Boil the granulated sugar and water together for a few minutes and leave to cool: syrup from preserved ginger, sweet chow-chow or fruit in brandy can be substituted when these flavourings are being used.

When the cream is solid, but not rocklike, transfer it to a bowl. Mix the bread crumbs or oatmeal with the syrup and immediately stir into the ice cream, beating the mixture well. Refreeze. Serve with thin biscuits or oatcakes. A stiffly beaten egg white may also be folded in after the crumbs or oatmeal. This makes the mixture lighter (and bulkier).

To make vanilla sugar: Put a vanilla pod [bean] and plenty of superfine sugar into a large screw-top jar. Leave for a week or two, and always keep the jar filled up, as the vanilla pod will impart its wonderful flavour for many months.

For quick vanilla sugar, pulverize a 3-inch piece of vanilla pod with ½ cup sugar. This produces a fine, black-speckled powder which should be mixed with superfine sugar until the flavour is insistent but not overpowering.

Biscuit Tortoni

Tortoni's was an Italian establishment which opened in Paris at the very beginning of the nineteenth century. Victor Hugo, Dumas *père* and Alfred de Musset all came to enjoy the delicious food, which was served buffet style. Outside in the street, ladies ate the famous ices, brought to them in their carriages (it was not yet respectable for women to be seen in restaurants). Ices which were better and creamier than any served in Paris before. This particular recipe was invented by Tortoni's son in honour of his father—a "biscuit" is an oblong ice cream, which is cut down into slices for serving.

> 1 cup heavy cream
> 1 cup light cream
> ¼ cup confectioners' sugar
> pinch of salt
> ½ cup hard macaroon crumbs
> ⅓ cup sweet brown sherry
> extra confectioners' sugar & macaroon crumbs

Whip the creams with the confectioners' sugar and the salt, and freeze until just firm. Transfer to a bowl and fold in the macaroon crumbs and sherry. Add more sugar if necessary. Freeze in an oblong plastic box or metal loaf tin. Turn out and decorate with a sprinkling of macaroon crumbs.

The best way of turning out the ice cream is to invert the whole thing onto a serving dish, and then to put a cloth wrung out in very hot water round the metal mould. This should free the ice cream. Dipping the mould into a bowl of hot water, or running it under the hot tap, can soften the ice cream too much.

Cream & custard ices

This recipe makes the best-textured and best-flavoured ice cream. It takes longer to make than the pure cream ices above, and it's more expensive, but there's no better recipe. Milk can be substituted for the light cream, but it brings a watery granular element into the mixture which is out of place.

> 1 cup light cream
> 4–6 egg yolks
> ⅔–¾ cup vanilla sugar (see p. 347)
> 1 cup heavy cream

Bring the light cream just up to the boil, then pour it onto the egg yolks, beating vigorously. Stir in about ½ cup of the sugar. Set the pan over a basin of simmering water, and whisk or stir until the mixture thickens to a custard. Strain and leave to cool. Whip the heavy cream, fold it into the custard and add more sugar (or the flavouring you have chosen; see below). Freeze at the lowest possible temperature in a metal mould. Turn the sides to middle when they begin to harden. Serve with thin almond or vanilla biscuits.

Variations

Chocolate: flavour the custard with coffee essence or instant coffee. Tia Maria may be added when the mixture is cold. Fold in ⅓ cup of chocolate chips, or grated chocolate, after adding the whipped cream.

Prune: soak, stew and purée ½ pound dried prunes. Sweeten slightly and flavour with rum when cool. Mix in with the cooled custard, before adding cream. Taste and add more rum if necessary. Serve with walnut (p. 320) or almond biscuits (p. 354).

Walnut and rum: add 4 oz. shelled and grated walnuts (about ¾ cup) to the light cream before heating it. When the custard has cooled, spin in the blender, then sieve it (this extracts the maximum flavour from the nuts, and removes the gritty bits that always seem to remain). Or put the custard through the finest plate of the vegetable mill. Beat in the whipped cream, and flavour discreetly with rum—just enough to enrich the flavour without being really recognizable.

Other nuts can be substitutued for walnuts. With almonds, kirsch is a better flavouring than rum.

Honey and orange: add a tablespoon of honey to the hot custard. When the mixture is cool, add the juice of a large orange, some orange liqueur and the whipped cream. Do not overdo the honey.

Nesselrode: said to have been invented by M. Mouy, chef to the great Russian diplomat and foreign minister Count Nesselrode. He was a friend of Talleyrand, the French foreign minister—both men were devotees of good food. No doubt it drew them together. This is an ice for a special occasion.

To the ingredients for the cream and custard ice, you must add:

> ½ cup unsweetened chestnut purée
> 1 tablespoon each seedless raisins & sultanas
>   [or yellow raisins]
> 1 tablespoon each chopped glacé cherries & orange peel
> ½ cup Malaga wine (or sweet sherry)
> additional whipped cream & marrons glacés to garnish

Add the chestnut purée to the custard when hot, and mix to a smooth paste. Soak raisins and sultanas in hot water for 1 hour, then put with the chopped cherries and orange peel into the Malaga for a further hour (drain off the surplus water first). Add the whipped cream to the custard and fold in the fruit and peel and wine. Freeze in the usual way, stirring up from time to time. Serve decorated with whipped cream and marrons glacés.

Mulberry: flavour to taste with mulberry syrup (p. 361).

Praline: flavour with praline powder (p. 329). The best ice cream of all.

COOKED FRUIT ICE CREAM

When one thinks of fruit being used to flavour ice cream, one thinks of strawberry, raspberry, peach or black currant ice cream. In these the uncooked fruit is sieved to a purée and blended with cream or cream and custard (see second recipe following). One does not think of the hard fruits or the dried fruits and fruits which need cooking as being suitable for ice cream. But they are. In combinations they make unusual and delicious flavours which sometimes puzzle people.

Apple (or pear) & quince
ice cream

Water ice and whipped cream are the best ingredients for most soft-fruit ice creams. For hard fruits such as apples and pears and quinces, or for dried fruits such as apricots and peaches, this is a good method:

½ lb. eating apples or pears & ¼ lb. quinces
   or ¾ lb. apples or pears
4 tablespoons unsalted butter
2 tablespoons water
sugar to taste
2 eggs, separated
½ cup light cream
½ cup heavy cream
toasted almonds
optional: apricot jam or cinnamon or lemon juice

Wash and cut up the fruit. Stew it slowly in a covered pan with the butter and water. Sieve to remove peel and cores. Flavour with sugar (if you are using apples alone add some apricot jam as well, or some cinnamon; with pears, lemon juice and a piece of cinnamon stick may be added as they stew). There should be about 1 cup of purée. Stir in the 2 egg yolks, beat well and reheat gently, keeping below the boil, for 5–10 minutes until the mixture thickens. Cool. Beat the two creams together until thick, fold into the egg mixture, then freeze. When the mixture is almost solid, beat the egg whites and add spoonfuls of the frozen mixture until you have a thick frothy mass. Refreeze. Serve garnished with toasted almonds.

The beaten whites are an optional addition, but they lighten the ice cream in a very agreeable way. It's worth making an effort to find a supply of quinces (see p. 354); they are a wonderful flavouring for apples and pears.

Variation

> **Iced gooseberry fool:** substitute gooseberries for apples and
> quinces. Flavour with a muscatel dessert wine such as Fron-
tignan. Or put a head of elderflowers in with the gooseberries as they
stew (p. 273). Serve almond biscuits, and omit the garnish of toasted
almonds.

Strawberry ice cream

This is a simple way of turning soft fruit, which doesn't need
cooking, into ice cream. It can be adapted to raspberries, peaches (weigh
the fruit after skinning and removing pits) or mulberries. The quantity
of sugar and citrus juices needs to be adapted to the sharpness or sweetness of the fruit.

> ½ lb. strawberries
> ½ cup confectioners' sugar
> juice of ½ lemon
> juice of ½ orange
> 1 cup heavy cream

Purée the fruit in the blender, or put it through a food mill, then put it
through a fine sieve to catch the seeds. Sweeten with sugar and sharpen
with lemon and orange juice to emphasize the flavour. Whip the cream
until it's stiff. Fold in the fruit purée, and freeze, at the lowest possible
temperature, as usual. Garnish with fine strawberries.

Camembert ice cream

This unusual recipe from the thirties makes a good ending
to the meal. The ice and hot biscuits are an important part of the recipe:

1 Camembert, soft & mature, not overripe
½ cup heavy cream
½ cup light cream
cayenne pepper or Tabasco
salt

for serving: cracked ice
          hot-water biscuits

Mash up (or put in blender) the cheese with the two creams. Season well with cayenne or Tabasco, and salt to taste. Freeze until just firm, but not hard. No need to stir. Serve sliced on a bed of cracked ice cubes, with the heated water biscuits in a separate dish.

Biscuit flowers

I am not one for fiddly cooking (particularly when the results are fattening), but I make an exception for these biscuit flowers to hold ice cream. The first ones you try may come to disaster. Don't despair; the quantities are enough for twelve flowers, which leaves plenty of chance for improvement.

6 tablespoons butter
⅓ cup vanilla sugar (see p. 347)
1 egg
2 egg whites
1 cup plain [all-purpose] flour

Cream butter and sugar, and add eggs and flour until the mixture turns to a smooth, thick batter. Cut vegetable parchment to fit a baking tray: on it, draw three circles with a 5-inch saucer. Turn the paper over and brush lightly with oil. Spread a generous teaspoon of batter over each circle. Bake at 300°, for 10–20 minutes, watching the biscuits to see that they turn brown, not black, at the edges. Meanwhile oil the exterior of a Thermos mug (or something else of the same shape), and invert it on the table to act as a mould for the biscuits. When they are cooked, remove one of them and quickly slap it right side down on the oiled mould. Press gently with a cloth, concentrating on the centre, and you will find that the edges cool into a wavy-edged flower. Transfer to an inverted cup and start on the second biscuit (keep the waiting biscuits warm in the oven, with the door ajar so that they don't overcook).

Store in an airtight tin.

Almond biscuits

Unwanted egg whites are a problem in the mayonnaise and ice cream season. Here's a delicious solution. These biscuits go so well with mousses and creams and all kinds of ices that no one could accuse them of being made from leftovers.

4 egg whites
4 oz. ground almonds
½ cup superfine sugar
1 tablespoon plain [all-purpose] flour

for baking: about 4 sheets rice paper or vegetable parchment

Beat the egg whites until they are firm. Mix the almonds, sugar and flour together and fold into the whites lightly but firmly.

Lay the rice paper on a baking tray (with the brand I buy, it takes two sheets to line the tray). Using a pastry bag, pipe the mixture on top in cat's tongue shapes. Bake at 300°, for 10–20 minutes. Cool on a wire rack, then tear off the surplus rice paper.

The mixture can also be baked on vegetable parchment-lined trays, and then rolled into "cigarettes," keeping the top side outside.

Store in an airtight tin.

FRUIT LIQUEURS & RATAFIAS

Fruit ratafias—fruit liqueurs made with brandy, not *eau de vie* distilled from the fruit itself—came to England from France, like the word itself, in the seventeenth century. Brandy then was infinitely cheaper.

In France they are still abundantly made, particularly in the wine-growing areas. But the old habit may soon be on the way out. Little by little the right to have *eau de vie* distilled from marc, except commercially, is being phased out to reduce alcoholism, the extent of which is pretty terrifying in some French villages. Nowadays the licenses die with their present owners. They can only be inherited by a widow or widower, not by the children or other relatives. Nor can a license be sold with a vineyard: the previous owner must retain it, and cannot dispose of it to anyone else. One sees the point. But it will mean an impoverishment of the hospitality which has always been so marked in poor households in the wine districts of France. (It will also mean an end of the travelling marc maker with his antique-looking still.)

One sits at an oilcloth-covered table, eating asparagus, *omelette aux fines herbes,* chicken cooked with morel mushrooms, salad, strawberries, fresh goat cheese, and drinking wine and liqueurs of quality. Hens walk in and out, dogs snore at one's feet with an eye half-open for chicken bones. Apart from bread, oil, coffee, sugar, everything has come from garden, vineyard, farmyard or commune woods. There will be no book, bathroom, television set or easy chair in the house. The normally divisive effect of poverty is not felt, because the host is well aware that few people in France can be offering their guests better food, and—more important —better drink.

Here are fruit liqueurs to make at home if you are prepared (1) to spend the money on brandy or *eau de vie de marc,* and (2) to wait for at least two months.

But then consider, you are turning one bottle of brandy into two or three bottles of liqueur, and you are storing up summer and autumn for midwinter and Christmas. And the basis is not three-star cognac, but the cheapest brandy you can find. Or gin, or better still vodka, which has no taste.

I shall be heretical and say that these fruit drinks (though admittedly you don't have the fun of creating the alcohol) are finer flavoured and more rewarding than the vast number of homemade "wines" (which aren't wines, because ipso facto a wine is something made from the fruit of the vine). As with wines, though, you must not try to sell them, or you'll be in trouble with government agents.

I find myself making bottles of one kind or another, and then putting them at the back of the cupboard and forgetting about them. The discovery months later is wonderful, promising a cordial end to meals and one which can be relied upon to delight other people.

There is little skill involved. Nothing can go wrong, unless you leave the bottles in too warm or too sunny a place.

These liqueurs are very good-tempered. One friend tops up his sorb apple liqueur with brandy and syrup from time to time, particularly in a year when the sorbs have been very good. In another bottle he has finely pared orange peel submerged in brandy and syrup: every time he eats an orange, he adds to his bottle, putting in more brandy and syrup as the peel level rises. I have a bottle of prunes in Armagnac; when I take out a few to serve with cream to an unexpected visitor, I replace them with unsoaked prunes and leave the bottle for at least another ten days before raiding it again.

It's worth making your own experiments. There are few fruits that can't produce a good liqueur; and some of the most unpromising—I'm thinking particularly of the fruits, the clustered berries, of the wild service tree—make the best ones of all. The guiding principle is that dry-textured fruits and peel need preserving in syrup and brandy, soft fruits need only sugar and brandy (their juice supplies the place of water in syrup).

Sloe (and mulberry) gin

It may seem difficult to be enthusiastic about anything made with sloes.[1] They set the mouth on edge. They nestle into a fakir's bed of thorns. One wonders how the welcomed blackthorn flowers of March and April could produce finally such bitter fruit. But, if you live in the United Kingdom, don't be discouraged: sloes are easy to find (blackthorn grows all over northern Europe, but it's in England that it most flourishes), and sloe gin is easy to drink.

For those lucky enough to pick sloes on a dry day when they have been mellowed by an early frost: remove the stalks and prick them all over with a darning needle.

To each ½ lb. of fruit, allow 1 pint gin, ¼ cup of sugar and 6–10 blanched, bruised almonds. Bottle and leave for 3 months before straining and rebottling (large widemouthed bottling jars are the best to use for fruit liqueurs, though small fruit such as sloes and cherries can be put into ordinary wine bottles and corked firmly).

Mulberries make a finer drink, but they are more difficult to come by. Lucky the owner of an old garden with an ancient mulberry tree.[2] Pick them when ripe and sweet and follow the above proportions. They will not need pricking.

---

[1] *The fruit of the Eurasian blackthorn tree. In the U.S. the same word is sometimes used in reference to various wild plums, but these fruits are not to be considered substitutes.*

[2] *Most Americans consider the mulberry an ornamental tree only, and some Southerners go so far as to use the fruit of red mulberries exclusively as food for pigs and poultry. "Because of the persistent stem and an axis that goes part way into the fruit," naturalist Euell Gibbons says, "many people do not like to bring fresh mulberries to the table, but they are better food than much that comes there. . . . I still prefer to eat my fresh mulberries directly from the tree, and use the ones I gather to make some delicious pies, jellies and cooling summer drinks."*

Apricot or peach ratafia

Choose fruit which is ripe and has a good flavour. Avoid woolly apricots or watery peaches. The kernels add a delicate almond flavour, which is very good; it can be increased by adding some blanched and bruised almonds.

> 12 large apricots,
>   or 1 generous lb. peaches
> 2 cups brandy
> 1 cup sugar
> ½-inch piece cinnamon stick
> 4 cloves
> ¼ teaspoon mace

Quarter the fruit (only the peaches need be peeled). Remove the pits and extract and bruise the kernels. If peaches are used, cut the pieces in half again. Add the kernels and the rest of the ingredients to the fruit, mixing well. Keep in tightly closed bottling jars for at least a month before using; three months is better still.

As with cherry brandy, there is no need to strain off and rebottle the liqueur. Many people like eating a piece of brandy-soaked fruit with the drink; it can also be used in fruit salads, mincemeat, or water ices.

Cherry brandy

Sweet dessert cherries are not used for this favourite English liqueur, but more acid-flavoured kinds like the morellos. There is, if you can find it, a very suitable variety called ratafia. In France, where they are more popular than in Britain, varieties of sharp, tangy-tasting *guignes* are used for liqueur making. These small crimson-to-black-heart cherries grow in many cottage gardens—sometimes a deserted site will have a tree of *guignes* still surviving, although the cottage is in ruins or has long disappeared.

Cut the cherry stalks down to a quarter or half inch. Prick each cherry five or six times with a darning needle as you put it into the bottling jar, which should be filled. Pour granulated sugar into the jar until it comes just under halfway up the fruit. Add brandy to cover it. Fasten the lid and leave for at least three months—or twenty years. The fruit will be almost as delicious as the liqueur, which acquires the desirable almond flavour from the cherry stones.

This recipe can be followed using grapes, but the entire stalk should be removed.

Ratafia

To the small wine-growers of the Loir, who boast no *appellations controlées*, there is only one fruit brandy deserving the name ratafia. Inevitably it is made from that fruit of fruits, the grape, when its cold, sweet juice pours from the *pressoirs* in an opaque purple stream. Four litres are taken from the barrel, and a litre of *eau de vie* marc is added. This stops the juice fermenting. Sugar is not required with the high proportion of fruit juice to brandy. Of all the ratafias it tastes the freshest and most invigorating.

The best home *pressoir* is the food mill (or the blender for 3 or 4 seconds only). Mill the grapes until they are mangled, pips and all, but not reduced to a purée. Strain debris and juice through a double muslin, squeezing until the residue, the marc, is dry. Measure the juice and add a quarter or more of its volume in brandy. Bottle and leave to clear.

In his great cooking dictionary, Alexandre Dumas gave a slightly different recipe for a ratafia of muscat grapes. Mangle, squeeze and measure the fruit as above, but add an equal quantity of brandy, plus sugar to taste. Leave to clear. The liqueur can then be poured off into clean bottles or jars.

Orange liqueur

6 very large oranges
4½ cups brandy
2 cups sugar
½ teaspoon coriander
1-inch cinnamon stick

Peel the oranges thinly—there must be no white pith adhering—and cut the peel into strips. Squeeze the oranges, and add the strained juice to the peel with the other ingredients. Put into bottling jars and cover tightly.

As I mentioned above, extra peel can be added to the liqueur when you eat an orange.

Quince ratafia

Anything made with quinces is bound to be delicious, and this ratafia is no exception. If the only ones you can buy are still green, let them ripen to yellow in the house. A word of warning—handle them carefully, as they are easily bruised.

Take 2 large quinces. Rub the grey down off them with a cloth, rinse and grate them, peel and core included. Put into a 1-quart bottling jar. Pour in granulated sugar to come about a third of the way up the bottle, add ¼ teaspoon each cinnamon, ginger and mace, then fill the bottling jar with brandy or vodka.

The reader who sent me this recipe remarks that the flavour of the quinces begins to predominate after only a week, that all fruit expel their flavours surprisingly soon. This is true, but I think that if these ratafias are left for a month or two or three, their taste seems to mellow and become more subtle.

Ratafia of red fruits

Assemble a medley of summer fruits—cherries, red currants, raspberries and mulberries. Bruise them and leave in a cool place for 3 days. Strain and add to the juice an equal quantity of brandy. To each pint of this mixture add ¼ cup sugar and a piece of cinnamon stick about 1 inch long. Leave for two months.

Sorb, medlar and wild service liqueurs

"Chestnuts in their spiky cases, squashy medlars, and tart-tasting sorb apples—the autumn drives before it a profusion of modest fruits which one does not pick, but which fall into one's hands, which wait patiently at the foot of the tree until man deigns to collect them." I like these lines of Colette's (and recommend you to search out the medlar and wild service[3] or sorb trees of your neighborhood) because small tawny gold sorb apples and medlars and the clusters of wild service-berries make the best of fruit liqueurs. One important point—make sure that the fruit is bletted before it goes into the bottling jars, i.e., that it is darkening and bruised in appearance, almost rotten, one might think, with perhaps the beginnings of a white mould. Should the fruit be hard when it's gathered, it should be laid on flat dishes in a warm room until it reaches the desired state.

Make a syrup for these liqueurs by simmering together 1½ cups of sugar and 1¼ cups of water for five minutes. Leave to cool.

Fill bottling jars with the fruit. Add syrup, according to the sweetness of the sorbs, medlars, or berries, either up to a third of the height of the fruit, or to just under half. Top up—make sure the fruit is covered—with

---

[3] In the U.S. serviceberries go abegging now in spite of their use by pioneers in pies, muffins, etc. They still spread over vast areas in the East, the Rockies and the Northwest.

brandy. Keep tightly covered for at least two months. Better still for a year and two months.

Eau de vie de poire

We have one friend, a resourceful Gaul of the Asterix breed, who is always busy with some new project connected, ultimately, with the pleasures of the belly. He may be smoking a ham from the family pig, or showing the children how to bottle the cider.

One day our daughter watched him tying wine bottles over several barely formed pears on the espalier pear tree. What was he doing? Well, the pears would grow and ripen in their individual greenhouses. Then he would break the stems and fill the bottles up with a mixture of syrup (see recipe above) and marc. At Christmas and New Year, his pear liqueur would cause a sensation—like a ship in a bottle, but much better, because the contents of these bottles would be drinkable.

Even if you have no pear tree, there is no reason to go short of pear liqueur. Buy fruit of a good-flavoured variety such as Williams, and let them ripen in a warm kitchen. Cut in quarters, fill a bottling jar and add a mixture of one-third syrup and two-thirds brandy. Fasten tightly, and leave until Christmas, or for two months.

Pineapple liqueur

Choose a fine ripe pineapple, pare it and slice it thinly. In a widemouthed bottling jar arrange one slice on top of the other, following the shape of the pineapple. Pour in any juice that came out while preparing the pineapple, and then sugar to come up to half the height of the fruit. Then cover with brandy (the jar need not be full, but there should be more brandy than sugar, and the fruit must be covered as in all these recipes).

Leave for at least two months.

Prunes in brandy

This is a delicious preserve for the storecupboard. The prunes can be served in small glasses with the liqueur, or they can be presented as a dessert on their own and served with whipped cream and almond biscuits (p. 354). Use giant prunes, which can be bought at health food stores.[4]

Fill a widemouthed jar three-quarters full of prunes, unsoaked prunes, pushing a few curls of orange peel and a small stick of cinnamon, about 1 inch long, well down among the fruit. Make up a syrup by boiling sugar and water together, in the proportion of 3 to 2, i.e., ¾ cup of sugar and ½ cup of water, for five minutes. Cool and pour into the jar so that it is between a third and half full. Top up with Armagnac if possible, or with marc or grape brandy. I think vodka is too neutral.

Crème de cassis

Although Canon Felix Kir, who died in 1968 at the age of ninety-two, was a hero of the French resistance, the immortality of his name is assured not by his courage but by an apéritif which bears his surname. He is said to have invented it with the idea of helping black-currant growers around Dijon, of which he was for many years the mayor, to find a wider market for their fruit, or rather the liqueur made fom it. (French children are not brought up on cordials of the Ribena type).[5] Kir consists simply of a glass of chilled, dry white wine—preferably from Burgundy—spiced with a teaspoonful of black currant liqueur. For this alone it is worth trying a homemade crème de cassis; it's also a wonderful improver of black currant sorbets (p. 341), summer pudding or properly made black currant jellies.

[4] As well as most supermarkets in the U.S.

[5] Ribena is the brand name for what Mrs. Grigson judges to be the best English black currant drink, "much vaunted," she says, "for its vitamins!" In the U.S. no great

> 1 lb. black currants
> 2 cups brandy or gin
> 1½ cups sugar
> ½-in. piece of cinnamon stick
> clove
> optional: 5 young green black currant leaves

Break up the black currants with your hands, or a fork, or with a food mill. Mix juice, debris and all the other ingredients together in a large bowl. Put in ordinary bottling jars, fasten and leave in a warm place (ideally the sun) for a month. Strain through a double muslin cloth, squeezing out the juice. Rebottle. It's now ready for use.

Tarragon liqueur

The important thing about this recipe is to get the right tarragon in the first place. You need the true French variety, *Artemisia dracunculus,* and not the coarse hardy Russian variety which has little flavour. It will flourish in a sunny window or balcony; the more warmth it gets the better it will taste.

> 2 good handfuls of tarragon
> 2 cups brandy or marc
> 1½ cups sugar
> 1 cup water

Put the tarragon, picked on a hot dry day, into a bottling jar. Pour on the brandy, fasten the jar tightly, and leave in a cool place for at least a month. At the end of this time make a syrup by boiling sugar and water together for 5 minutes. Let the syrup cool. Strain off the tarragon brandy into a bowl, and add the syrup to it gradually, tasting from time to time— no hardship. When the flavour appeals to you, stop adding syrup. If both tarragon flavour and sweetness seem too strong, add a little water.

---

emphasis is placed on vitamin properties of black currant cordials distilled here, but they bear the same nom marchand as that which comes from Dijon, crème de cassis.

Throw away the tarragon, and pour the liqueur back into the bottling jar. One fresh tarragon branch may be added for appearance. Fasten up the jar, and use as required.

This liqueur is a pale green colour, not as bright as true Chartreuse, but the flavour is not dissimilar.

NOTE: Black currant and other soft fruit liqueurs can also be made by this method.

List of U.S. Sources

Fennel plants:
Check herb growers in your own area; or write Pine Hills Herb Farm, P.O. Box 307, Roswell, Georgia 30075.

Stoneware rillette mugs:
Stoneware half-gallon milk jugs:
Any stoneware jug will do, which you may find in shops selling pottery; order according to size desired. Or try The Pottery Barn, 231 10th Avenue, New York, N.Y.

Squabs:
Available at good butchers and poulterers in all major cities.

Wild-game birds:
Friends who hunt are the best source. Or send for list from Maryland Market, 412 Amsterdam Avenue, New York, N.Y.

Larding needles:
Any supplier of gourmet cookware should carry these. In New York, The Bridge Company, 212 East 52nd Street; Bazaar de la Cuisine, 160 East 55th Street; The Kitchen Galerie, 25 Scotland Road, South Orange, New Jersey; and in San Francisco, Williams & Sonoma, 576 Sutter Street, and Bazaar Français, 666 6th Avenue, are all good sources and will handle mail orders.

Vension:
If hunters or local sources fail you, try in New York Maryland Market, 412 Amsterdam Avenue, or Hammacher Schlemmer, 147 East 57th Street; and in Chicago Czimer Foods Co., 953 West 63rd Street.

Asparagus boiler:
Local gourmet cookware shops, or send to any of those listed above under larding needles.

Sea salt:
Local fancy foods stores, or send to Colonial Country Kitchen, 270 West Merrick Road, Valley Stream, New York.

Bean pot (fagiolara):
Same as sources for stoneware mugs above.

Moutarde de Maille:
Local fancy foods stores, or write to Bloomingdale's, 59th Street and Lexington Avenue, New York, N.Y.

Parsmint herb mill:
Moulinette chopper:
Heart-shaped moulds:
Gourmet cookware stores, or any of the above sources for larding needles.

Walnut oil:
Now available at local health-food stores; or write to Bloomingdale's, 59th Street and Lexington Avenue, New York, N.Y.

Suchard chocolate:
Try local shops that handle imported nuts and candies; or write to Fox's Nut Shoppe, 1263 Lexington Avenue, New York, N.Y.

Index

A NOTE ON THE AUTHOR

Jane Grigson was born in Gloucester, England, and studied at Cambridge University, Florence University, and the Courtauld Institute of Art in London. She has worked in art galleries and publishing houses and has translated a number of books from Italian (one of which received the John Florio translation prize in 1966).

The background to this book (as to The Art of Charcuterie, published by Knopf in 1968) is a cavehouse in Touraine, France, where Jane Grigson spends summer and autumn vacations with her family, and a seventeenth-century farmhouse in Wiltshire, where they live the rest of the time, engulfed in a library of books on every subject from literature, art, and archeology to natural history, gardening, and—of course—cooking. She contributes articles regularly to the London Observer Colour Magazine and it was from these pieces that Good Things emerged.

A NOTE ON THE TYPE

This book is set in Electra, a Linotype face designed by W.A. Dwiggins (1880-1956), who was responsible for so much that is good in contemporary book design. Although much of his early work was in advertising and he was the author of the standard volume *Layout in Advertising*, Mr. Dwiggins later devoted his prolific talents to book typography and type design and worked with great distinction in both fields. In addition to his designs for Electra, he created the Metro, Caledonia, and Eldorado series of type faces, as well as a number of experimental cuttings that have never been issued commercially.

Electra cannot be classified as either modern or old-style. It is not based on any historical model, nor does it echo a particular period or style. It avoids the extreme contrast between thick and thin elements that marks most modern faces and attempts to give a feeling of fluidity, power, and speed.

This book was composed, printed, and bound by The Haddon Craftsmen, Inc., Scranton, Pennsylvania. Typography and binding design by Anthea Lingeman.